FOLK LITERATI, CONTESTED TRADITION, AND HERITAGE IN CONTEMPORARY CHINA

FOLK LITERATI, CONTESTED TRADITION, AND HERITAGE IN CONTEMPORARY CHINA

Incense Is Kept Burning

Ziying You

INDIANA UNIVERSITY PRESS

This book is a publication of

Indiana University Press
Office of Scholarly Publishing
Herman B Wells Library 350
1320 East 10th Street
Bloomington, Indiana 47405 USA

iupress.indiana.edu

Manufactured in the United States of America

Cataloging information is available from the Library of Congress.

ISBN 978-0-253-04635-2 (hardback)
ISBN 978-0-253-04636-9 (paperback)
ISBN 978-0-253-04639-0 (web PDF)

1 2 3 4 5   25 24 23 22 21 20

*To the brilliant and
kind villagers (laoxiang) in Hongtong,
Shanxi, China.*

CONTENTS

ACKNOWLEDGMENTS

IN HONGTONG, SHANXI, CHINA, FIRST AND FOREMOST I would like to thank the participants of local annual ritual processions and temple fairs for their passion, devotion, generosity, kindness, patience, and trust. In the village of Yangxie, I would like to express my sincere appreciation to Wang Wei and Miao Hongjun, who hosted me in their home, guided me to local culture, shared many precious local sources collected by Wang's family with me, accompanied me to numerous interviews, and kept me nourished with all kinds of delicious foods. In Yangxie, I am also grateful to Qiao Longhai; his wife, Miao Hongmei; and other members of Qiao's family, who kindly showed me Qiao Guoliang's manuscripts and told me his stories. In addition, I thank the Wei family, Wang Wenhua, Yan Zhenghong, Pei Beiji, Shao Caiwang, Qiao Bao, Su Jilin, Zhang Zhongyi, Wang Mandou, Su Wenkui, Chai Yufeng, Zhang Wenjin, Wang Zhizhong, Wang Jincui, Yan Quansheng, and numerous other local people who shared their values, beliefs, and stories with me. In Lishan, I would like to express my sincere appreciation to Li Xuezhi for his enthusiasm and perseverance in publicly reviving local traditions over the past several decades and for his support of my research. I also thank Yang Biyun, Qin Sanyou, Li Miaotiao, Li Chunwen, Yang Jianli, Li Genwa, Wei Tianxing, Fan Wenxuan, Shi Ling'er, Li Desheng, Sun Laixi, Shi Haiyu, Li Hongxing, Sun Guangsheng, Li Deshan, and many others for their generous help and lively conversations about local tradition. In Wan'an, I am grateful to Du Baiwa and his family, Chen Baozi, Chen Zhongwei, Han Xiaomao, Shi Menzi, Hu Zhikan, Zhao Changzi, Hu Bingxian, Wang Tianguan, Du Dongxi, and many others. I would like to thank Zhou Xibin and Wang Chunliang for their help throughout my fieldwork in Hongtong. And finally I would like to thank Liu Kuili, Chen Yongchao, and many other folklorists in China who introduced me to the lively living traditions in Hongtong and helped in so many ways, both in furthering my studies and research and also in keeping me happy and sane throughout the process.

I would like to thank Mark Bender for offering his continued and unwavering support throughout all stages of the writing of this book and for being such a wonderful mentor and friend. I also owe many thanks to Dorothy Noyes, Meow Hui Goh, Kirk Denton, Amy Shuman, and Jeffrey H. Cohen for their guidance, advice, and patience during my writing process. I also owe a debt of gratitude to the great folklore community and the Department of East Asian Languages and Literature community at the Ohio State University for their overwhelming support.

I benefited greatly from the help, advice, and resources of many other scholars and friends during my fieldwork and research: Chao Gejin, Lü Wei, An Deming, Gao Bingzhong, Xiao Fang, Shi Aidong, Yang Lihui, Michael Dylan Foster, Lisa Gilman, Ina Asim, Sue Tuohy, Zhang Juwen, Jessica Anderson Turner, Li Jing, Levi Gibbs, He Man, Li Mengjun, Anne Henochowicz, Thomas Barone Beardslee, Cheng Anxia, Wang Junxia, Zhao Yuanhao, Wang Yao, Zhong Jian, Yao Huiyi, Sun Chunfang, and Yuan Bo.

The research for this book was conducted with the financial support of the Ohio State University Office of International Affairs, Center for Folklore Studies, and Department of East Asian Languages and Literature. Funding, space, and time for writing and research from 2015 to 2017 were provided by an Andrew W. Mellon Postdoctoral Fellowship, and in my position as visiting assistant professor of Chinese Studies at the College of Wooster from 2017 to the present.

I am blessed with family who has offered much love and support over the years, particularly throughout all stages of my research and writing. I am particularly indebted to my father, You Shicai, and my mother, Cao Chuanxiu, in China. They encouraged me to pursue my own destiny and fight for my dream, even though I could not live close to them and take care of them while I did so. I am forever grateful for my husband, Zuchao Shen, who has been my strongest support on this project and so many others. His sacrifice of time and his unwavering dedication to my work leave me deeply touched. I am also grateful to my son, Enle Lucas Shen, who was born when I wrote the final chapter of my dissertation in May 2014, and to my daughter, Enxi April Shen, who was born when I was revising my book manuscript in April 2017. These two little individuals changed my life profoundly and strongly motivated me to succeed in my career.

Last but not least, thanks are due to members of the Indiana University Press for considering this book for publication. I am very grateful to Gary Dunham and Janice E. Frisch for their encouragement, support, and professional work. In addition, I am thrilled and honored to have worked with René Rodgers, my developmental editor, who put a great deal of time and effort into polishing this book from a stone to precious jewelry. I am also grateful to my anonymous reviewers for thoughtful comments at crucial stages of this book's production.

None of the above-mentioned people or institutions are responsible for the interpretations or any shortcomings in the book.

Part of my discussion in chapter 6, "Making Intangible Cultural Heritage: Folklore, Tradition, and Power," appeared in the *Journal of Folklore Research* 2–3 (2015): 253–68. Part of my discussion in chapter 3, "Contested Myth, History, and Beliefs: Worshipping Yao and Shun at Village Temples in Hongtong," appeared in my chapter in the edited book volume *Chinese Folklore Studies Today: Discourse and Practice* (2019), Bloomington: Indiana University Press.

A NOTE ON ROMANIZATION, CHINESE CHARACTERS, AND ENGLISH TRANSLATION

THE ROMANIZATION USED IN THIS BOOK IS THE Hanyu Pinyin system now in use in the People's Republic of China. For Chinese characters, I use both traditional and simplified ones in exactly the same way that the authors have used them in their original texts. I do not transform traditional Chinese characters into simplified ones or vice versa, because the coexistence of both systems indicates the tension between traditionalization and modernization as well as the shifting status of Chinese written systems.

When referring to Chinese names, places, and terms, I provide the English translation, Hanyu Pinyin, or Chinese characters. I am clearly aware of the "linguistic compromise" that I have to make when I translate some words and texts from Chinese into English (Chau 2006, 61). My goal is to convey the basic ideas from Chinese into English in an interactive transcultural communication.

FOLK LITERATI, CONTESTED TRADITION, AND HERITAGE IN CONTEMPORARY CHINA

INTRODUCTION

THIS BOOK ADDRESSES THE ROLE OF FOLK LITERATI in transmitting, producing, and reproducing local traditions, as well as controversies and conflicts over the reconstruction of tradition and the safeguarding of intangible cultural heritage (ICH) within local contexts in contemporary China. In the twenty-first century, with the influence from the United Nations Educational, Scientific and Cultural Organization (UNESCO), the project to protect ICH has spread all over China, greatly contributing to the current boom in cultural restoration, reconstruction, and tourism. Scholars often examine this global cultural landscape top-down and emphasize the role of extra-state and state institutions and powerful individual actors in the process of producing and managing heritage. However, it is important to recognize the perspectives of practitioners and local social actors who often became disempowered in this dynamic bureaucratic process of heritage making. With this book, I will explore grassroots perspectives and individual agency in the process of cultural reproduction and the safeguarding of ICH. Through a focus on collaborative and bottom-up approaches, I will illustrate local, regional, and national conflicts regarding the discourse and practices of tradition-reconstruction and ICH-protection efforts in contemporary China and discuss the role of folk literati who have been important in continuing and reproducing local tradition before, during, and after the ICH project.

I coin the term *folk literati* to describe a group of people who are skilled in classical Chinese, knowledgeable of local traditions, and capable of representing them in writing. Generally, the ultimate goal of folk literati is to maintain cultural continuity, as expressed in the vernacular concept that "incense is kept burning" (*xianghuo buduan*) in the face of the many tensions and ruptures associated with practicing local folk traditions, especially during periods of political upheaval. The literati, as a significant social group in cultural production, have been widely studied in premodern Chinese history and literature (Yu 1987; Holcombe 1994; Huang 1995; Roddy 1998; Gerritsen 2007; Tan 2010), but this social group and the surrounding cultural milieu are believed to have disappeared in China during the twentieth century (Yung 2008; Shang 2010). Little attention has been paid to the living conditions of folk literati or their important role in remaking local traditions in contemporary China. Therefore, I draw on my ethnographical research to present the important role of folk literati in reproducing local traditions and continuing stigmatized beliefs in a community context, underlining why they should not be excluded from the fields of folklore studies and cultural studies.

My ethnographic case study concerns the living beliefs of those worshipping the ancient sage-kings Yao and Shun as well as Ehuang and Nüying (who are Yao's daughters and Shun's wives) in several villages in Hongtong County, Shanxi Province, China. Named as an item of China's national ICH in 2008, the official title of the local tradition that I study is *Hongtong zouqin xisu*, "the custom of visiting sacred relatives in Hongtong." I explore the ways different social actors have competed and negotiated with each other in the process of transmitting, reproducing, and representing local beliefs, legends, and history. Combining ethnography with history in my research makes my ethnographic observations in the present more meaningful because history is crucial to the communities that I study.

In particular, I show how a wide range of intertwined social actors and institutions—including *shè* (the primary folk group that sponsors local festivals and celebrations; see chap. 1 for more detail about this group), temple reconstruction associations, folk literati, local cultural institutions, the national government, and UNESCO—construct the dialectics of cultural continuity and change in China. Shè organize the annual ritual processions and temple fairs, while the temple reconstruction associations, which also function as general shè, oversee the reconstruction of local temples and the management of incense donation money collected in the temples. The folk literati play an important role in transmitting, reproducing, and representing local history, legends, and beliefs in local communities. Local cultural institutions, such as cultural centers and ICH-protection centers, both regulate and profit from folk tradition, and they even represent local communities to protect local heritage. China's national government has promoted local tradition as a means of bolstering its own legitimacy and developing its economy since the reform era, and although UNESCO does not play a direct role in preserving local traditions, its agenda has influenced the Chinese government to launch big campaigns to preserve local cultural heritage countrywide. All of these actors have interacted and competed with each other in reproducing and promoting local traditions in

Hongtong, Shanxi. My main purpose with this book is to show how these various actors have reconstructed, shifted, contested, and negotiated local traditions in both discourse and practice and how the conflictive relationships among them have both shaped and reflected cultural reproduction and ICH protection on the ground.

Theorizing Tradition, Cultural Heritage, and Grassroots Agency

As a point of scholarly debate, *tradition* undoubtedly has been one of the most common as well as most contested terms in folklore studies (Ben-Amos 1984; Bronner 1998, 2005, 2011; Noyes 2009; Silva 2012; Oring 2013). It used to be conceived of as past-oriented, static, fixed, bounded, and homogeneous, with a seemingly endless perpetuation of cultural forms through time and across space. However, with a changing view of culture and cultural transformation, such a conception has been problematized (Handler and Linnekin 1984; Hobsbawm and Ranger 1983). Tradition is no longer perceived as a natural essence or a given but as a social and cultural construction, a dynamic process that embodies both continuity and discontinuity, and the process of creating and recreating tradition entails negotiation and power struggles among local dwellers and on-site actors.

Tradition is always in the crossfire of competing agents (Bronner 2005; Jing 1996), and making the past serve the present involves constant power struggles among different actors. These actors may have different agendas and motivations for employing cultural constructions to turn a combination of distant myths, historical representations, and imagined realities into collective beliefs (Jing 1996), and they may even compete with one another to gain control of constructed traditions in both discourse and practice. Within these constant negotiations, different agents and their concept of tradition may dominate at different times—this concept can be constantly changing, and so the historical process is open, the connection between the past and the present always changing, and the relationship among local actors fluid.

Theorizing Tradition in Folklore Studies

Tradition is one of the core terms in American folklore studies and is itself traditional in the field (Oring 2013). Elliott Oring tracks its usage by John

Aubrey in his *Miscellanies* in 1696 and W. J. Thoms's use of *local traditions* in his 1846 letter to the *Athenaeum* in which he proposed his neologism *folklore* (Oring 2013, 22; Dorson 1968a, 1:53). E. Sydney Hartland character-ized folklore as the "science of tradition" in the last years of the nineteenth century (Dorson 1968a, 2:231). Since then tradition has remained central to most definitions of folklore and is regarded as one of a few key words in American folklore studies (Oring 2013, 22).

Francis Lee Utley (1965) establishes *tradition* as the prominent word in his proposed conglomerate definition of folklore. Dan Ben-Amos (1971) has challenged this criterion in the definition of folklore, arguing that "the tra-ditional character of folklore" is an analytical construct by scholars instead of a cultural reality. In his essay "The Seven Strands of Tradition: Varieties in Its Meaning in American Folklore Studies," Ben-Amos (1984) identified a variety of ways that folklorists have used *tradition*: as lore, canon, pro-cess, mass, culture, langue, and performance. By drawing on sources from different publications during different periods, Ben-Amos intends to con-struct an intellectual history of the construction of the term by folklorists. In conclusion, he writes:

> The seven strands of tradition are exposed not for choice nor for pref-erence; none is more adequate than the other, none is more proper than the other. Together they reveal the meanings tradition has had in American folklore studies, and together these meanings constitute the history of the term. As a key word, it has served students of differ-ent periods and different persuasions. All retained the term but pre-ferred to shift and twist the meanings for their own theoretical and methodological purposes. Like selective tradition itself, tradition has accumulated its own traditional meanings through a process of selec-tion and combination of ideas and references. Tradition has survived criticism and remained a symbol of and for folklore. It has been one of the principal metaphors to guide us in the choate world of experi-ences and ideas. As a metaphor that has been in such common use, tradition also accumulated a patina of meanings with its own luster. But behind the shine there is also an accumulation of frustrations, ambiguities, trends and directions for which the history of folklore could be a guiding map. (Ben-Amos 1984, 124)

Oring continues to explore the important questions left by Ben-Amos, pro-posing that "the major problem of tradition in folklore studies is that it has not sufficiently been regarded as a problem." (2013, 43) For instance, he criticizes the way *tradition* has been used as a label to mark new territories of folklore studies such as digitalized and online communication, and he suggests that folklorists should think deeply about the term to shape substantive questions for the field.

The reframing of tradition as a symbolic construction instead of a core of inherited essences was intertwined with the paradigm shifting in the humanities and social sciences in the 1970s and 1980s. Since the early 1980s, scholars in different fields began to focus on a set of interrelated terms—"practice, praxis, action, interaction, activity, experience, performance"—while a second interconnected set of terms related to "the doer of all that doing: agent, actor, person, self, individual, subject" (Ortner 1984, 144). Sherry Ortner mentions that an English translation of Pierre Bourdieu's book *Outline of a Theory of Practice* was published in 1977, and it was about that time that "a more practice-oriented approach" began to spread in many academic fields. In general, this approach was situated to oppose the dominant, essentially Parsonian/Durkheimian, narrative that saw the world as ordered by rules and norms. Scholars who espoused this approach intended to examine the interaction between the system and human action. Under these trends, the concept of tradition itself has been deconstructed and reconstructed as a historical process in folklore studies.

In the book *The Invention of Tradition*, six historians and anthropologists argue that traditions that appear or claim to be ancient can be quite recent in origin and are sometimes literally invented in a single event or over a short time period (Hobsbawm and Ranger 1983). In the introduction, Eric Hobsbawm defines *invented tradition* as follows:

> "Invented tradition" is taken to mean a set of practices, normally governed by overtly or tacitly accepted rules and of a ritual or symbolic nature, which seek to inculcate certain values and norms of behavior by repetition, which automatically implies continuity with the past. In fact, where possible, they normally attempt to establish continuity with a suitable historic past. . . . However, insofar as there is such reference to a historic past, the peculiarity of "invented" traditions is that the continuity with it is largely fictitious. In short, they are responses to novel situations which take the form of reference to old situations, or which establish their own past by quasi-obligatory repetition. (1983, 1–2)

Hobsbawm states that there is probably no time and place that has not seen the invention of tradition, although he also argues that invented traditions occur more frequently at times of rapid social transformation when old traditions are disappearing. Furthermore, Hobsbawm distinguishes between three types of invented traditions, which each have a distinctive function: (1) those establishing or symbolizing social cohesion and collective identities; (2) those establishing or legitimatizing institutions and social hierarchies; and (3) those socializing people into particular social contexts (Hobsbawm 1983, 9). The power of invented traditions is significant, but it is intertwined with the power of genuine traditions (Oring 2013). The invention does not come from nowhere; instead it is rooted in the inheritance of the past, which is crucial to connect people together in the present.

Richard Handler and Jocelyn Linnekin (1984) suggest that *tradition* refers to an interpretive process that embodies both continuity and discontinuity and that it must be understood as a wholly symbolic construction. Their statement has challenged the intellectual discourses and common concepts about tradition. The dichotomy between tradition and modernity is unjustified, and the distinction between authenticity and fakeness is blurred. However, they do not exhaust the possible roles that the past may play in the contemporary world, nor do they engage with the interpretation of tradition as a process of cultural reproduction (Oring 2013). They adapt emic perspectives to study what is claimed as traditional by practitioners, but they fail to show the conflicts between the etic and emic perspectives and the negotiation process between scholars and practitioners.

Dorothy Noyes (2009) summarizes three key words from the historical interpretation of tradition: *communication*, *ideology*, and *property*. Indicating change and separation, the second key word in the view of tradition as "a temporal ideology" is elaborated with the binary contrast to the theory of modernity. As Bengt Holbek (1992) points out, the changing attitude toward tradition derived from a change in ideology. For example, in the nineteenth century, the church gradually lost its status in Europe, and people began to explore a new focus of identification, finding it in the nation and the conception of progress. This change in ideology provided a revolutionary basis for the bourgeoisie, which became the leading class during that time (Holbek 1992, 10). In this historical process, tradition was first viewed as pure, natural, and original, and it was used as an alternative way to establish a new identity for the nation; later on, it had to be discarded in a modern society, where the main goal was progress (Holbek 1992, 11). Of course, this statement is a little oversimplified, but it reveals the vulnerability of tradition to outside influences in the modern world. Confronted with the dilemma between preservation and progress, scholars discover that tradition is not necessarily opposite to modernity but is mixed with it as an integrated body: "Just as the traditional is modern, so the modern is traditional. . . . Closely examined, all culture is recycled" (Noyes 2009, 244).

Despite its central role in American folklore studies, the idea of tradition has not helped folklorists to frame new questions or to think about how the study of cultural products and practices could contribute to an understanding of tradition as a process of "cultural reproduction" (Oring 2013, 25). An ethnographic approach will enrich our understanding of tradition as a process and help us to highlight how both etic and emic concepts matter on the ground. The key issues to explore include the following: "How are beliefs and practices taught and learned; what is the source of the authority of tradition and how does its force make itself felt; how do past practices continue to operate in the present and how and why do new practices come to destroy or marginalize the old?" (Oring 2013, 42). Folklore fieldwork can address these problems in considerable ways.

From Tradition to Heritage

Since the early 1990s, *tradition* as a term has been problematized by Barbara Kirshenblatt-Gimblett (1995, 1998a, 1998b) in many of her works. In her presidential address to the American Folklore Society in 1993, Kirshenblatt-Gimblett (1998b) argued that folklore must reimagine itself in a transformed disciplinary and cultural landscape. She explored why the field of folklore studies, historically constituted as "the science of tradition," had so much difficulty coming to grips with the contemporary. Her objective is to return to the problem of tradition—not to defend folklore's canonical subject but rather to take the popular "misperceptions" of folklore as indicative of the truths of heritage as they emerge from contemporary practice (Kirshenblatt-Gimblett 1995, 1998b).

Kirshenblatt-Gimblett's "Theorizing Heritage" (1995) reconsiders folklore studies as "the science of tradition" and builds folklore's contemporary subject as the study of "heritage." She problematizes the concept of tradition, while also attempting to capture the different truths of heritage as they emerge from contemporary practice. She defines *heritage* for the sake of her argument as "the transvaluation of the obsolete, the mistaken, the outmoded, the dead, and the defunct" and claims that "heritage is created through a process of exhibition (as knowledge, as performance, as museum display)" and that exhibition "endows heritage thus conceived with a second life" (Kirshenblatt-Gimblett 1995, 369). She examines the historical process of "producing heritage" and the political economy of the heritage industry in a contemporary world.

According to Kirshenblatt-Gimblett (1995, 369), heritage produces something new "in the present that has recourse to the past," it adds value to existing assets that either have ceased to be viable or were never economically productive, and the heritage industry exports its product through tourism. Furthermore, she questions what was at stake for those whose heritage is represented and exhibited in new productions. Basically, heritage for insiders is estranged and exhibited for outsiders, and new meanings are produced in the process. The interface, the means by which heritage is represented onstage, such as in folk festivals, museum exhibitions, and historical villages, thus became a powerful engine of meaning and cultural form. Authenticity became irrelevant or incapable of explaining anything in these cases, and whatever concerned insiders and outsiders at present was reviewed as important.

Despite its social and cultural advantages, heritage has also been problematized in intellectual discourse. Denis Byrne (2009) advocates for resisting the tendency of heritage discourse to reduce culture to things and for countering its privileging of physical fabric over social life. As an archaeologist working in the heritage field, Byrne understands that, in addition to the problems of what survives and what is recoverable, there is the problem of what, in any given political and social context, will be given attention. In his eyes, *heritage* is "a certain way of knowing archaeological objects and sites, a certain way of drawing attention to them, of bringing them forward and valorising them" (Byrne 2009, 230). He argues that the selectivity of heritage discourse can serve to bury or efface certain places at the same time as it reveals and celebrates certain others. He specifically considers the case of mass graves belonging to the era of the Cold War by looking at how people remember and commemorate past events behind the scenes. In some of his cases, this constitutes a kind of "counter-heritage" in which places are commemorated despite official heritage discourse. This kind of heritage is also termed *negative heritage*, illustrating how whole categories of heritage can lie hidden in the landscapes of everyday life. Whether they truly are hidden or not does not matter—in these contexts they are unmentionable, and that is the point. As Byrne shows, in many countries of the world, quite significant parts of the history of the modern era, and the sites associated with this history, remain in the category of the unmentionable, primarily because they convey important meanings to a part of the population who are disempowered. Therefore, heritage is always produced as a historical process mired in the politics of tangibility and visibility.

I agree with Byrne's insightful interpretation of the politics of heritage, and I choose to still use the term *tradition* in my own research despite its problems in discourse and practice. I intend to define *tradition* as a historical process of different actors' making, deconstructing, remaking, and negotiating cultural continuity and change between the past and the present, mired in the integration of power struggles and individual agency.

In "Cultural Heritage," Valdimar T. Hafstein writes that "heritage says more about us than it does about past generations or what they've left behind" (2012, 512). Similar to heritage, tradition is also a construction that is recreated anew in response to contemporary needs and ideas. Hafstein compares *heritage* with *environment* and reviews both as "a new category of things, lumped together in novel ways under its rubric," and he further points out that both seek not to "describe" the world but to "change" it (Hafstein 2012, 502). Therefore, heritage is about change, and about the question of who has the power to make a change.

Heritage Regimes and Global and State Actors

The broad ethnographic literature on heritage production and heritage management records the various dimensions of ideological logics and processes that transform tradition into heritage (e.g., Smith and Akagawa 2009; Bendix, Eggert, and Peselmann 2012; Hafstein 2012). Discussing the results of patrimonial interventions, Dorothy Noyes highlights the bureaucratic power of heritage regimes that create tensions in the understanding of culture and that change the uses of traditions (Noyes 2006). Heritage as an ideological process is "a regime in rapid expansion" (Hafstein 2012, 502), and this expansion depends on the particular institutional nature of heritage regimes that are organized according to western bureaucratic logics (Bendix, Eggert, and Peselmann 2012). Bureaucracies expand in a notorious manner as soon as they are created. Consequently, bureaucratic institutions continuously legitimize their existence and their search for new fields of action, and their expansion is accompanied by the need for money, which requires further legitimation. In this process, a vast number of social actors have seized upon the new fields to legitimize their institutional existence. UNESCO, established in 1946, is the most influential actor in heritage making and management, and it has been enormously successful in making local, regional, national, and international discourses on and practices of heritage.

One of UNESCO's original achievements was to adopt the Convention for the Protection of Cultural Property in the Event of Armed Conflict in 1954. In the several decades following this, UNESCO developed separate legal instruments and bodies for the protection of cultural property and the safeguarding of cultural heritage. Today UNESCO is well known for its 2003 Convention for the Safeguarding of the Intangible Cultural Heritage, resulting in a Representative List of the Intangible Cultural Heritage of Humanity, which was changed from the original Masterpieces of the Oral and Intangible Heritage of Humanity. Since 2003, many member states have ratified the convention, and states find varied ways to shape their preexisting efforts to protect or promote local culture in terms of UNESCO's global efforts and to operate selection processes and administrative policies locally. Therefore, heritage regimes have been shaped dynamically at the state level and have interacted with international heritage regimes (Bendix, Eggert, and Peselmann 2012).

When tradition is turned into heritage, or cultural property, it receives a number of new dimensions and meanings and gives rise to new owners and actors, often in conflict with old meanings, perspectives, owners, and actors. In the process of heritage making, global, national, and regional actors have come to actively interplay and compete with each other, therefore causing a series of transformations that disempower old owners and users (Hauser-Schäublin 2012b).

Intangible Cultural Heritage

The concept of intangible cultural heritage (ICH) emerged in the 1990s as a counterpart to world heritage, which focuses mainly on tangible aspects of culture. In 2001 UNESCO made a survey among states and nongovernmental organizations to try to agree on a definition, and the Convention for the Safeguarding of the Intangible Cultural Heritage was drafted in 2003 for their protection. According to the 2003 convention, ICH is the mainspring of humanity's cultural diversity, and its maintenance is a guarantee for continuing creativity. It is defined as follows:

> The "intangible cultural heritage" means the practices, representations, expressions, knowledge, skills—as well as the instruments, objects, artifacts and cultural spaces associated therewith—that communities, groups and, in some cases, individuals recognize as part of their cultural heritage. This intangible cultural heritage, transmitted from generation to generation, is constantly recreated by communities and groups in response to their environment, their interaction with nature and their history, and provides them with a sense of identity and continuity, thus promoting respect for cultural diversity and human creativity. For the purposes of this Convention, consideration will be given solely to such intangible cultural heritage as is compatible with existing international human rights instruments, as well as with the requirements of mutual respect among communities, groups and individuals, and of sustainable development . . . The "intangible cultural heritage," as defined in paragraph 1 above, is manifested inter alia in the following domains:
>
> (a) oral traditions and expressions, including language as a vehicle of the intangible cultural heritage;
> (b) performing arts;
> (c) social practices, rituals and festive events;
> (d) knowledge and practices concerning nature and the universe;
> (e) traditional craftsmanship. (UNESCO 2003)

In reality, the construction of the concept of ICH has been a long historical process with debates and controversies (Aikawa-Faure 2009). Since World War II, UNESCO has supported a series of world heritage initiatives, starting with tangible heritage, both immovable and movable, and expanding to natural heritage and most recently to intangible heritage. Although there are three separate heritage lists, there is increasing awareness of the arbitrariness of the categories and their interrelatedness (Kirshenblatt-Gimblett 2004). Over several decades of attempts to define intangible heritage—previously and sometimes still called folklore—there has been an important shift in the concept of intangible heritage to include not only the masterpieces but also the masters. The earlier folklore model supported scholars and institutions who documented and preserved a record of disappearing traditions. The most recent model aims to sustain a living, if endangered, tradition by supporting the conditions necessary for cultural reproduction. This means according value to the carriers and transmitters of traditions, as well as to their habitus and habitat (Kirshenblatt-Gimblett 2004).

On May 18, 2001, after decades of debate over terminology, definition, goals, and safeguarding measures for what had previously been designated "traditional culture and folklore," UNESCO finally announced the first nineteen Masterpieces of the Oral and Intangible Heritage of Humanity. The list, the most tangible outcome of decades of UNESCO's negotiation, then became the most controversial issue in the project. Scholars problematized the nature of this list and the logic in making it, and many who participated in the development of the intangible heritage initiative wanted to focus on actions that would directly support local cultural reproduction rather than on those that would create such metacultural artifacts as the list (Kirshenblatt-Gimblett 2004).

After the establishment of the 2003 convention on ICH, UNESCO changed the masterpieces list to the Representative List of the Intangible Cultural Heritage of Humanity, which is claimed to be made up of "those intangible heritage practices and expressions that help demonstrate the diversity of this heritage and raise awareness about its importance" (UNESCO 2008). Since 2009, the List of Intangible Cultural Heritage in Need of Urgent Safeguarding has also been produced, and it is composed of "intangible heritage elements that concerned communities and States Parties consider require urgent measures to keep them alive" (UNESCO 2017). Every year the Intergovernmental Committee for the Safeguarding of Intangible Cultural Heritage meets to evaluate nominations proposed by the states who joined the 2003 convention and to decide whether those cultural practices and expressions of ICH should be inscribed on the convention's lists. As UNESCO's ICH list is made and released annually, the power relations behind its construction become central to a variety of controversies and debates. Within these, there are several key issues related to ICH: What happens when the UNESCO ICH convention is ratified by a specific state? How do UNESCO's global efforts interact with local, regional, and state efforts to conserve and preserve expressive culture? How does the recognition of a form of expressive culture as ICH create changes in the presentation and expression of the nominated traditions, and how do those changes affect local communities? How do local communities respond to those changes? How do they become the active agents for the safeguarding of their own cultural heritage? (Bendix, Eggert, and Peselmann 2012; Foster and Gilman 2015; Adell, Bendix, Bortolotto, and Tauschek 2015; Kuah and Liu 2017). As Khun Eng Kuah and Zhaohui Liu write: "While the state and UNESCO are interested in selected intangible cultural heritage for listing purposes that would bring them national and global prestige, to the local people and community, their intangible cultural heritage is what they consider as their living cultural traditions and they continue to practice them irrespective of whether the state or heritage bodies take notice of them or not. They are less concerned about the hype that surrounds heritage conservation and preservation and they continue to live their life around them" (2017, 2–3). With that in mind, this book sets out to explore the grassroots agency in the process of transmitting, producing, and reproducing tradition, as well as in the process of ICH protection.

Contested Tradition, Cultural Heritage, and Grassroots Agency in China

If *tradition* is an overworked term in Western scholarship, then it is also an overloaded term in Chinese. My main purpose here is not to track comprehensively how *chuantong* (传统), a term equivalent to *tradition* in Chinese, has been constructed, contradicted, and negotiated in Chinese scholarship, since the meanings and functions of this word have changed through time and across space and it would be impossible for me to exhaust all the important sources to achieve that goal. Instead, I will track some major interpretations of the Chinese concept of *chuantong* and define the term for the purpose of my localized ethnographical research.

Chuantong is a "return graphic loan," a Japanese Kanji term derived from classical Chinese that was used to translate the modern European term of *tradition* and that was then reintroduced into modern Chinese (Liu, Lydia He 1995, 302). *Chuantong*, as a classical compound, first appeared in *The Book of the Later Han* (*Hou Hanshu*, 后汉书), which is an official Chinese historical text covering the history of the Han dynasty from 6 to 189 AD. In this text, *chuantong* is used as a verb. It could be translated as "hand down," "pass on," or "transmit." It refers primarily to the inheritance of the imperial system and the transmission of knowledge from one generation to the next, so the sense of continuity in time is crucial. Another word, *chuitong* (垂统), with the same reference as *chuantong*, can be found as early as in the *Mencius* (*Mengzi*, 孟子), which was written by Mencius (ca. 372–289 BC). Like *chuantong*, *chuitong* contains the word *tong*, which means "gather into one," "interconnected system," "together." The concept of *tong* and its usage in classical Chinese language is probably similar to what we refer to as *chuantong* (noun) in modern Chinese. In *Mencius*, *chuitong* is used as a verb that means to hand down what the founder has made, to inherit the imperial throne. This verb is also used in other important historical documents, such as *Records of the Grand Historian* (*Shiji*, 史记) and *Comprehensive Mirror in Aid of Governance* (*Zizhi Tongjian*, 资治通鉴). Like *chuantong*, *chuitong* means to hand down, and the main things handed down for generations are the kingdom and the imperial throne. In these texts, the term *chuantong* conveys the intertwining relationship between political hegemony and continuity in ancient China.

In *Collected Essays from the Shaoshi Shanfang Studio* (*Shaoshi Shanfang Bicong*, 少室山房笔丛) (1589), Hu Yinglin (胡應麟) (1551–1602) differentiated *jiuliu* (九流), nine different schools in the pre-Qin period, and pointed out the domination of Confucianism in intellectual history, writing: "The 'Nine Schools' [classification] revised by myself consists of: first, the Confucians; second, the Miscellaneous School (I have put the Logicians and the Legalists into one school and have named it the Miscellaneous School; I have also included the ancient Miscellaneous School here); third, the Military Strategists; fourth, the Agriculturists; fifth, the Diviners; sixth, the Arts; seventh, the Xiaoshuo School; eighth, the Daoists; and ninth, the Buddhists. The Confucian School contains mainly subsidiary orthodox teachings; and the doctrines of learned scholars and famous sages are included in appendices" (余所更定九流一曰儒二曰杂[总名法诸家为一故曰杂古杂家亦附焉]曰兵四曰农五曰术六曰艺七曰说八曰道九曰释儒主传统翼教而硕士名贤之训附之) (Hu 1958, 345). *Chuantong* here could be translated as "orthodox teachings," among which Confucianism is the dominant teaching—in this context, the term has clear ideological indications.

Confucianism had been established as the official state ideology of China since the Han dynasty, but it was challenged and attacked after the overthrow of the imperial system in the revolution of 1911. The May Fourth intellectuals[1] believed that the Confucian tradition stifled the progress of China and that the corrupt bureaucratic system increased the political and military crisis in the nation. Within the new ideological and political order established by the new Republic of China (1912–49), Chinese intellectuals attempted to find an alternative ideology to guide China and ensure its prosperity. They suggested that this new teaching should not be based on either Confucianism or Western thought. In their search for new ideas, the intellectuals "discovered" previously ignored folklore (Schneider 1971; Hung 1985). In this folk literature movement, folklorists identified the entire Chinese tradition with Confucianism and launched a fierce attack on it. Gu Jiegang was a pioneer in this movement, and he was also a leading force in the Doubting Antiquity School (*Yigu pai*, 疑古派). On the basis of the historical skepticism of his mentor Hu Shi, Gu put forward a "stratification theory" to explain the limited and contingent knowledge contemporary historians possessed about China's distant past. He argued that as time passes, historical myths become longer and more elaborate and mythical figures take on increasingly heroic and superhuman features. Because of this natural process of mythmaking, it is impossible for us to know the actual truth of ancient historical events and peoples; rather, historians can know only the situation relating to the most recent written examples of these legends. For Gu and other "doubters of antiquity," the essential question was not "What really happened in ancient China?" but rather "Why did past historians write what they did?" (Leibold 2006, 193–99).

On March 20, 1928, Gu Jiegang gave a famous lecture entitled "Sages' Culture and People's Culture" (*Shengxian wenhua yu minzhong wenhua*, 圣贤文化与民众文化) at Lingnan University (岭南大学). In this lecture, he first pointed out that the whole of Chinese history was recorded by and for the ruling class, while the common people were voiceless in this grand history. Gu's goal was to change this situation and construct the history of the common people. His motto was "study old culture and create new culture" (*yanjiu jiu wenhua, chuangzao xin wenhua*, 研究旧文化，创造新文化), which is a continuation of the May Fourth intellectuals' goal. Furthermore, Gu's classification of "Sages' Culture and People's Culture" corresponds to the May Fourth intellectuals' idea of two literatures—that is, aristocratic literature and people's, or folk, literature. Although this dichotomy in Chinese literature and culture is a little oversimplified and not clearly defined, the critique of the dominant ideology and the promotion of common people's traditions reflected Chinese intellectuals' ideals of democracy and social equality, particularly at a chaotic time of foreign aggression, internal disorder, and dissatisfaction with old ideology. However, is aristocratic literature really in opposition to folk literature? Is sages' culture opposite to folk culture? Who are aristocrats and sages, and who are the folk? All these questions hadn't been fully explored by Chinese scholars. Moreover, China underwent dramatic changes and transformation in the twentieth century. The ruling class was first overturned by the 1911 Revolution, and then by the revolution launched by the Chinese Communist Party. If the class of aristocrats did dominate in imperial China, it was overthrown and oppressed in Maoist China. The old ruling class became subordinate, relegated to the bottom of society during the Cultural Revolution. Under these circumstances, how should we define what is high and what is low? And how may we conceptualize its reversion and hybridity in the twentieth century?

The Mao era was an anti-traditionalist period (Chau 2006), and many traditional activities, such as temple fairs and incense burning, were attacked and banned as "feudal superstitions" during the Socialist Education Movement (also called the Four Cleanups) (1963–66). During the Cultural Revolution (1966–76), the dismantlement of local traditions reached its height, and many practitioners of tradition were attacked and even sent to labor camps or prisons. In the late 1970s, the policy of anti-traditionalism started to change. In the reform era, many people rebuilt or renovated temples and other important traditional places that had been dismantled during the Cultural Revolution, and they also revived traditional activities that had once been banned as feudal superstitions. Many practitioners of old traditions resumed their practice, and many new actors emerged.

Tradition, targeted for eradication from the New Culture Movement to the Cultural Revolution, has become an important resource for capitalist development, political legitimization, and cultural identification in the twenty-first century, especially with the widespread promotion of ICH protection throughout China. Tradition has been frequently used in academic works and general publications. It also became the key word used to define ICH.

The definition of ICH promoted by UNESCO overlaps with the idea of folklore in general, and folklorists have laid a good foundation for the construction of this concept and made great contributions to its development and promotion worldwide (An 2008, 14–17). China officially joined the Convention for the Safeguarding of the Intangible Cultural Heritage in August 2004, and on March 26, 2005, the State Council of the PRC issued the official document "Recommendations on the Strengthening of the Safeguarding of China's Intangible Cultural Heritage" (*Guanyu jiaqiang woguo feiwuzhi wenhua yichan baohu gongzuo de yijian*) (2005a), which recommended establishing a list of China's national ICH and protecting "representative transmitters" (*daibiaoxing chuancheng ren*) of national items of ICH. In 2005 the State Council also issued the "Circular on the Strengthening of Protection for Cultural Heritage" (*Jiaqiang wenhua yichan baohu de tongzhi*) (2005b), which further established the principles and policies of the safeguarding of ICH and established the second Saturday of June as Cultural Heritage Day (*wenhua yichan ri*). The Intangible Cultural Heritage Law was enacted in China in 2011. It put forward normative requirements of ICH protection as three aspects: survey system, directory system, and transmission system. With this law, China now has a legal framework to protect ICH (Ye 2015). With the participation and promotion of the Chinese central government and local governments, this project soon spread as a national political campaign all over the country. Since Xi Jinping's election as president of China in 2012, he has promoted the dream of "the great rejuvenation of the Chinese nation." This program reveals the strong appeal of using both tangible and intangible heritage as a platform for nation-state building and nationalist imagination in contemporary China.

One of the most tangible and representative outcomes of the ICH protection in China is the existence of national lists of ICH made by the Ministry of Culture and approved by the State Council. Up to 2015, four national lists of ICH have been released: the first list of 518 items was released in May 2006, the second list of 510 items was released in June 2008 (with an extended list of 147 items), the third list of 191 items was announced in May 2011 (with an extended list of 164 items), and the fourth list of 153 items was publicized in November 2014 (with an extended list of 153 items). In total, 1,372 elements are designated as China's national ICH. In addition, 13,087 ICH elements were designated at the provincial level by 2016 (CICHPC 2016).

All the elements in the national lists have been categorized into ten genres: "folk literature" (*minjian wenxue*, 民间文学), "traditional music" (*chuantong yinyue*, 传统音乐), "traditional dance" (*chuantong wudao*, 传统舞蹈), "traditional opera" (*chuantong xiju*, 传统戏剧), "performing arts" (*quyi*, 曲艺), "traditional physical activities, games, and acrobatics" (*chuantong tiyu, youyi yu zaji*, 传统体育、游艺与杂技), "traditional fine arts" (*chuantong meishu*, 传统美术), "traditional craft skills" (*chuantong jiyi*, 传统技艺), "traditional medicine" (*chuantong yiyao*, 传统医药), and "folklore" (*minsu*, 民俗). *Chuantong* is primarily used as an adjective on the lists and is translated as "traditional," indicating the construction of connections from the past to the present. Originally, the genres contained the term *folk* (*minjian*,

民间), but this term was gradually replaced by *chuantong* in the lists, since the high and low dichotomy has been blurred in the new context of ICH preservation. In particular, traditional music, traditional dance, and traditional fine arts were originally categorized as "folk music" (*minjian yinyue*, 民间音乐), "folk dance" (*minjian wuda*, o 民间舞蹈), and "folk fine arts" (*minjian meishu*, 民间美术), in the national list of 2006; *traditional* (*chuantong*) replaced *folk* (*minjian*) and became a dominating key word in the lists that came out in 2008, 2011, and 2014. *Folk* was problematized in these cases because it could not cover a variety of genres that were favored by the ruling class in ancient China. For instance, the *guqin*, an ancient seven-string Chinese musical instrument played by scholars and literati in ancient China, was proclaimed as one of the Masterpieces of the Oral and Intangible Heritage of Humanity by UNESCO in 2003, and it was selected as an item of national ICH under the genre of folk music in 2006. It stands juxtaposed to many regional and ethnic folk songs on the national list. It is not convincing to place the *guqin* under the category of folk music, but *traditional music* makes sense.

In my research, I intend to explore the grassroots and individual agency in the process of reconstructing tradition and protecting ICH, especially in its relation to powerful heritage regimes, from collaborative and bottom-up approaches. Like tradition, the individual is not a natural given but is constructed from a dynamic process of making and remaking. As Ray Cashman writes: "The individual is best understood not as a bounded, natural, static entity but as an on-going work-in-process—enacted, maintained, and revised through performance, recursive and changeable over time" (2011, 303). Cashman draws on the ethnography of communication to illustrate the interrelationship between tradition and the individual, and he shows us how his star uses narratives from traditional resources to interpret and criticize his own society as well as articulate and project "a coherent moral self" (2011, 303). The remaining issue that I seek to address is how to review the role of power and agency in this individual-as-process. What motivates an individual to reconstruct tradition and protect heritage? Is individual action determined by tradition and power? Do actors act for their own identifiable reasons?

Among individuals who make tradition, I focus on the cultural group of folk literati. Gu Jiegang once named this group "the intellectual class among the common people" (*minzhong li de zhishi jieji*, 民众里的知识阶级) when he examined their creation of "song books" (*chang ben*, 唱本) and "popular songs" (*su qu*, 俗曲) in the context of folklore studies (Gu 1929). However, some scholars disagreed with this characterization. They called this cultural group "low-class literati" and argued that their creations should not be included in the field of folklore studies (Gu and Wu 1931). This controversy has never been completely resolved (Hung 1985). In my book, I draw on my ethnographic research to argue for the important role of folk literati in remaking local traditions, and I support the idea that they should not be excluded from the field of folklore studies.

The Shifting Role of Literati in Modern China

Wenren (men of culture, 文人) is the Chinese term used for the concept of literati I survey in this book; they were also called *shi* (仕 or 士) in earlier times (Jin 1984; Yu 1987). These terms generally refer to those who were well trained in classical Chinese literature and culture and who felt a sense of social responsibility toward cultural production and cultural transmission. In Chinese history, *wenren* generally aspired to political office, and many of them passed the national examinations and became scholar-officials, actively engaging in governance and politics (Yu 1987). The distinction between *wenren* and *shi* was not particularly important during the Tang and the Northern Song dynasties because most *wenren* were in one way or another admitted into the official world. However, the situation started to change dramatically during the Yuan dynasty (1271–1368), when the Mongol rulers ranked the literati near the bottom of the hierarchy of social classes and restrained their role in politics (Huang 1995). According to Yoshikawa Kōjirō (1989), it was during the Yuan dynasty that *wenren* was first used to describe those literati who were not officials and who devoted themselves to literature and art while often displaying a distance from Confucian morals or accepted social norms. Although the social position of the literati improved during the Ming dynasty (1368–1644), the intensified competition in the civil service examinations kept most of them out of officialdom. With the Manchu rule during the Qing dynasty (1644–1912), the social status of literati diversified and fragmented. Some *wenren* chose to concentrate on literary writing and other cultural activities, and some became professional scholars who contributed to the eventual rise of a new intellectual movement, the so-called "evidential scholarship" (*kaozheng*, 考证) movement (Huang 1995).

Yu Yingshi defines literati as the intellectual class and summarizes their essential goal as "transmission and creation of culture and thought" (*wenhua he sixiang de chuancheng yu chuangxin,* 文化和思想的传承与创新) (Yu 1987, 1). Citing the philosopher Zengzi (505–436 BC), he lays out the goal of literati in Chinese culture: "Literati may not be without breadth of mind and vigorous endurance, for his burden is heavy and his course is long. Practicing and spreading the teaching benevolence is his responsibility—is it not heavy? Only with death does his course stop—is it not long?" (士不可以不弘毅，任重而道遠。仁以為己任，不亦重乎? 死而後已，不亦遠乎?) ("Taibo" in *Lunyu;* Yu 1987, 3). He points out that the literati tradition continued in China for more than two thousand years, starting from Confucius's time (551–479 BC); however, this social group was never homogenous or stable through Chinese history. According to Yu, those identified as literati varied during different periods, and the literati tradition was thus a dynamic one. The purpose of Yu's research was to situate literati within particular political, economic, social, cultural, and intellectual contexts and to examine their specific roles during certain periods through premodern Chinese history (Yu 1987). He also extends his theoretical framework to study the changing social status of Chinese intellectuals through the early twentieth century, after the collapse of the Qing dynasty and after the May Fourth Movement (Yu 1997, 1993). Picking up where Yu leaves off, I explore the shifting social status of literati after the establishment of the new revolutionary regime in China in 1949. I also want to highlight the fact that this group of people is still known as literati in local communities, instead of intellectuals (*zhishi fenzi,* 知识分子).

The differentiation and connection between traditional literati and modern intellectuals have been widely discussed by scholars from different perspectives. Since the late Qing dynasty, the literati, associated with tradition and classical literature, have been viewed as the polar opposite of modern progressive intellectuals (Jin 1984; Denton 1996). The term *intellectuals* or *zhishi fenzi* was borrowed from the West (Jin 1984), and it indicates a break with the traditional literati both structurally and ideologically (Hao 2003). Hao Chang dates this break to the 1890s, when the new intelligentsia challenged Confucianism's basic morals and its concept of social order (Chang 1971). Yu Yingshi symbolically marks 1905—the year when the old examination system was abolished—as the dividing line between the traditional literati and the modern intellectuals "because the latter was no longer linked to state power as the former was" (Yu 1993, 143). Li Zehou and Vera Schwarcz (1983–84) viewed the first generation of modern Chinese intellectuals as beginning with the generation of 1911, the year when the 1911 Revolution overthrew the Qing dynasty and established the Republic of China.

Despite different theories about the circumstances of the rupture between traditional literati and modern intellectuals during the early twentieth century, some scholars highlight the connection and the continuity between them. Hao Zhidong argues that the transition from literati to intellectuals did not mean that the modern intellectual was a completely different breed from the traditional literatus; they might have parted with tradition, but they were still deeply rooted in it (Hao 2003). His argument is an extension of Robert Scalapino and George Yu's statement: "The 'new intellectual' remained the keeper of the old as well as the bearer of the new. Skill in calligraphy, poetry, painting, and knowledge of the great Chinese literary classics remained the mark of the educated man" (Scalapino and Yu 1985, 486). Hao raises the example of Mao Zedong (1893–1976) to foster his argument, illustrating that Mao was "the most revolutionary of all" but "was deeply immersed in traditional literature, loved calligraphy and poetry, and practiced the traditional ways of ruling the country" (Hao 2003, 383). Hao emphasizes the continuity between traditional literati and modern intellectuals, making it clear that the modern intellectuals had expanded their roles by incorporating Western thinking into their traditional learning; however, they also kept carrying on their social responsibility and sometimes served in the official world as the old literati class did (Hao 2003). Although this social group has been reshaped and reoriented through time, they tend to embody the combination of new trends and traits with old ones, instead of completely breaking with tradition.

One of the most dramatic changes happened to Chinese literati or intellectuals after the establishment of the People's Republic of China (PRC) when this social group was continuously reformed by the Communist Party of China (CPC) and suffered during a variety of political movements, including the Anti-Rightist Campaign (from roughly 1957–59), the Socialist Education Movement (1963–66), and finally the Cultural Revolution (1966–76). During these political movements, old literati and new intellectuals were marginalized and relegated to the bottom of society, some were sent to prison, and some were executed or committed suicide (Hao 2003). The goal of these movements was to purge dissidents from within the party and beyond, reinforce the hegemony of Marxism-Leninism-Mao Zedong thought, and create a high degree of "political uniformity" (Hao 2003, 74). Independent thinking and even the mildest criticism were suppressed, and some intellectuals were labeled "counterrevolutionary." With political uniformity dominating the Mao era, intellectuals seemed voiceless in public under the new revolutionary Communist regime. In reality, the situations were much more complicated than what we could imagine. Yang Kuisong draws on three important case studies of Chinese intellectuals—the philosopher Zhang Dongsun (张东荪) (1886–1973), the journalist Wang Yunsheng (王芸生) (1901–80), and the sociologist and eugenicist Pan Guangdan (潘光旦) (1899–1967)—to examine how Chinese intellectuals had conceptualized and adapted to dramatic political transformation in China after 1949, how they differed in their adaptation, and how those differences led to different endings in their personal lives. Yang does not give an overview of the interaction between intellectuals and politics during the Mao era; his purpose is to situate Chinese intellectuals within particular changing political contexts after 1949, unfolding their struggles and contested ideas about new ideology. He attempts to argue against the idea that most Chinese intellectuals changed their political standpoints simply because of brainwashing by the Communists. Instead, he points out that their real situations varied case by case in practice and argued that we cannot draw any final conclusions from their different personal experiences.

Interestingly, Yang Kuisong uses the concept of scholars (*shusheng*, 书生) to refer to China's intellectual class, and this concept is interchangeable with the term *literati* in his book. Yang defines this social group broadly as "those who read books and pursue spiritual goals in their lifetime" (*yi jingshen mubiao wei bisheng zhuiqiu de dushu ren*, 以精神目标为毕生追求的读书人) (2013, iv). He further points out that *shusheng* had many weaknesses and problems in their individual lives, such as cowardice, irresolution, and the inability to deal sensibly with practical matters and build social networks. However, they couldn't help caring about local people and carrying out their social responsibilities at crucial moments in history. Unlike other scholars who were inclined to suggest that Chinese intellectuals had completely lost their independence and ability to think critically during the Mao era (Li and Ying 1999; Wei 2004), Yang makes no moral judgments about those Chinese intellectuals. Rather, he attempts to put forward a nuanced understanding of their ideas and situations within particular political contexts and to view them as normal human beings who experienced one of the most dramatic political changes in Chinese history.

Literati and intellectuals were relegated to the bottom of the hierarchy of social classes during the Mao era, but their low status changed after Mao's death in 1976. In the reform era, the CPC shifted its focus from class struggle to economic development, and the intellectual class began to have relative freedom of expression (Hao 2003). Hao Zhidong argues that intellectuals as a group become fragmented after 1978, and the processes of fragmentation and reorganization have accelerated since the democracy movement in 1989. Within these new political and cultural contexts, the school of New Literati Painting (*xin wenren hua*, 新文人画) emerged in the 1990s, and the term *literati* has been resurrected in the post-Mao era, reflecting a new traditionalism (Chen 1999).

Are these new literati playing the same roles as their predecessors? Or are they a new kind of cultural group? What has changed and what has not changed in their cultural production and transmission? With this book, I will examine a group of people who are perceived as literati in village communities and illustrate their roles in producing and remaking local traditions within local contexts. Some of these people passed away before I conducted my fieldwork, but they left behind their manuscripts and a legacy of influence on local people. Some have long engaged in local cultural production, and others are new actors in representing local traditions. The focus will be on eight folk literati in Hongtong as I explore their life narratives and their significant role in tradition revival and reconstruction.

Doing Fieldwork in Hongtong County, Shanxi Province

My work in Hongtong began in spring 2007 when I joined a group of Chinese folklorists to help local communities apply for the nomination of their tradition as China's national ICH (see chap. 6 for further discussion of the ICH application). Then in 2012 and 2013 I conducted six months of fieldwork studying the living beliefs of those worshipping the ancient Chinese sage-emperors Yao and Shun as well as Ehuang and Nüying (Yao's two daughters who married Shun) in several villages in Hongtong County, Linfen City, Shanxi Province, located in the North China region. Archaeological findings at the ruins of Taosi in Linfen stand a good chance of indicating the location of the capital of the Yao period (traditionally ca. 2356–2255 BC). The Old Temple of Emperor Yao was located in Yangxie Village, where local residents call Yao "grandpa" and call his two daughters "aunties." Every year on the third day of the third lunar month, villagers in Yangxie carry Ehuang and Nüying's divine sedan chair to Lishan, where the sisters' memorial temple was located, to receive their two aunties and bring them back to visit the home of their parents in Yangxie. On the twenty-eighth day of the fourth lunar month, which is believed to be Emperor Yao's birthday, a temple fair is held in the Old Temple of Emperor Yao in Yangxie, as villagers from Lishan escort the two sisters back home.

Yao and Shun's age was established as the early beginning of the history of Chinese culture in the *Book of Documents* (*Shangshu*)—the earliest Chinese work of history, thought to have been compiled by Confucius—and in the *Records of the Grand Historian* (*Shiji*), as well as in other historical and literary documents (Chen 2000). Both Yao and Shun have been represented in Chinese history as morally perfect sage-kings. Yao's benevolence and diligence and Shun's filial piety and modesty were highly extolled by Confucian philosophers in later centuries, and they served as a model for Chinese kings and emperors. Nüying is believed to have been born in Hongtong (Yu and Cai 1731), and the base temple for her and her older sister, Ehuang, was built in present-day Lishan. Both of them are worshipped as important deities in Hongtong.

During the annual ritual processions of receiving Ehuang and Nüying in both the third lunar month and the fourth lunar month, the parades usually pass more than twenty villages, where local people burn incense, provide free tea and snacks, genuflect toward the divine sedan chair of Ehuang and Nüying, and ask for blessings. In large villages, local people also play drums and gongs, competing with the players from Yangxie or Lishan. In some villages, free lunches and afternoon meals are provided for the participants in the parade. Residents of Lishan and Wan'an accommodate Yangxie residents respectively on the second and third day of the third lunar month, and Yangxie residents host Lishan and Wan'an residents respectively on the twenty-seventh day and the twenty-eighth day of the fourth lunar month.

This local tradition was listed as one element of China's national ICH by the State Council on June 7, 2008. In the application materials, the original title of the tradition was "'receiving aunties and greeting *niangniang*' visiting relative activities" ("*Jie gugu ying niangniang*' zouqin huodong") (Chen Yongchao 2015, 35). Yangxie residents, viewing themselves as the offspring of Emperor Yao, call Ehuang and Nüying aunties, while the residents around Lishan call Ehuang and Nüying *niangniang* because they view themselves as the offspring of Emperor Shun. Yangxie residents use *receiving aunties* to refer to their annual ritual processions of receiving the deities on the third day of the third lunar month. *Greeting niangniang* is used by residents around Lishan to name their annual ritual processions of welcoming Ehuang and Nüying back on the twenty-eighth day of the fourth lunar month. Because of their distant connections with Yao and

Shun, Yangxie and Lishan residents refer to each other as relatives or sacred relatives, believed to be more intimate and important than secular relatives. In the officially released ICH list, the title was changed to *Hongtong zouqin xisu* (洪洞走亲习俗), the custom of visiting sacred relatives in Hongtong.

In summer 2012 and spring and summer 2013, I went back to Hongtong to conduct my dissertation fieldwork (You 2015a), staying in Yangxie Village with my host family during the majority of my fieldwork. My host "elder brother" Wang Wei and his wife, Miao Hongjun, were extremely hospitable and generous, and they accompanied me as I interviewed many villagers and traveled in the neighborhood. Local shè and temple reconstruction associations also provided me with many sources for study and assistance. I stayed in the Lishan temple complex for two weeks in summer 2012, and the temple reconstruction association there kindly provided me with meals and a place to sleep; my hosts in Wan'an also took very good care of me when I stayed there for one week in summer 2012. I accompanied the annual ritual parades to travel throughout the county over the course of my fieldwork, and many villagers opened their homes to me, generously offering delicious meals and clean beds. I built strong relationships throughout the period of my fieldwork, and my hosts and the villagers I met became like my relatives.

My main fieldwork sites were in the temples of Ehuang and Nüying in Yangxie, Lishan, and Wan'an. I met many local people who came to burn incense and ask for protection from the deities, and some of them were willing to share their personal stories, beliefs, and practices with me. Our conversations flowed naturally, and I got to know their concerns, desires, and wishes. The hundreds of people I encountered and talked with included heads and members of local shè and temple reconstruction associations, opera troupe members, cultural workers, vendors, local officials, ritual specialists, and villagers. In addition to casual conversations, I conducted formal interviews with folk literati, local officials, temple heads, and villagers. Participant observations were also important for my data collection.

I conducted my fieldwork without the accompaniment of any Chinese officials—being native Chinese helped me avoid the official restrictions that often hinder foreign researchers. Even though I am from Henan Province, not far from Shanxi, I still have difficulty in understanding the local dialect in Hongtong. I speak Modern Standard Mandarin, or *Putonghua*, the official language in China, which is comprehensible to most of the people in Hongtong that I encountered, primarily because of the use of Modern Standard Mandarin in television broadcasting. It took me some time and effort to understand the local dialect; fortunately my host family was extremely helpful in this process.

Chapter Outline

My study of local traditions covers a wide range of issues, and therefore a chapter outline will prove helpful. In addition to this introduction and the conclusion, where I revisit the central themes of my study and make a proposal about some trends for further research, the book has six chapters focused on setting the context for my study area, exploring the interaction between folk literati and local traditions, and examining the development of ICH in broader and more local situations.

In chapter 1, I present a general introduction of the history, society, and culture of Hongtong County, Shanxi Province. I describe local beliefs surrounding Ehuang and Nüying and illustrate how beliefs, history, and place are closely integrated by local people. Particularly, I examine intertwined beliefs and local practices regarding Ehuang and Nüying in three places: Yangxie, Lishan, and Wan'an. I introduce the temples of Ehuang and Nüying in these three places as key fieldwork sites.

In chapter 2, I explore the role of folk literati in the process of transmitting, producing, and reproducing local tradition in Hongtong, Shanxi. First, I present the vernacular concept of cultural continuity—"incense is kept burning" (*xianghuo buduan*, 香火不断)—that I encountered during my fieldwork in Yangxie and explore the important role of folk literati in continuing and representing local tradition. Qiao Guoliang (乔国樑), an important folk literatus I learned about during my fieldwork in Yangxie, continued the annual ritual processions of receiving Ehuang and Nüying by himself during the Cultural Revolution and was sent to prison because of it. I draw on my interviews with his family members and his friends to narrate his life stories, and his composed poetry served as a way to explore how he represented himself as a literatus and how he reflected on his shifting role under changing regimes in the twentieth century. Furthermore, I introduce his manuscript "E Ying Zhuan" (Biographies of Ehuang and Nüying), in which he chronicled important events surrounding Ehuang and Nüying and their beliefs in local communities. Particularly, I analyze how he represented local place and space in his writing and how he represented local history and beliefs with a clear understanding of cultural continuity within local contexts. Finally, I demonstrate his political standpoint and examine his role in continuing local traditions as a member of the common people, acting with and for the common people in local communities.

The era of Yao and Shun has been constructed as the early beginning of Chinese cultural history, and their stories have been recorded as an essential part of ancient history in China. However, this long-enduring construction was challenged and overturned by revisionist historians in the early twentieth century; in the process, Yao and Shun's stories were transformed from history into myths (Gu et al. [1926–41] 1982). In chapter 3, I problematize this process of deconstructing ancient history and reconstructing it into myth. My purpose is to draw on my ethnographic case study to explore the living traditions of the worship of Yao and Shun in Hongtong, using locals' points of view to interpret written and oral narratives concerning Yao and Shun that scholars see as myths and analyzing the dynamics of the construction of preliterate history in Chinese local contexts. In particular, I examine how Li Xuezhi, an influential folk literatus, remade Yao and Shun's stories in Hongtong in the 1990s, how he has perceived himself through the reconstruction of contested ancient history, and how he has competed and negotiated with other local folk literati in the process of mythmaking on the ground. I interpret myth as a metadiscourse on the basis of which social actors can construct social borders and also as "a discursive act" through which actors pursue certain cultural, political, and economic goals in practice within constructed communities (Lincoln 2014, 23).

In chapter 4, I draw on a new model of "tradition ecology" to reinterpret the balance of both cultural continuity and innovation in tradition reconstruction as well as the competing agency of folk literati in remaking local legends in Hongtong. In particular, I examine how folk literati have debated and negotiated with each other in remaking the legends about the conflicts between Ehuang and Nüying. I first present the warring relationships between folk literati in Hongtong and their representation and negotiation of Ehuang and Nüying's conflict legends within a community context. Second, I analyze how local common people view the roles of these folk literati in remaking the warring legends and how they receive Ehuang and Nüying's changing conflict legends in local communities.

I explore the relationships that exist between local legends and folk literati in chapter 5, examining how folk literati are constituted as a social group within local contexts, how they are differentiated from and connected with their native fellows, which roles folk literati have played in transmitting and reproducing local legends and beliefs, how they review each other's work, and how they and their work are received in local communities. I also analyze how folk literati interact with other local social actors, including shè, temple reconstruction associations, ritual specialists, and ordinary people. I propose that tradition be conceptualized as a dynamic process of the transfer of appreciation, an ability to understand the meaning or importance of a valued practice or cultural process.

Chapter 6 addresses the dilemma faced by Chinese folklorists in the safeguarding of ICH and the contentious local responses to ICH protection in Hongtong in the late 2000s and the early 2010s. First, I introduce the notion of ICH in the Chinese context and explain how it overlaps with and differs from discourses of *folklore* in China. Second, I discuss the national ICH framework and the applied administrative system in China. Then I draw on my case study to illustrate how *Hongtong zouqin xisu* was selected as an element of ICH at county, provincial, and national levels and which actors played important roles in the process of heritage making. I highlight local conflicts over the designation of ICH and the nomination of "representative transmitters" and discuss why folk literati did not receive the particular designation of "transmitters." Furthermore, I explore the ways local people have responded to the safeguarding of ICH, with a focus on shifting actors and power relations in the process of heritage making. In particular, I analyze shifting power relations among shè, the temple reconstruction associations, and the local state in the process of protecting local traditions as ICH. I argue that the heritage-making process has not empowered the key folk institutions (including shè and the temple reconstruction associations) and folk literati to protect local traditions with and for local people, but has disempowered them and put local communities at the bottom of the power relationship, therefore exaggerating preexisting inequalities between folk society and the local state.

Note

1. The May Fourth Movement was an anti-imperialist, cultural, and political movement growing out of the student demonstrations in Beijing that took place on May 4, 1919. The broader use of the term *May Fourth Movement* often refers to the period of 1915–1921 that is more commonly known as the New Culture Movement, during which scholars such as Chen Duxiu, Cai Yuanpei, Li Dazhao, Lu Xun, Zhou Zuoren, and Hu Shi launched a revolt against Confucianism and called for the creation of a new Chinese culture based on democracy and science.

1

BACKGROUND

Situating Local Beliefs about Ehuang and
Nüying in Hongtong, Shanxi

General Introduction: Hongtong County, Linfen City, Shanxi Province

The northern province of Shanxi in China is known for its long history, its temple architecture, and its rich coal resources (see map 1.1). The province's name literally means "west of mountains," a reference to its location west of the Taihang Mountains. Shanxi borders Hebei to the east, Henan to the south, Shaanxi to the west, and Inner Mongolia to the north, and its landscape primarily consists of a plateau bounded by mountain ranges, along with a central area of valleys where the Fen River runs. Shanxi's name is abbreviated with the character Jin (晋), after the state of Jin that existed in the region during the Spring and Autumn period (approximately 771–476 BC). During the early Warring States period (475–221 BC), the state of Jin was divided into three parts, known as the Three Jins, and this name has been used in many historical documents up to the present.

Linfen is located in the southwestern part of Shanxi (see map 1.2), on the lower reaches of the Fen River, bounded by Changzhi and Jincheng to the east, the Yellow River to the west, Jinzhong and Lüliang to the north, and Yuncheng to the south. Hongtong is a county in the prefecture-level city of Linfen in the southwestern part of the province.[1] The most recent census data from 2010 shows Hongtong as the most populated county in the city of Linfen, occupying an area of 1,563 square kilometers and containing a population of 733,421.[2] It has 7 townships (*xiang*) and 9 towns (*zhen*),[3] including 463 villagers' committees (*cunmin weiyuanhui*), which govern 902 natural villages (*zirancun*)[4] (Zhang and Wang 2005, 19–30).

Map 1.1. Map of China, © Daniel Dalet, https://d-maps.com/carte.php?num_car=11572&lang=en.

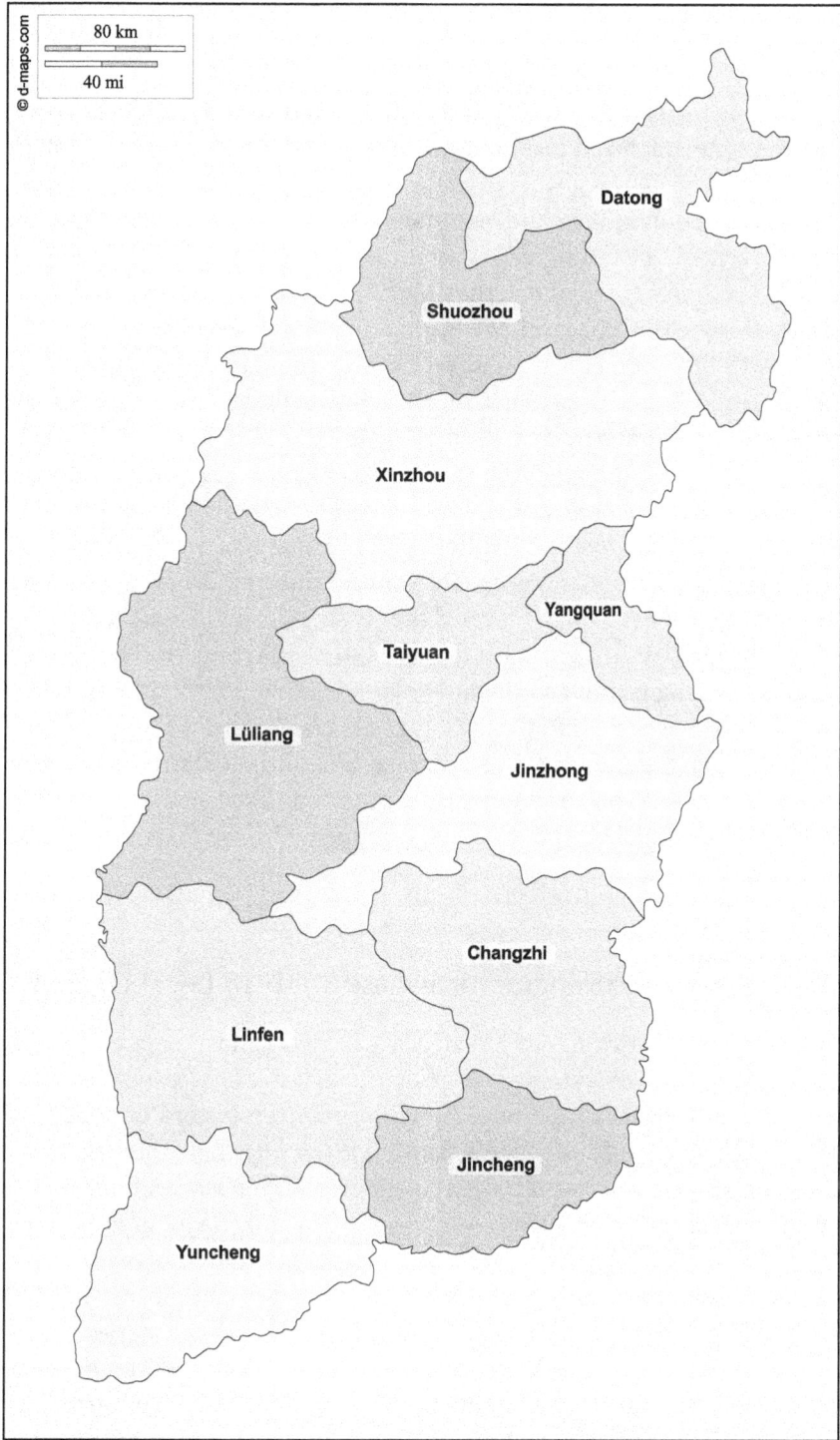

Map 1.2. Map of Shanxi, © Daniel Dalet, https://d-maps.com/carte.php?num _car=17817&lang=en.

During the Hongwu (洪武) (1368–98) and Yongle (永乐) (1403–24) periods, the state organized mass migrations to replenish losses of population in other provinces brought about by the continual wars during the late Yuan and early Ming dynasties, and Hongtong was used as a major immigration transfer center. The immigrant experience was traumatic for many people, as they were forced to abandon their old homelands and leave for unknown places. Despite this upheaval, the immigrants continued to remember and feel ties to their hometowns, and they passed these memories on to their descendants. Today a popular Chinese folk song asks: "Where is my old hometown? The big pagoda tree in Hongtong, Shanxi. What is the name of my ancestors' old home? The stork nest under the pagoda tree" (问我老家在何处, 山西洪洞大槐树。祖先故居叫什么, 大槐树下老鹳窝。) (Zhang and Lin 1988, 1). The pagoda tree and the stork nest in Hongtong became important symbols of roots for many people of Chinese ancestry all over the world. In 1991 the local government revived the yearly sacrifice to ancestors under the old pagoda tree—a tradition that used to be held only by the common people—making it into an annual "seeking roots and offering sacrifice to ancestors" (*xungen jizu*) festival (Zhang and Wang 2005, 194–95). This sacrificial festival, held during the traditional Clear Bright Festival (*Qingming jie*), continues to the present day. This custom was also listed as an element of China's intangible cultural heritage approved by the State Council on June 7, 2008.

Situating the Ethnographical Case Study in Local History

My historical research has included local gazetteers and annals, along with the text engraved on extant steles. Even though the local people in Hongtong claim that their traditions have an unbroken history of about five thousand years, as old as Chinese cultural history itself, neither their rituals nor their festivals are recorded in the local gazetteers and annals. As Sun Huanlun (1887–1958) notes in his preface to *Hongtong County Annals* (1917), the introduction of local famous people generally starts from Gao Yao (皋陶) and Shi Kuang (师旷) (572–532 BC)[5], not from Emperor Yao and Shun (Chen Yongchao 2015, 40) (I will further discuss the stories of Yao and Shun in chap. 3). Gao Yao is believed to be the chief minister of crime during Emperor Yao's time (traditionally ca. 2356–2255 BC). His birthplace and memorial temple are in Shishi Village, Hongtong. In the 1731 edition of

Hongtong County Annals, the name of Yangxie and the Temple of Ehuang and Nüying were listed as follows:

> Yangxie Old Relics: Twenty-five *li* away in the south of the county. It was said that during Yao's time a goat gave birth to *xiezhi*, a sacred goat, and the village was thus named after it. Around it, there were plenty of sands; no grass or plants could be grown on it.
>
> The Temple of Emperor Shun, Ehuang, and Nüying: In the second year of the Tianyou period of Emperor Zhao (905), it was deemed to be an Esteemed Integrity Shrine. The shrine was on the Shun Ling, twenty *li* away in the west of the county. (Yu and Cai 1731, vol. 8: 1)

The first entry introduced how Yangxie Village was named after a sacred *xie* that was born during Yao's time. This legend has become a dominant narrative in present-day Yangxie Village, where almost everyone knows this story and takes it seriously. The second entry describes how the Temple of Ehuang and Nüying at the Shun Ling got its imperial title during the late Tang dynasty. If the Shun Ling is in the present-day Lishan area, the worship of Ehuang and Nüying there can be tracked back more than 1,100 years.

The local tradition of worshipping Yao and Shun, as well as Ehuang and Nüying, can primarily be found among people from three places in Hongtong: Yangxie, Wan'an, and Lishan. Yangxie is the name of an old village that now includes three natural villages: North Yangxie, South Yangxie, and Ertai. Wan'an is an old town, a significant market center in the past and today. Lishan, or Li Mountain, is believed to be the place where Emperor Shun plowed during Yao's time. The current Lishan in Hongtong was originally known as Yingshan (英山, Ying Mountain) or Yingshen Shan (英神山, Ying Sacred Mountain), named after Nüying. Hongtong is believed to be the place where Nüying was born during Yao's time, and therefore, the memorial temple to Nüying and her older sister, Ehuang, was built in Yingshan.

As an important historical site, Yingshan was marked clearly on the map of Hongtong County in the 1731 edition of *Hongtong County Annals*. There were also two poems and one essay commemorating the site in the ninth volume, "The Treatise on the Classics and [Ordinary] Writings" (*Yiwen zhi*) (Yu and Cai 1731). One poem, entitled "Ying Mountain," was written by Liu Yingshi during the Ming dynasty; the other, entitled "Visiting the Memorial Temple of Shun's Two Royal Wives" (*Ye Shun erfei ci*), was written by Liu Chengchong, a native of Hongtong, also during the Ming dynasty.

The poem "Ying Mountain" reflects on Ehuang and Nüying's tragic tale as follows:

> Looking at the mountain of immortals west of Yang City,
> It is the place where Nüying and Ehuang were born and grew up.
> They went to Xiao and Xiang Rivers, where clouds were misty and dim,
> Leaving the Wei and Rui Rivers alone, with the murmuring of flowing water.
> Their appearances and statues look familiar, as they were made in their days.
> Who knows when their spirits and souls will come back?
> Their hearts were broken on the "Stone of Watching for Husband" at
>   Cangwu,
> Even up to today, the long bamboos are spotted with their tears.
> (Yu and Cai 1731, vol. 9, pt. II: 35)

Liu Yingshi does not narrate Nüying and Ehuang's stories in detail in the poem. Instead, he expresses sorrow for their deaths and describes how local people in Hongtong later memorialized the two women. According to historical records (Sima 1959 [91 BC]; Liu 2007 [18 BC]), Nüying and Ehuang were wed to Shun by their father, Emperor Yao, near the Wei and Rui Rivers. After occupying the imperial throne for many years, Emperor Shun went on an expedition to the south, where he died at Cangwu, a mountain near the Xiang River. Nüying and Ehuang rushed from their home to find his body and cried by the river for days. Their tears turned into blood, staining the bamboos by the river. Overcome by deep grief, both women threw themselves into the Xiang River and drowned. The first chapter of *The Biographies of Exemplary Women* (*Lienü zhuan*)—"The Two Consorts of Youyu" (*Youyu erfei*)—states: "While making an expedition, Shun died at Cangwu. His honorary title was Chonghua (Double Splendor). The two royal wives died in the region between the Yangtze and the Xiang rivers. Therefore they were commonly called the 'Ladies of the Xiang,' or 'Goddesses of Xiang'" (Liu 2007 [18 BC], 31).

The poem "Visiting the Memorial Temple of Shun's Two Royal Wives," written by Liu Chengchong, is translated as follows:

> With the turnings of mountains and the twists of peaks, green and luxuriant
>   are trees,
> People all said that it was the palace of Yu Shun in old times.
> In the past the miraculous queens frequently made rain,

and occasionally girls made wind by themselves.
Waves are still green in Xiang River in late autumn,
Flowers are still red in Gui and Rui River in late spring.
For thousands of years, the building is magnificent,
[I] worship Chongtong by burning incense and offering jade.
(Yu and Cai 1731, vol. 9, pt. II: 48)

The poet Liu Chengchong was named "Shao yin" (少尹) when composing this poem, and he once served as civil official, or "zhu bu" (主簿), in Feng
County, Shaanxi Province, in late Ming dynasty (Chang 2010, 126). During
his time, the Liu family in Hongtong boomed and grew into a renowned
one. Besides recording his own family's genealogy, Liu Chengchong also
worked to preserve local history through his writings (Chang 2010, 128). In
this poem, written during the late Ming dynasty, he recorded local beliefs
and practices, including people apparently praying to Ehuang and Nüying
for rain.

The essay in the 1731 edition of *Hongtong County Annals* was written
by Xing Dadao (邢大道), a native of Hongtong, for County Magistrate Luo
Renzhong (駱任重) during the Ming dynasty. Entitled "Record of the Sacred
Ancestral Temple in Ying Mountain" (*Yingshan shenci ji*), it introduces
local people's beliefs toward Ehuang and Nüying in Hongtong at that time,
recorded from Luo's perspective. Luo, Hongtong County magistrate from
1610 to 1611, visited the temple in the winter of 1610, and his son was born
in June 1611. He participated in the ritual of thanking the deities on the
thirteenth day of the twelfth lunar month in 1611 and provided his account
sometime after the ritual. The full text is as follows:

To the west of Fen River, there stands the tall Ying Mountain; on the
top of Ying Mountain, there stands the tall Temple of Ehuang and
Nüying, who were Yao's two daughters and had been married by Yao
to his chosen successor, and eventual emperor, Shun. The historians
said that Emperor Shun went on an expedition to the south and died
in the desert of Cangwu. His two wives wept by the Xiang River, their
tears staining bamboo permanently with their spots. They became
deities after they drowned themselves in the river, and up to today
their souls and spirits, which went to heaven, still exist. I am a native
of Sichuan. The memorial temple was built on Ying Mountain; why
did Hongtong become the place of worship? Yao established Pingyang as his capital, and Pingyang was less than one hundred *li* away

from Hongtong, while nearby is the place where Ehuang and Nüying were born. Therefore, the natives called the two deities "aunties," just as if they were the offspring of the maternal family of the two ladies.

In the winter of the Gengxu year of the Wanli reign (1610), I went through the western part of the county to disperse bills and dropped by this place. I paid my respects and visited the temple. The memorial temple was built during the past dynasties, and it had been a long time. The wood and the stone were not ruined, but the golden statues were peeled off, and it was not caused in one day. I felt compassion for it; then I made my promise and said: "As a humble official my salary is not high, but I will make some donations to decorate the statues of the deities." Soon a Daoist priest invited me to sit in a guest room and drink tea, as he continuously said how miraculous the deities were. People prayed because of droughts, prayed for rain, prayed for children; none of them was not responded to and blessed. I thus rinsed my hands, burned incense, and asked for blessings. I said I was more than forty years old but still had no children. If I got blessings from the deities, and my Luo family lineage was continued without ceasing, I would not forget their great virtues! The next year, in the June of that summer, I really did have a son, so wasn't it a reward from the deities? What the Daoist priest said was not a lie.

In the December of that winter, the decoration of the statues was complete, and the statues were clearly and brightly new. Two days before the fifteenth full-moon day, I killed sacrificial animals and brought alcohol, to genuflect a hundred times in the temple, in order to repay the blessings of the deities. Therefore, I recorded it in written words here. (Yu and Cai 1731, vol. 9, pt. I: 74)

The beliefs and practices recorded in this text are very similar to what I have observed from my own fieldwork in Hongtong. Ordinary people often visit the temple to pray for good luck and ask for blessings from the deities. What they usually pray for are healthy children, followed by health, fortune, and high status. When their wishes come true, they take gifts to the temple and perform rituals to repay the blessings from the deities. Their offerings include food, alcohol, and decorations for the statues or the temple.

Based on records from the *Hongtong County Annals*, the Temple of Yao in Yangxie can be traced back to 1354, and the Temple of Shun in Lishan can be traced back to 1029 (Sun et al. 1917). We have no other extant evidence to prove the earlier history of local temples in Yangxie, but two items stand out in a local museum in present-day Lishan. One is a fragmental stele from the Song dynasty discovered in Lishan, marking the year 1029 (the text is unrecognizable). The other is a tomb brick discovered in a Yuan tomb in Lishan, with the following signature: "Zhang Zhirui, the abbot of Shang Ying Temple in Juantou Village, Hongtong County, Pingyang Prefecture" (Chen Yongchao 2015, 44). These are the earliest extant records about the temples in Lishan.

The Stele Texts in the Temple of Ehuang and Nüying in Wan'an

Currently, the earliest historical document concerning local annual ritual processions of receiving Ehuang and Nüying is found inscribed on a stele in the Temple of Ehuang and Nüying in Wan'an. The stone tablet was erected in 1674, and it tracks the temple back to 1648. The main part of the stele text is not a full statement about the history of the local tradition but a list of objects in the temple. These objects were used in local festivals, rituals, and parades focused on the worship of Ehuang and Nüying, particularly on the third day of the third lunar month and on the twenty-ninth day of the fourth lunar month, as they are today. The full stele text reads as follows:

> After opening, the Public Property in the Palace of Ehuang and Nüying [include]
>
> One Divine Sedan Chair[6] Two Yellow Umbrellas[7] Two Tall Flags[8] Ten Flags with Five Colors[9]
>
> Eight Large Gongs, Each Weighs Five *Jin* Twelve *Liang*
>
> Four Small Gongs, Each Weighs Two *Jin* Six *Liang*[10]
>
> Two Opera Gongs, Weighing One *Jin* Four *Liang* in Total
>
> Two Drums[11] Three Altar Tables One Single Table
>
> Six Long Tables Two Cloth Curtains Ten Reed Mats One Hundred and Thirty Big and Small Bowls
>
> Ten Iron Spoons Ten Ladles Two Iron Pots Eight Pottery Pots Fifty-Eight Pairs of Chopsticks
>
> One Pair of Bamboo Lanterns
>
> On the Fifth Year of Shunzhi (1648), Four Cypresses Were Planted in front of the Open Chamber[12]
>
> On the Ninth Year of Kangxi (1670), Two Cypresses Were Planted in front of the Sacrifice Hall[13]
>
> Newly-Elected *Xianglao* Ji Xuesi Qiao Wansong Du Chenggui

Inscribed on the Lunar May Fifth Jiayin Day of the Thirteenth Year of
Kangxi (1674)
Old *Xianglao* Li Tianzhi Du Yingrui Li Xianxiang
(Li, Wang, and Zhang 2008, 168; Wang Xuewen et al. 2009, 257)

According to the stele text, the tablet was made by the old and new *xiang
lao* (incense people), who were in charge of burning incense and managing
incense money in the temple. Also known as *xiang tou* (incense heads), *shè
tou* (*shè* heads), or *miao tou* (temple heads), people managing incense run
a variety of temple affairs, such as coordinating temple fairs and parades,
leading local people in burning incense and making sacrifices, managing
incense money in the temple, and so on. Temple heads are usually old people, and therefore, they were referred to as *lao*—"the old"—in the stele text.

In addition, another stele inscribed in 1788 has been preserved in the
temple:

A Stele Inscription for the Celebration of the Sacred Birthdays of
Ehuang and the Goddess of Fertility
It has been many years since the temples of Ehuang and the Goddess of Fertility were built here. Predecessors sincerely worshipped
them . . . their offerings and sacrifices were bright and clean. There are
normal rituals for sacrifice in four different seasons, but the offerings
are unknown during the sacred birthdays of deities. It is a pity in our
hearts that the big ceremony is missing. We live in different places, far
away from each other. But we all receive generous favor and prosperous blessings from deities. Thus we would like to return their favor
and show our respects sincerely, and we are willing to make sacrifice
during the sacred birthdays of deities. We have curved wooden drinking cups, and connect people together to form a group [by drinking
alcohol]. There are sixty-two individuals who live in different places
but share the same thought. Each person contributed two *liang* of
gold, many small amounts accumulated to make a large amount. In
total, we got more than four hundred *liang* of gold, and it is enough
to run our business. We use the annual interests that we receive to
pay sacrifices. On the twentieth day of the third lunar month, it is
the sacred birthday of the Goddess of Fertility, we offer sacrificial
animals and opera performance. On the eighteenth day of the sixth
lunar month, it is the sacred birthday of Ehuang, we provide banquets
and chant sutras. Although things are different in complexity and

essence, we make our rules based on particular times and situations. We do not intend to be unfair, but to live in the moment. When the group is formed, we record particularly what happened, inscribe it in this stele, and expect that it would be remembered in the future. The names of the group members are inscribed in the back of this stele.

> Written by Qiao Ningmi, a scholar who lives on prefecture-level government grants
> Calligraphy by Ji Xingyi, a young scholar
> Inscribed by Wei Linhe, a stonemason
> Abbot Zong Dao
> On the twentieth day of the sixth lunar month, the fifty-third year of Qianlong
> Established by the whole group
> (Li, Wang, and Zhang 2008, 299)

Sixty-two benefactors erected this stele in 1788, and they used the annual interests accumulated from personal donations to make offerings to celebrate the birthdays of both Ehuang and the Goddess of Fertility in the temple. Abbot Zong Dao was probably a Buddhist monk who supervised various affairs in the temple in the late Qing dynasty. The birthday of Nüying was not mentioned in the stele text, but Nüying's birthday is now widely celebrated on the ninth day of the ninth lunar month in Yangxie and Lishan.

Shè

Shè, the key folk groups sponsoring local festivals and celebrations, provide a way to connect people together to serve deities in the temples. As a micro-geographic unit common in Shanxi, a shè could be identical to a natural village, several small villages could combine to form a shè, or a single large village could include several groups of shè (Johnson 2009). Each shè serves a particular god in a particular temple, and different shè sometimes rotate to take turns serving the same god in the same temple. In my case study, six small villages combine to form three shè directed toward Ehuang and Nüying and their temple in Lishan. The six villages include Three Religions Village (Sanjiao Cun), Song Family Valley (Songjia Gou), Eastern Fence (Dong Juantou), Lan Family Village (Lanjia Jie), Western Fence (Xi Juantou), and West to the Sacred Temple (Shenxi). Three Religions Village and

Song Family Valley combine to form the Eastern shè since they are located east of the Temple of Ehuang and Nüying in Lishan; Eastern Fence and Lan Family Village surround the temple and therefore form the Middle shè; and Western Fence and West to the Sacred Temple make the Western shè as they are located west of the temple. These three shè take turns running temple affairs, with each shè serving once every three years. The takeover process begins on the first day of the fifth lunar month and is finalized on the fifth day of the fifth lunar month when shè heads from Yangxie arrive in Lishan.

Wan'an, an important center of trade in Hongtong, is very large in size and population, and it is divided into two shè: the Northern shè and the Southern shè, a division based on the location of the participants' residences. In Wan'an, the Temple of Ehuang and Nüying was built outside the North Gate of the old town: residents near the North Gate form the Northern shè, and residents living in the south make up the Southern shè. Even though older residents might have moved to different places in the village, their children or grandchildren inherit the shè titles from them and serve Ehuang and Nüying in the temple. Because of the large population, each shè is further divided into four teams (*ban*). Thus, there are eight teams serving the deities, and each team assumes responsibility every eight years. Nowadays, the handover between the Northern shè and the Southern shè takes place on the fifteenth day of the twelfth lunar month, fifteen days before the Spring Festival or Chinese New Year.

During the late Qing dynasty, shè and the divided teams functioned effectively in the Temple of Ehuang and Nüying in Wan'an. An old commemorative plaque in the temple notes that it was donated by "followers in the second team of the Southern shè" (*nan shè er ban di zi*), dated "good days of the fourth month, wuzi year of the Daoguang reign" (*Daoguang wuzi qinghe yue gudan*, 道光戊子清和月穀旦) (1828). The inscription further indicates that shè and divided teams existed from early times and that the "followers" (local ritual specialists) were devoted to glorifying the miraculous efficacy of the deities, as expressed in the phrase "containing magnificence, enlarging grandeur" (*hanhong guangda*, 含宏光大) (see fig. 1.1).

However, the organizational structure and operation of shè in Wan'an changed after 1949, influenced by the rapid succession of social changes in China. With the start of the Socialist Education Movement in 1962, the activities of local shè were attacked as "feudal superstitions," and they were banned during the Cultural Revolution (1966–76). After China instituted

Fig. 1.1. The commemorative plaque, hung on the Open Chamber in front of the main temple hall in the Temple of Ehuang and Nüying in Wan'an (August 11, 2012).

the reform and opening policies in 1978, public local traditions were revived, and shè activities were resumed in 1990, thanks to the efforts of several local cultural activists. Their first project, completed in 1991, was to rebuild the ruined Temple of Ehuang and Nüying in its original location, and after the rebuilding project was completed, the general shè was established to supervise Wan'an's Southern shè and Northern shè in order to coordinate temple affairs effectively. There are usually six people in the general shè: one head in chief, one head of the Southern shè, one head of the Northern shè, one accountant, one treasurer, and one custodian.

There used to be one main shè in Yangxie, but this shè was divided into two—the Northern shè (bei shè, 北社) and the Southern shè (nan shè, 南社)—after the village itself was divided into two villages with the expansion of population in 1978. The shè alternate to run the temple affairs, and the annual shifting ceremony is held on the first day of the first lunar month, the Chinese New Year.

Villages and Temples

According to the *Hongtong County Annals* of 1917, there were four temples devoted to Ehuang and Nüying in Hongtong: one was outside the old County City, one was in Yangxie, one was in Wan'an, and the other was in Yingshan, now present-day Lishan (Sun et al. 1917, vol. 8, 18). Today the Temple of Ehuang and Nüying outside the old County City does not exist, but the other three temples are still extant. In addition to these three temples, a new Temple of Ehuang and Nüying was built halfway between Yangxie and Lishan in Xiqiao Zhuang in 1936 (Xiqiao Zhuang Miaoweihui 2006). My fieldwork took place primarily in Yangxie, Lishan, and Wan'an, and it is worth exploring the history and contemporary context for each of these villages here.

Yangxie

Yangxie is a very old village in Hongtong County that was named after the *xiezhi* (獬豸), a sacred one-horned goat believed to have been born there during Emperor Yao's time. According to local legend, Emperor Yao's minister of justice, Gao Yao, reported the birth of the sacred goat to the emperor, who took his wife to see it. When they arrived, Emperor Yao's wife, who was pregnant, gave birth to a baby. The baby was brilliantly beautiful, and she spoke after only three days and walked several days later. Because of these

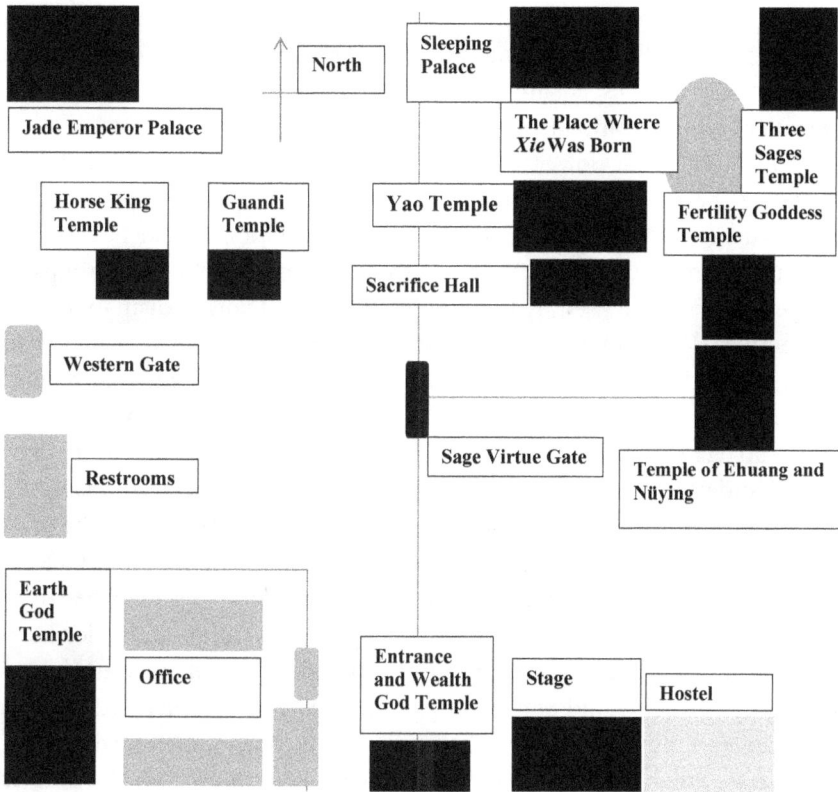

Map 1.3. Schematic map of the Old Temple Complex of Emperor Tang Yao in Yangxie, Shanxi, in 2013.

auspicious events, Emperor Yao renamed the village Yangxie (*yang* means "goat"), called his newborn daughter Nüying, and moved his whole family to Yangxie. Because of this local legend, Nüying and her sister, Ehuang, are worshipped as aunties in Yangxie, and temples to Yao and his two daughters are also built in the village (for a map of the present-day Old Temple Complex of Emperor Tang Yao, see map 1.3).

Although Yangxie is very old, its population is not stable and fixed. At least two-thirds of its inhabitants were immigrants from Henan, Hebei, Shandong, and other provinces. When the warlord Yan Xishan (1883–1960) ruled Shanxi from 1911 to 1949, he carried out a policy of "protecting the borders and giving people peace" (*baojing anmin*) (Jing 2008, 78–87). With the implementation of this policy, even during the disastrous years of the Second

Sino-Japanese War and other internal conflicts, Shanxi's economy and agriculture prospered and its education system excelled. These factors attracted many immigrants, especially from bordering provinces such as Hebei and Henan, and immigration from these areas continued into the 1960s.

In Yangxie, the power struggles between "the established" and "the outsiders" have been intense (Elias [1965] 1994), and these struggles sometimes turned bloody during the Cultural Revolution. Local beliefs and practices were at the core of some of these tensions, and newer groups of residents, who were used by the dominant political power, dismantled the old temples. The dismantlement exaggerated the tensions between these two groups, and the established residents later went to great lengths to rebuild the temples and revive traditional beliefs and practices. In the long series of power struggles between these two groups, local traditions have both continued and changed, remaining open to shifting actors and relationships.

Because of water conservancy projects in the 1950s and 1960s, the original Yangxie Village became saturated with saline and alkaline, making it no longer suitable for living, and so from 1958, local residents began to move south and north of the village, relocating to higher and drier locations (Yan 2012, 140). As the population expanded, the village was divided into North Yangxie and South Yangxie in 1978. The former is still named Yangxie, and the current South Yangxie also includes another natural village, Ertai, which is to its south. Despite its divisions, I use Yangxie to refer to the old village and the new villages, including the natural villages of North Yangxie, South Yangxie, and Ertai, and I use the specific name when referring to a natural village.

Today 2,585 residents live in North Yangxie, at least two-thirds being outsiders; around 1,700 people live in South Yangxie, most of whom are established residents; and around 700 people live in Ertai. After the division, both North Yangxie and South Yangxie organized their own shè—the Northern shè and the Southern shè—which alternate in the running of temple affairs.

Geographically, Yangxie is about eleven kilometers away from Hongtong County City (the capital of Hongtong County) and about fifteen kilometers away from the Yaodu District of Linfen. The Huohou First Class Highway passes across the east of the village, connecting Yangxie with both Hongtong County City and Linfen. Southern Tongpu Railway,[14] a main railway in Shanxi Province, passes along the east of the village. The Fen

River, one of the largest tributaries of the Yellow River, flows south through the west of the village.

In Yangxie, residents attach great importance to the well-being of families, and they frequently pray to their "aunties" for the health and safety of their children or grandchildren. Villagers used to get married in their early twenties, having children very soon afterward. They then became grandparents in their forties and great-grandparents in their sixties or seventies. I encountered many households made up of four generations. Family is the most important thing to most villagers, and women in these households give birth to children at an early age and bear the responsibilities of taking care of both the old and the young in the family. Their daily routine usually includes cooking three meals a day for the whole family, keeping the house clean, and doing some work in the field. The men are expected to make a living and support the multigenerational family, usually by working in a factory, on a construction site, or at a market outside the village. Currently, many young people leave to make a living in cities in Shanxi, such as Linfen and Taiyuan, and some even go to prominent national cities such as Beijing, Guangzhou, and Shenzhen. In order to take care of their families, some villagers choose to work temporarily in Hongtong or Linfen, commuting between home and the workplace.

Until recently, most villagers in Yangxie were peasants who relied on agricultural production to earn their living. In China, the government has ultimate ownership of the land, with peasants only having the right to use it. However, since summer 2012, many villagers have lost their access after the town-level government sold the land of North Yangxie, South Yangxie, and several other bordering villages to a local company in order to develop the local economy and tourism. The company has made plans to build a tourist park and related accommodation facilities centered on the Old Temple Complex of Emperor Tang Yao in Yangxie, and it paid local residents 1,200 yuan annually for each acre of land bought. Unfortunately, households might get less than 1,000 yuan since they generally had less than an acre of land—a payment too small to buy flour for a whole family for a year. Moreover, in several years local residents will have to relocate in accordance with the company's construction plan. Most villagers are unwilling to sell their lands and relocate, but the local government has absolute power to make the decision for them. Needless to say, the villagers are very dissatisfied with the new development plan and feel exploited.

In addition to the challenges presented by the development of the villagers' land, a human-caused disaster occurred during the Spring Festival in 2013. On the morning of Friday, February 15, 2013, the irrigation pipeline of Quting Reservoir in Hongtong caved in, causing about 300 meters of the 460-meter dam walls to collapse the next day. Nineteen million cubic meters of water in the reservoir flowed through Yangxie before entering the nearby Fen River. The flood destroyed at least sixteen houses and flushed away many properties in South Yangxie Village. Although villagers received compensation from the county government, their anger toward official corruption as well as toward the cleanup and relocation project was exacerbated after this disaster. To make matters worse, the compensation money for the village land was embezzled by some village officials, and local residents did not get what they were owed. On June 21, 2013, Yangxie residents launched public protests against corrupt village heads and party secretaries as well as against the land expropriation, and the conflicts between the local government and the underrepresented villagers intensified. Even though the Yangxie villagers did not know what outcome these protests would bring, they chose to fight for a better future.

Lishan

Today six villages are located around Lishan, with approximately 3,150 residents: around 730 people live in Three Religions Village, 530 in Song Family Valley, 650 in Eastern Fence, 412 in Lan Family Village, 570 in Western Fence, and 250 in West to the Sacred Temple (Cheng 2011, 21). Compared with Yangxie, Lishan is not a densely populated area, and their transportation options are not as convenient. There is only one road—Wan Zuo Xian (万左线)—crossing the area, and it starts at Wan'an and ends at Zuomu Xiang (左木乡), a town in a deep mountain area (Zhang and Wang 2005, 361). Driving on the steep, curvy mountain road is difficult and sometimes very dangerous, and travel is often by bike or motorcycle, or even by foot, especially for older villagers.

Lishan is about twenty kilometers away from the downtown area of Hongtong and about ten kilometers away from Wan'an. Residents in the mountain area have plenty of vegetables from their own gardens, and they may go shopping once or twice a month in Hongtong or Wan'an for meat and other foods. The mountainous land is not good for agricultural planting. Crops such as wheat and corn often require extra labor there, with the resulting harvest being very low. In addition, water is rare, making it hard to live there. In order to survive, most villagers have to go out to work at nearby construction sites and factories or find temporary jobs in cities.

The Temple of Shun in present-day Lishan is the most famous and influential temple in the local area. The temple, which has been destroyed and reconstructed many times, was rebuilt in 1992. Currently Lishan has the largest temple complex in Hongtong, a site that took about twenty years to build (see map 1.4); this complex provides a place for all the important gods from Confucianism, Daoism, and Buddhism to reside. In addition to the Temple of Ehuang and Nüying and the Temple of Shun, the temples of Heavenly Jade Maiden (*Bixia Yuanjun*), Dragon King (*Long Wang*), the Jade Emperor (*Yu Huang*), Grand Supreme Elder Lord (*Taishang Laojun*), Divus Guan (*Guandi*), Queen Mother of the West (*Xi Wangwu*), Truly Martial Grand Emperor (*Zhenwu Dadi*), God of Mount Tai (*Dongyue Dadi*), Mercy Goddess or Avalokiteśvara (*Guanyin*), Earth Treasury or Kṣitigarbha (*Dizang*), Confucius (*Kongzi*), Earth God (*Tudi Gong*), and other popular gods or goddesses were all built in the temple complex on the top of the present-day Lishan. Li Xuezhi, one of the important founders of the temple complex in Lishan, clearly stated to me that the construction of these temples embodied the concept of "three teachings mixed into one" (*sanjiao he yi*). The Temple of Ehuang and Nüying has been kept in its original place, but most of the other temples were relocated from their old sites in the six villages around Lishan. After the relocation, the old temples in the villages were destroyed, and villagers had to go to the temple complex to burn incense and genuflect before their gods and goddesses. In addition, some temples in the Lishan complex, such as the Temple of Confucius, were invented places of worship; Palaces of the Netherworld (*diyu*) is another. There were no such temples in old villages; the Confucian temple and the Buddhist Hell were all built to embody the concept of three-teachings-into-one.

In general, the architecture of the temples in Lishan followed the model of Beijing's Forbidden City, which was the imperial palace during most of the Ming and Qing dynasties. These sacred places of worship are easily distinguished from the vernacular architecture of the area (see fig. 1.2). However, the continuous reconstruction projects on the temple complex have forced local people to bear heavy financial burdens because the temple reconstruction executors in 2002 decided to take illegal loans from local people and promise them high interest rates (1% monthly). Because of their strong beliefs in Ehuang, Nüying, and the other deities, many local people

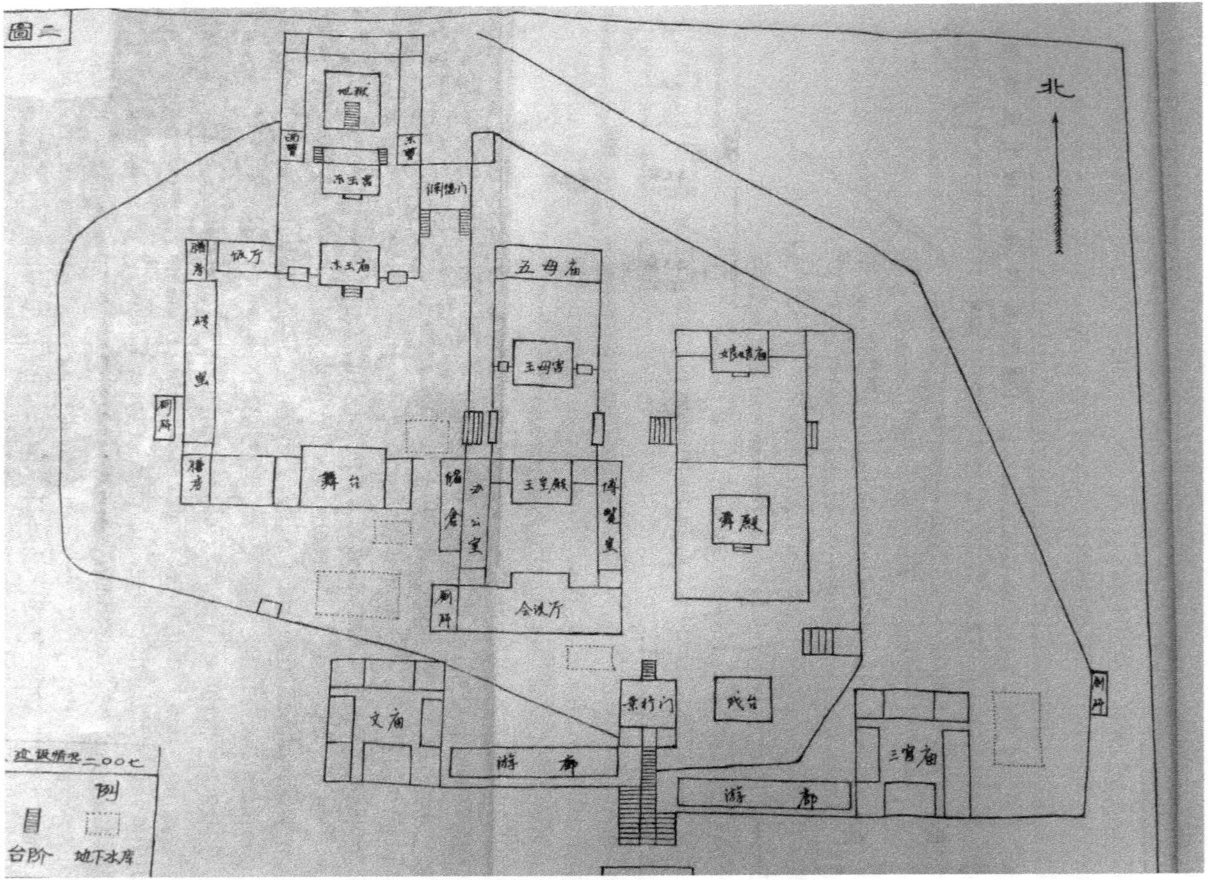

Map 1.4. Schematic map of the temple complex (from 1992 to 2007) in Lishan, Hongtong. Drawn by Li Chunwen in 2012.

Fig. 1.2. The entrance of the Temple of Shun in Lishan, Hongtong, Shanxi (July 15, 2012).

took the opportunity to support the temple projects, hoping too that they would benefit financially from the offered high interest. As a result, more than 420 households from about twenty local villages in Hongtong lent their money—often earned in the hundreds of local illegal coal mines—to temple executors. Unexpectedly, the source of the loans came to an end when the government forcibly closed these illegal coal mines in 2008. With the exhaustion of this source of revenue, the lenders were eager to get their money back from the temple reconstruction projects, but they soon learned that they could not get any of the promised interest or their original capital back. The lenders then found out that the temple was in debt for more than 9,000,000 yuan, and nobody in the temple complex could clearly explain where the money had gone. With anger building, the affected people got together to protest in front of the temple complex in 2010 on the Double Ninth Festival, when the temple fairs celebrated Nüying's birthday. When town- and county-level government officials learned of the urgent situation, they pacified the protesters and asked the temple supervisor, Yang Biyun, to handle the "debt crisis." Yang had been assigned as the official general director by the Hongtong County government when the temple reconstruction association was established in Lishan in 1992. She has not only donated a lot of money to the projects but also raised a large amount of funding for temple reconstruction. She became the director of the temple reconstruction association in Lishan in early 2011 when she took over after the start of the debt crisis. The old director, Li Yinzi, quit and left the temple in late 2010 after the protest; some old executors left with him at the same time.[15]

Yang Biyun was in her early sixties and had been the director of an official county-level grain administration station for many years before she retired several years ago. Her husband used to be the president of People's Procuratorate in Hongtong, and he also retired several years ago. After Yang took over as director of the temple reconstruction project, she promised to pay off the enormous debt left behind by the former executors. Her main strategy was to fight against corruption in the temple and strictly manage the temple accounts; she also attempted to raise as much money as possible from the local people. However, Yang's leadership was not well received in Lishan and Yangxie. Former temple executors in Lishan accused her of appropriating donations and temple funds, and village party heads in Yangxie disagreed with her about her management of temple affairs. Instead of solving the problems related to the debt crisis, the power shift in Lishan exacerbated existing conflicts and tensions. Not only were local people's savings and donations sacrificed in the situation, but their autonomy to run temple affairs by and for themselves was also negatively affected. However, today local villagers are still actively fighting to get back their money and rights.

Wan'an

Wan'an is not only the name of a town but also the name of a village in Hongtong. Wan'an Town is to the west of Hongtong County City, ten kilometers away from the downtown area. The government center of Wan'an Town is located in Wan'an Village. Currently, the town has sixty village committees, governing eighty-seven natural villages. There are 13,713 households in Wan'an Town, with 62,406 people residing there, about 10,000 of which are living in Wan'an Village. All the inhabitants are Han people, the majority ethnic group of China.[16] To the west of the town is a mountainous region, including the current Lishan area, which is about ten kilometers away from Wan'an Village; the rest of the town is situated on plains. The Sanjiao (三交) and Jian (涧) Rivers flow through the town from the west and then turn east to pass through the Xincun Township before joining the Fen River. Transportation options in Wan'an are convenient, with one freeway, several highways, and several roads. Half of the land in the town is arable farmland, and the main crops are wheat and corn.

Wan'an Village has been an important market center since the Ming and Qing dynasties. The old city walls and five gates were rebuilt by a member of the local gentry during the Jiaqing (嘉庆) period (1796–1820) of the Qing dynasty (Zhang and Wang 2005, 404). As an important economic center in Hongtong, it contains a variety of public institutions, factories, shops, and markets. Because of the fast social, political, and economic changes after 1949, a large number of old buildings and the city walls have been destroyed, with only a few preserved up to the present.

The Temple of Ehuang and Nüying was built in Wan'an during the Yuan dynasty (Wang Xuewen et al. 2009, 790), and it was totally destroyed during the Cultural Revolution. The shè was revived in 1990, and the temple was rebuilt in 1991. Two shè and eight *ban* had functioned very well until 2011, when local conflicts related to money and accounts management between shè arose. Formerly, the Southern shè and the Northern shè took turns running temple affairs, but after a temple renovation project began in 2003, a general shè was established to run the two shè. At the end of the year, the shè on duty was supposed to hand in all the money left in the temple accounts to the head of the general shè. However, in 2010, when the Northern shè received a 100,000-yuan donation from one donor, the temple executors on duty were not willing to accept the leadership of the general shè and hand in the donation; instead, they decided to open an independent temple account and manage the money by themselves. Meanwhile, the first *ban* in the Northern shè was on duty in 2011, but the head was very old, and therefore he was not able to supervise a large number of people and run temple affairs effectively. Nobody was willing to take responsibility and replace the old head, and so the executors in the Northern shè decided to merge the four teams into one, and the whole Northern shè became independent from the supervision of the general shè.

Conflicts between the general shè and the traditional shè, like those seen in Wan'an, are also common in Yangxie and Lishan. The general shè in Yangxie was officially established in 2004, and the general head was chosen from the Northern shè, which aroused tensions between the traditional Southern shè and Northern shè. The general shè was first formed in Lishan in 1992, with the official initiation of the temple reconstruction association. Today tensions among shè, temple construction associations, and local state officials are ongoing in Yangxie, Lishan, and Wan'an, and the power struggles are still intense (see chap. 4 and 6 for elaboration on these issues).

Differentiation and Interaction among Yangxie, Lishan, and Wan'an

Separated by the boundary of the Fen River, Yangxie residents (to the river's east side) call Ehuang and Nüying *aunties* (*gugu*) as if they were the offspring of Emperor Yao, while people from Lishan, Wan'an, Xiqiao Zhuang, and most other villages (to the river's west side) call them *niangniang* (empresses, goddesses, or grandmothers) as if they were the offspring of Emperor Shun. In this way, the Fen River functions not only as a geographical marker but as a cultural marker noting different generational status in the sacred family. This differentiation sounds arbitrary, and the influential local figure Li Xuezhi in Lishan explained it to me in my first interview with him on April 18, 2007. He told me that Ehuang and Nüying's marriage with Shun was interpreted as "thousands-of-years marriage" (*qianqiu yinyuan*) and that Lishan people called Yangxie people *biaoshu* (表叔, uncles), sons of one's grandmother's brother, as if Yangxie villagers were the sons of Ehuang and Nüying's brother, while Yangxie people called Lishan people *biaozhi* (表侄, nephews), one's maternal cousin's sons, as if Lishan people were the sons of Ehuang and Nüying's son. Li furthermore stated that people from Yangxie and Lishan were banned from marrying each other, as otherwise it would be regarded as incest.

The construction of kinship through historical and geographical bonds is not stable among different groups of people in Hongtong. In practice, Yangxie people and Lishan people just call each other *qinqi* (relatives), and their relationships are interpreted as *shengqin* (圣亲) or *shenqin* (神亲), "sacred relatives." In my fieldwork, I have never encountered anyone from Lishan calling Yangxie people uncles or Yangxie people calling Lishan people nephews. Li Xuezhi's interpretation may be his reification of longtime historical connections between Yangxie and Lishan, which is used by Li to prove the legitimacy of local beliefs and practices after they were attacked as feudal superstitions. Moreover, Li's reification functions to bridge the huge rupture between the distant past—that is, Yao and Shun's time—and the present.

In reality, of course, everything keeps changing, and Li Xuezhi's reification is a case of "objectified objectification," when "the dialectic of objective structures and incorporated structures which operates in every practical action is ignored" during the process of remaking cultural continuity in local contexts (Bourdieu [1980] 1990, 30–41). Most residents in Yangxie were immigrants from other places, and no villagers claim that their ancestry in the village can be traced back for more than five hundred years, although they do claim that their beliefs and practices have continued for more than four thousand years. Over time, new residents kept moving in, and some local inhabitants moved out. The populations in Yangxie, Lishan, and Wan'an were never stable or fixed. The beliefs surrounding Ehuang and Nüying function strongly as forms of local identification; whoever immigrated to the places around the temples gradually came to believe in the deities and then actively joined "native" inhabitants to participate in the local annual temple fairs and ritual processions.

Five Festivals Centered on Local Beliefs

Centered on the beliefs of Ehuang and Nüying in Hongtong, five festivals are marked for local annual ritual processions in the lunar calendar: (1) the festival on the third day of the third lunar month, when Yangxie residents receive their aunties back home from Lishan; (2) the festival on the twenty-eighth day of the fourth lunar month, when people from Lishan, Wan'an, Xiqiao Zhuang, and other places come to Yangxie to celebrate Emperor Yao's birthday and then receive their *niangniang* back; (3) the Double Fifth Festival on the fifth day of the fifth lunar month, when Yangxie temple executors go to celebrate Emperor Shun's birthday and participate in the shè rotation in Lishan; (4) the festival on the eighteenth day of the sixth lunar month, when women from Yangxie come to celebrate the birthday of their older aunty, Ehuang, in Lishan; and (5) the festival on the ninth day of the ninth lunar month, when women from Yangxie come to celebrate the birthday of their younger aunty, Nüying, in Lishan.

During the first festival, a large temple fair is held in Lishan; during the second annual festival, Yangxie residents host a large temple fair in the Old Temple of Emperor Yao, celebrating Emperor Yao's birthday. During the celebration of Nüying's birthday, a large temple fair is also held in Lishan. During the first two festivals, people from more than twenty nearby villages participate in the celebrations, receive the deities along the processions or make pilgrimages to the temple, and donate incense money to the temple. During the other annual festivals, Yangxie pilgrims pass through the Temple of Ehuang and Nüying in Xiqiao Zhuang on their way to Lishan for celebrations and then go to the Temple of Ehuang and Nüying in Wan'an before going back to their own village temple. These festivals are ritualized, and the processions on these occasions are similar to the one on the third day of the third lunar month, although the participants are different. The shè heads and core members coordinate and participate in all the festivals if their shè takes over temple affairs that year. Only men participate in the processions during the first two important festivals, whereas women make the processions to celebrate Ehuang's and Nüying's birthdays during the last two festivals. The annual temple fairs usually attract tens of thousands of people from all over Shanxi and nearby provinces, such as Henan and Shaanxi.

During these festivals, people from Yangxie, Lishan, and Wan'an receive and accommodate each other warmly in their houses. Of course, not all the residents treat their "relatives" with hospitality and honor; only those who strongly believe in Ehuang and Nüying would provide free meals and sleeping space to host sacred relatives, and they would ask for blessings from Ehuang and Nüying when they treat their sacred relatives during these rituals. At the domestic banquet before they eat and drink together, the host family and the guests often burn incense and genuflect before the domestic altar of Ehuang and Nüying, which enshrines the statues or pictures of the two deities and which is usually located in the main hall of the household. Local people also make offerings to Ehuang and Nüying at home on the first and fifteenth days of every lunar month and during important festivals.

Contested "Sacred" Social Bond and Local Tension

In "The Social Base of Folklore," Dorothy Noyes writes: "The imaginary that bonds communities may be freely chosen. . . . It may be imposed from above. . . . It may be imposed from outside. . . . Mobile moderns tend to idealize communal attachments, but belonging is ambivalent in practice, a source of both comfort and tension" (Noyes 2012, 24–25). In my ethnographical case study, locals draw on the distant past to reconstruct their "sacred" social bond and reify it as bounded and stable. In practice, however, this "sacred" social bond has always been challenged and negotiated within interconnected village communities.

Conflicts between Wan'an and Lishan arose in the early 1990s, when the local traditions were revived after the Cultural Revolution. The local tension primarily centered on the legitimacy of the Temple of Shun in these two places. The Temple of Shun used to be located in Lishan, but some Wan'an residents built a new Shun temple near the old temple of Ehuang and Nüying in the 1990s. Liu Baoshan, a local influential cultural figure, even claimed Wan'an to be Shun's birthplace. Li Xuezhi from Lishan challenged Liu's claim and initiated a huge project to rebuild the Temple of Shun in Lishan in 1992 (the debates between Liu Baoshan and Li Xuezhi will be elaborated on in chap. 3). In his work, Li Xuezhi often emphasizes the "sacred" social bond between Yangxie and Lishan. The exclusion of Wan'an offended Liu Baoshan and other Wan'an residents, prompting them to argue against Li Xuezhi in an attempt to earn back their legitimate status in the "sacred" social bond. In the struggle, Yangxie temple heads stood with Li Xuezhi, only recognizing the legitimacy of the Temple of Shun in Lishan.

The role of Wan'an in local traditions became a key issue in local debates and controversies. People from Yangxie and Lishan state that Wan'an is just "a way station for resting horses and eating meals" (*xiema liangdian*, 歇马粮店) during the annual ritual processions of receiving deities on the third day of the third lunar month, whereas Wan'an residents argue that

Emperor Shun was a native of Wan'an and that one of Shun's wives lived permanently in her temple in Wan'an. Thus, people from Wan'an believe that they help escort one of their *niangniang* back to her temple in Wan'an on the twenty-ninth day of the fourth lunar month. People from Lishan and Yangxie argue against this claim and say that those from Wan'an just come to do some cleaning in the Temple of Ehuang and Nüying in Yangxie after Lishan residents receive their *niangniang* back.

The local controversies have lasted for many years, even though some powerful local people like Yang Biyun have attempted to solve them. During the course of my fieldwork in Hongtong in 2012 and 2013, some Wan'an informants still told me that Shun was born in Wan'an and that one of their *niangniang* was living in her temple in Wan'an, whereas people from Lishan and Yangxie insisted that Wan'an residents had changed history to support their argument. Even though people in Wan'an treat their "relatives" very well during annual festivals and parades, they do not really get along with each other. Based on what I observed during the Double Fifth Festival in 2012 and 2013, and during the eighteenth day of the sixth lunar month in 2012, the temple heads in Wan'an always tried to lead Yangxie "relatives" to the newly built Temple of Shun and tempt them to burn incense and genuflect there, in order to acknowledge the legitimacy of the new temple; however, the Yangxie "relatives" always stopped in front of the Temple of Shun and never entered. The tension worsened during a local conflict over regional opera performances at the temple fairs. During the ninth day of the ninth lunar month in 2012, when people from Yangxie went to celebrate Nüying's birthday in Lishan and to have lunch in the Temple of Ehuang and Nüying in Wan'an, the local Puju opera was performed onstage. The episode "Shefan" (舍饭), a classic *zhezixi* (episode) in Puju, was especially selected by local sponsors. *Shefan* literally means "to give meals in charity," and this title offended the Yangxie participants because it seemed to suggest that the Wan'an participants were handing out meals to those from Yangxie as if they were beggars. Traditionally, this opera piece was forbidden from being performed onstage at local temple fairs because of its offensive implications. The shè heads from Yangxie asked the Wan'an shè heads to change the performance, but the Wan'an shè heads said that local sponsors, not themselves, had chosen the episode. After some negotiations, another opera piece was performed onstage, and it caused even more offense. The title of the new opera episode was "Duan Qiao," literally "broken bridge." Although this episode was from the well-known opera

The Legend of White Snake Lady (*Bai She Zhuan*), the title indicated to the Yangxie participants that the road ahead was broken and inaccessible. This bad omen insulted them, and they assumed that the Wan'an residents had chosen the episode on purpose. Consequently they did not stay for lunch but went directly back home. Some of the Yangxie participants even suggested breaking the "sacred" social bond with Wan'an, but most people rejected this idea because they believed that the connection was created by, with, and for the deities.[17]

The "sacred" social bond between Yangxie, Lishan, and Wan'an has been contested over and over, but it has never been broken because it is intertwined with the locals' sense of place, history, beliefs, and identity. People from these villages do not interact with each other in daily life, but their social bond is constantly and continuously maintained because of local beliefs and practices surrounding Ehuang and Nüying. This "sacred" connection strengthens the relationship among local people, especially during times of calamity. After Yangxie was flooded on February 16, 2013, the Wan'an Communist Party Branch, representing the village committee and Wan'an residents, delivered more than two hundred large bags of flour and other supplies to South Yangxie. Their slogan was "disaster relief by family bond" (*qinqing jiuza*). In order to thank the people of Wan'an for their help, the Yangxie Communist Party Branch and village committee sponsored Yangxie villagers to make a plaque and deliver it to Wan'an on the third day of the third lunar month in 2013:

> Transmitting the Sage's Virtues: Being Sacred Relatives through Thousands of Years, Lasting through Tens of Thousands of Years.
> 传承圣德: 千古圣眷, 万古延年

On this occasion, the "sacred" bond between Yangxie and Wan'an was recognized as having thousands of years of history, with hopes that the bond will continue for tens of thousands of years more.

However, old feuds and conflicts die hard, and they sometimes continue to influence local temple affairs. In 2013 some Wan'an residents wanted to come early to the Old Temple of Emperor Yao in Yangxie to participate in the official ceremony celebrating Emperor Yao's birthday. However, the old conventions did not allow for the Wan'an residents' participation in the ceremony, and they were only supposed to arrive at Yangxie after Lishan residents had passed the Fen River around noon. One day before Emperor

Yao's birthday, an emergency meeting was convened at the Old Temple of Emperor Yao with all temple heads and shè heads from Lishan and Yangxie participating. They decided to make arrangements to stop the Wan'an processions from crossing the Fen River until the ceremony was done and the Lishan parades had passed the river, and so on the twenty-eighth day of the fourth lunar month (June 6), 2013, three shè members from South Yangxie were sent to wait at the river bridge at Tunli. After the official ceremony was completed at Yangxie around 11:00 a.m. and the Lishan participants had begun to leave the village, some residents from Tunli Village who were prepared to receive their aunties at the ferry stopped the people arriving from Wan'an. They did not let them proceed until all Lishan participants had crossed the Fen River. The Wan'an processions arrived at Yangxie at almost 1:40 p.m., and their wish to change the time of the parades and to participate in the celebration ceremony failed.

Local traditions are always negotiated by different actors in a dynamic process. In this case, some actors were expected to show up onstage, like the Wan'an parade participants, but they tried to alter their role and thus were delayed for their performance. Other actors, like the Tunli participants, unexpectedly emerged to resolve the tension between the conflicting forces. The social bond between these actors was sometimes strengthened by natural disasters, but it was also sometimes worsened by conflicting interests, such as the struggle over the public celebrations. No matter what has occurred, these actors have actively played their relative roles and tried to earn their social status in the local traditions. Life comes to no end, and so too with the story.

Conclusion

This introduction—with its focus on the history, society, and culture of Hongtong County, Shanxi Province, and on the beliefs surrounding Ehuang and Nüying in local communities—provides context for my exploration of the ways ordinary people within local communities make sense of their places, history, beliefs, and selves, and the ways these elements are inseparably intertwined and negotiated. My introduction to intertwined beliefs and practices on Ehuang and Nüying centers on three places: Yangxie, Lishan, and Wan'an, where the Temples of Ehuang and Nüying are located. My observations of differentiation and interaction in their approach to the histories and beliefs among people from these three places demonstrates how they have made their "sacred" social bond through local beliefs and practices on Ehuang and Nüying, and how they have challenged and negotiated this connection on the ground within particular contexts. While the shè has been identified as an important social group who organizes the annual ritual processions and annual temple fairs at village temples, the role of folk literati in the transmission, production, and reproduction of local traditions will be explained in detail in the following chapters.

Notes

1. Generally speaking, the administrative divisions of China have consisted of five practical levels: provincial (province, autonomous region, municipality, and special administrative region), prefecture, county, township, and village.

2. "Sixth National Population Census of the People's Republic of China," National Bureau of Statistics of China, http://www.lfxww.com/xinwen/bsxw/2011/7/88582.shtml. Retrieved November 11, 2012.

3. A Chinese county is generally divided into *xiang* (townships) and *zhen* (towns), which are then divided into *cun* (villages). The difference between *xiang* and *zhen* is that the former is defined as a rural administrative center with the population predominantly engaged in agriculture, whereas the latter is defined as an urban administrative center with the majority of the population undertaking nonfarming activities. In reality, the difference in status between these two types of jurisdiction is determined by considerations that are not necessarily economic (Lin 2001; Bramall 2007).

4. Villagers' committees are the organizational entities of the Chinese state at the lowest level in the countryside. They have control over an administrative village (*xingzhengcun*), which may be made up of several natural villages (*zirancun*)—spontaneous, naturally grown settlements.

5. Gao Yao was the minister for law of Emperor Shun (Sima 1959 [91 BC], 39). Shi Kuang was a blind music master in the Jin Kingdom during the Spring and Autumn period. He was exceptional at playing *qin*, a seven-string Chinese musical instrument of the zither family. He is named as the deity of music in China, known for his musical achievements as well as his political insights. His tomb is believed to be in Shi Village, Quting Town, Hongtong County.

6. *Loujiao* (楼轿) is a holy wooden sedan chair that carries the statues of Ehuang and Nüying. It is believed to be the place where Ehuang and Nüying sit, and because it symbolizes their presence, the sedan chair has played a crucial role in the whole ritual and parade in honor of Ehuang and Nüying (Cheng 2011, 72).

7. *Huangsan* (黄伞, the Yellow Umbrella), also known as *wanmin san* (万民伞, Ten Thousand People's Umbrella), is an old royal canopy made with donations from ten thousand people, with all their names written on separate yellow belts, which were stitched together around the canopy.

8. *Gaozhao qi* (高招旗, the Tall Flag) is a high flag bearing the name of the village that the parades come from. In the annual parade of receiving Ehuang and Nüying from Yangxie to Wan'an on the twenty-ninth day of the fourth lunar month, the bearer carrying the Tall Flag walks ahead of the whole procession, and the flag shows where the parade is from.

9. *Wuse qi* (五色旗, Flags with Five Colors) are usually in red, pink, yellow, blue, and green. Today their bearers follow the bearer of the Tall Flag in the annual parade, and they are followed by the group of people who play *weifeng luogu* (威风锣鼓, the Awe-Inspiring Gongs and Drums), which are believed to have originated from Yao and Shun's age.

10. *Jin* and *liang* are traditional Chinese units of weight: 1 *jin* = 1/2 kilogram, 1 *liang* = 50 grams, and 1 *jin* = 10 *liang*.

11. Gongs and drums are important musical instruments in local festivals, rituals, and parades.

12. *Juanpeng* (卷棚, the Open Chamber) is a chamber without walls in front and back, where people are able to rest.

13. *Xiandian* (献殿, the Sacrifice Hall), is the main building of the temple, where the statues of Ehuang and Nüying are situated and where sacrifices are made. In the Temple of Ehuang and Nüying in Wan'an, the *Xiandian* was built during the Yuan dynasty but was ruined in the 1960s. It was rebuilt in 1991 (Wang et al. 2009, 790) and then again in 2010.

14. Tongpu Railway is a major trunk line in northern China. The railway, located entirely within Shanxi, diagonally bisects the province from Datong in the northeast to Fenglingdu, near the village of Puzhou, in the southwest corner. The line is often referred to by its northern and southern halves, with Taiyuan—the provincial capital—as the midpoint. Southern Tongpu Railway, from Taiyuan to Fenglingdu, is 513 km (319 mi.) in length and was built from 1933 to 1935. The Northern Tongpu Railway, from Datong to Taiyuan, is 351 km (218 mi.) in length and was built from 1933 to 1940.

15. This information is based on my interviews with local people in Hongtong in 2012 and 2013.

16. Refer to the Hongtong government website: http://www.hongtong.gov.cn/Dep_index .asp?id=84. Accessed December 25, 2012.

17. All the information above is based on my interviews with local people in Hongtong in 2012 and 2013.

2

INCENSE IS KEPT BURNING

The Role of Folk Literati in Continuing and Representing Local Traditions

I ENCOUNTERED THE VERNACULAR CONCEPT OF CULTURAL CONTINUITY— "INCENSE is kept burning" (*xianghuo buduan*)—during my fieldwork in Hongtong, and the exploration of that concept in this chapter presents the opportunity to analyze the important role of folk literati in continuing and representing local traditions. I focus particularly on Qiao Guoliang (乔国樑), a folk literatus who continued the annual ritual processions of receiving Ehuang and Nüying by himself during the Cultural Revolution and was sent to prison for it. Drawing on interviews with his family members and friends, I examine how Qiao represented himself as a literatus and how he reflected on his shifting role under changing regimes in the twentieth century. His manuscript "Biographies of Ehuang and Nüying" chronicles important events surrounding Ehuang and Nüying and their beliefs in Hongtong, and my analysis focuses on how he represents local place and space as well as local history and beliefs in his writing. Finally, I also explore Qiao's political important for the people and examine his role in continuing local traditions.

"Incense Is Kept Burning"

On July 2, 2012, I sat at the Temple of Ehuang and Nüying with several women from South Yangxie Village who were on duty that day. These women volunteered to serve their aunties in the temple once or twice every month when their shè took over temple affairs for that year. They came to the temple around seven o'clock in the morning, cleaned up the rooms, and prepared the sacrificial items on the altars. Most of them were in their sixties, and they formed a small group, rotating with nineteen other groups. They all strongly believed in their aunties and actively engaged in local traditional activities. After learning my purpose for being at the temple, they began to talk about the past. During the Cultural Revolution, local beliefs were attacked and banned as "feudal superstitions," and villagers from Yangxie were forbidden from receiving their aunties. However, several people still insisted on enacting local traditions and went to present-day Lishan under cover. One such folk hero was Qiao Guoliang, who once made his pilgrimage to Lishan and escorted the aunties back by himself in the early 1970s. Qiao's action was labeled "counterrevolutionary," he was sent to prison, and he lost his job in the local supply and marketing cooperatives (*gongxiaoshe*). After sharing stories about Qiao, a woman commented: "He suffered from hardships for his aunties. It was like fighting for sovereignty over rivers and mountains, that sovereignty is remarkably strong right now" (*Ta weile gugu zao le zui le. He da jiangshan yiyang, xianzai jiangshan dou dade haode liao-bude le*). Immediately, another woman in her early seventies said: "Rivers and mountains were won back, but he has gone. . . . At that time, the burning incense was not broken, the incense is kept burning" (*Jiangshan daxia le, ta zou le . . . nashi xianghuo meiduan, buduan xianghuo*).

The vernacular expression "incense is kept burning," a well-known metaphor widely used in China, was exactly the concept I was looking for to describe the cultural continuity within local contexts. The burned incense serves as a sacrificial offering to ancestors and deities and as a tool to help worshippers pray for what they desire. Burning incense is often the most fundamental ritual act in worshipping, and the fragrant smoke is thick nowadays in various temples, in lineage halls, and above familial altars. Although simple, the short phrase "incense is kept burning" encompasses all the cultural meanings of continuing local traditions, continuing a family line or clan lineage, and becoming a moral self in China. Through the burning of incense for ancestors and deities, those carrying on local traditions are carrying themselves on, physically and spiritually.

One of the essential issues explored here is how traditions are understood, reflected, and practiced on the ground by common people in northern rural China. Is there a less abstract concept than *tradition* in China to capture the sense of cultural continuity? In what ways do folk traditions differ from state-supported traditions? Are there any tensions associated with practicing these folk traditions? Most ancient Chinese scholars used the term *chuantong* to refer to state-supported traditions, and this usage has continued up to the present day. The voice of the common people was hardly heard throughout history until it was "discovered" and emphasized during the folk literature movement (1918–37), when young Chinese intellectuals under the spirit of the May Fourth Movement started to focus on the concept of the folk (mainly peasants) and elevated the status of common people to a level unprecedented in Chinese history (Hung 1985). These scholars developed a "romantic" perspective toward the folk, assuming that "this untapped, but rich, folk culture, if treated properly, could be used to convey new ideas and furnish urgent solutions to China's myriad problems" (Hung 1985, xii). They believed that an appropriate evaluation of the value of folk literature "was an essential part of obtaining a total view of China's culture, previously identified only as the elite tradition" (Hung 1985, xii). In the process, Chinese folklorists shifted the focus from high culture to low culture, choosing to reject the old values embedded in high culture and inculcate the new from the folk culture. Despite shifting the emphasis from high to low, these scholars also examined the two-way flow between the two cultures, illustrating their continuous interactions over the course of history (Hung 1985).

Who are the folk in the folk traditions? In the folk literature movement, the folk were primarily defined as Chinese peasants who planted their fields and harvested their crops for the ruling aristocrats. Intellectuals in the movement drew from the rebellious spirit embodied in folk literature to reject the social and moral values of the elite Confucian tradition. Understandably, they excluded the literati from their view of the folk. From 1962 to 1966, during the Mao era, folk literature was used to promote socialist education campaigns (You 2012). Within the Communist regime, the folk began to encompass workers, peasants, soldiers, and other working-class people, set apart from the bourgeois and landlord classes. After the Cultural Revolution, Chinese folklorists started to reflect on the dominant Marxist theory in folklore studies and realized that everyone should be included as a member of the folk without reference to class difference (Liu 2006). In this sense, the literati should not be excluded from the folk, even though too little attention has been paid to the role of these people in transmitting, producing, and reproducing local traditions on the ground.

Chen Yongchao draws on his fieldwork to track the dynamics of reconstructing folk legends in Hongtong about Yao and Shun as well as Ehuang and Nüying, illustrating the shifting forces in changing local legends through time and across space (Chen 2010). Chen differentiates seven different folk groups in the process of reconstructing local legends: (1) ordinary villagers; (2) exceptional villagers; (3) spiritual mediums; (4) temple executors; (5) folk intellectuals; (6) local officials; and (7) cultural outsiders. Chen points out that these different folk groups have played different roles in remaking local legends within specific contexts. In particular, he emphasizes the important role of "folklore elites" (*minsu jingying*) in the process of legend making. Chen defines this term as a particular group of people "who obtained certain power in producing local knowledge and discourse, leading the trends of integrating and changing local knowledge" (Chen 2010, 69). Chen further makes it clear that folklore elites could come from any of the first five folk groups he has classified, but they always include all folk intellectuals and extraordinary villagers. He acknowledges that the classification of folklore elites is his own theoretical construction and that this group of people is not homogenous or fixed in practice. His main concerns are with important local actors who have transmitted and invented local knowledge. In brief, the term *folklore elites* does not exist in practice; it is an analytical concept to describe the people who have played important roles in remaking local knowledge on folklore. Chen does not draw on local people's points of view to illustrate local experiences and perspectives on folklore elites, and he also does not study local responses to the reproduction of knowledge on the ground. In my research, however, I have worked to illustrate local people's own concepts and interpretations of those actors who have played important roles in transmitting, producing, and reproducing local knowledge and discourse on tradition, as well as local people's interactions with these actors. Drawing on the views of the villagers, I use the term *folk literati* to describe those people who have played important roles in making and remaking local history and folklore within their communities.

Mengzi categorizes the group of literati (*shi*) at different levels in ancient China: in a village, in a state, and in the world (*Mengzi, Wan Zhang xia*).[1] When examining the range of intellectual worlds in modern China, Timothy Cheek starts with three categories: "metropolitan" intellectuals active at the national level, "provincial" intellectuals influential in their province or region, and "local intellectuals" "with the skills, interests, and activities clearly representative of the everyday lives of most of China's thinkers and writers but not widely influential" (Cheek 2015, 11). The concept of folk literati is similar to Mengzi's concept of literati in a village and Cheek's concept of local intellectuals. However, what makes folk literati unique is their active role in remaking local folklore within their communities and their primary goal of maintaining cultural continuity—as expressed in the concept "incense is kept burning"—in the face of the many tensions and ruptures associated with practicing local folk traditions, especially during periods of political upheaval.

The story of Qiao Guoliang (1927–98), an influential folk literatus in Yangxie, is particularly relevant here. Many people mentioned Qiao to me during my fieldwork, and their comments made me curious about who he was and why he had been such a significant figure in the local communities, even after he passed away. With these questions in mind, I started to interview his children and grandchildren, who then guided me to some of Qiao's friends in Yangxie and Lishan. In addition, Qiao's oldest grandson, Qiao Longhai, kept his grandfather's unfinished manuscript, "E Ying Zhuan" ("Biographies of Ehuang and Nüying"), which he shared with me. These sources helped me begin to understand who Qiao Guoliang was, though the portrait I have of him is far from complete.

Qiao Guoliang's Story

Qiao Guoliang was born to a respectable family in old Yangxie Village on February 20, 1927, the only son of his parents. He received a very good education in his early years, studying the Four Books and Five Classics, ancient Chinese books used in Confucianism as the basis of studies.[2] He got married when he was eighteen years old and became a teacher when he was nineteen. Because of his training in classical Chinese language and literature, he taught Chinese in the elementary school in Xilu, a village close to Yangxie. Around 1951, Qiao passed the examination for a position and joined the newly established supply and marketing cooperative in Ganting Town. At that time, money was not easily available, so Qiao brought the goods to local villages for exchange.

During the New Land Reform Movement in 1952, Qiao's family was labeled as "rich peasants," a classification that later negatively influenced the whole family. During the Destruction of the Four Olds (Old Customs, Old Culture, Old Habits, and Old Ideas) in 1966, the annual ritual processions of receiving aunties were attacked as "feudal superstitions." Despite political suppression, a few Yangxie villagers still made their pilgrimage to Lishan to mark this annual ritual, and in the 1970s, Qiao started to receive aunties by himself after the old shè executors passed away. His fellow villagers reported his activities to the local government, and he was attacked as counterrevolutionary. Qiao was sent to prison for reeducation, and while there he suffered all kinds of humiliation. He also lost his official job. Despite these hardships, he never regretted what he had done to continue the traditions surrounding Ehuang and Nüying.

When the policy of "reform and opening up" was carried out in 1978, Qiao Guoliang was rehabilitated; he got his job back, and the local government compensated him for salary lost. Because his second son had been labeled a son of "rich peasants," no family wanted to marry their daughter to him. Eventually he got married, but he was put in the humiliating position of having to live with his wife's family. Later, he got divorced and left his son with his father to raise. He used his father's compensation money to marry again and formed a new family.

When Qiao Guoliang was fifty-four years old, his wife passed away, and his family was in desperate poverty. At that time, Qiao had to support his old parents, his third son, and his grandson from his second son, along with himself. He lost his official job again in 1983 because he participated in reviving the annual ritual processions in public. In order to earn a living for his family, he served as a handyman in the neighborhood and made a small amount of money by doing manual labor. No one in the family had a stable income, and they relied on their small plot of land to grow food. In the village, parents usually take the responsibility of arranging their sons' marriages. However, Qiao could not afford to pay for his third son's wedding; instead, his third son paid for it himself. Qiao also could not afford to hold funerals for his own parents, and he had to turn to his sons for help—his first son managed the funeral for Qiao's father, and his second son sponsored the funeral for his mother. Eventually his third son supported him in his final years and paid for Qiao's funeral.

No matter what happened to him, Qiao Guoliang felt a strong sense of responsibility to maintain cultural continuity and managed to practice the annual ritual processions of receiving aunties without interruption. He continuously tried to mobilize local villagers to participate in the pilgrimage and persuaded them that their participation would bring good luck and fortune to their families. Some of the villagers influenced by him later became core executors in local shè, and they played important roles in rebuilding local temples and reviving temple fairs in the 1990s and 2000s. Moreover, because of his influence, Qiao's sons, grandsons, and great-grandsons all became active participants in local traditions. His oldest grandson, Qiao Longhai, served as the shè head in South Yangxie from 2004 to 2006 and

Fig. 2.1. Qiao Jinming's wife (*left*), Qiao Jinming (*middle*), and the author (*right*) in Qiao Jinming's house on August 2, 2012. Qiao Jinming, Qiao Guoliang's third son, takes after his father.

later became the associate village head because of his strong capabilities in coordinating local affairs.

When he died of cancer in 1998, Qiao Guoliang left an important legacy to his communities, including a booklet to interpret divination sticks (*qian*) at the temple of Ehuang and Nüying, a booklet of music notations for the Awe-Inspiring Gongs and Drums, and his unfinished manuscript, "Biographies of Ehuang and Nüying." Qiao Jinming (乔金明), his third son, told me that Qiao also wrote an autobiography; unfortunately, it was lost after his death. During my interview with Qiao Jinming on August 2, 2012 (see fig. 2.1), he told me that he once read his father's autobiography but did not know all the characters that his father used in the work, since he was not very well educated. It was clear that Qiao Jinming had a lot of respect for his father's learning and writing. When commenting on his father's life, he emphasized its challenges: "He had never lived in ease and comfort, but endured hardships in his lifetime."

Self-Representation of Folk Literati

On July 10, 2012, I met Sun Laixi, a son of one of Qiao Guoliang's best friends in West to the Sacred Temple Village. When Qiao made the pilgrimage to Lishan by himself during the Cultural Revolution, Sun Laixi's father, Sun Yunliang, secretly received him in his village. Sun's family knew that Qiao was a person with strong moral virtues. Sun Laixi's father and Qiao maintained their sacred social bond but also kept up a good personal relationship. They met each other every year: when Qiao went to receive aunties in Lishan, he stayed in Sun's house, and when villagers from West to the Sacred Temple came to receive their *niangniang* in Yangxie, Sun stayed in Qiao's house. The two families maintained an intimate relationship because of their participation in local traditions. Sun Laixi viewed Qiao as a literatus (*wenren*) because Qiao was skilled in calligraphy and poetry and had knowledge of the Chinese literary classics. Before he died of cancer in 1998, Qiao gave Sun Yunliang a couplet and a poem done in his beautiful calligraphy (see fig. 2.2), and when Sun Yunliang passed away several years ago, his son kept Qiao's calligraphy. During my interview, Sun Laixi showed me the couplet:

> If the literati had the illustrious rank of nobility, people from thousands of miles away would inquire of them;
> If the literati fell down from the high rank, people living very close would dislike and avoid them.

爵顯千里詢
仕落咫尺嫌

This couplet reveals Qiao Guoliang's representation of his own personal experiences. Qiao conceived himself as literatus and represented his profoundly life-changing experience with ten Chinese characters. As this couplet indicates, Qiao lived in a rich family, received a good education, and obtained a good official position at an early age, and people from everywhere asked him for help and showed him their respect. However, after he was stigmatized as a counterrevolutionary and lost his job during the Cultural Revolution, he lived in abject poverty and his fellow villagers disparaged him in public.

His self-representation as a literatus and his reflections on the fickleness of human relationships were also conveyed in the poem that he wrote for Sun Yunliang:

Fig. 2.2. The poem and couplet written by Qiao Guoliang.

Sprouting in spring, shadowed in summer, from it the light did not pass
    through,
Literati, peasants, workers and artisans, and merchants all relaxed under it
    for shade.
When the cool wind in autumn blew withered yellow leaves falling,
Where were those that once relaxed under it for shade?
—A Poem Reflecting on an Autumn Tree, by Qiao Guoliang

春芽夏陰不透光
仕農工商俱乘凉
秋風吹落枯黄葉
乘凉之人在何方
—秋樹感詩一首　喬國樑書

This poem was written around 1996, and all the descriptions in it are about
a tree—about its growth, its shape, its practical use as a shelter in summer, and later its falling leaves. Qiao projected his feelings and identity onto
the tree: like the tree, he stood lonely in the cold fall, suffering from other
people's fickleness and indifference.

This poetic expression about the tree in fall was by no means new; it had already been developed by Chinese literati in poetry beginning with "Nine Changes" (*Jiubian*), the first poem on the sorrow of autumn, in the *Chu ci*, also known as *The Songs of the South* or *The Songs of Chu*, during the Warring States period (Hawkes [1985] 2011, 207–9). "Nine Changes" begins:

> Alas for the autumn air!
> Bleak and cold; plants and trees shake and lose their leaves, falling into decay. (*Jiubian*, chap. 1)

The poem is said to have been written by Song Yu, a well-known poet in the state of Chu (Hawkes [1985] 2011). It captures the sadness of autumn and the frustration of individuals—where the autumn season could seem joyful and filled with harvests for someone feeling happiness, for a person in distress, like Song Yu and Qiao Guoliang, every touch of autumn echoes one's own sadness.

The author's identification with a lonely tree was also not new in literati poetry. Bao Zhao (415?–66), a lower-class literatus during the Six dynasties (220 or 222–589), composed the poem "I Met a Lonely *T'ung* Tree on My Journey to the Mountain":

> A *t'ung* tree grows amidst a cluster of rocks,
> Its roots are buried alone beneath the cold, dark earth.
> Above, it leans against the receding bank,
> Below, it reaches deep into the cave.
> Rapid torrents shoot forth violently in the winter,
> Fog and rain are incessant in the summer.
> Before the autumn frost its leaves are already withered,
> Even without wind its branches moan by themselves.
> At dusk and in broad daylight sad thoughts pile up,
> Day and night, sorrowful birds call.
> The abandoned woman, looking at it, will cover her face and weep,
> The exiled official, facing it, will press his heart and sigh.
> Though it gives comfort to solitary and brave souls,
> Its own grief and loneliness cannot be borne.
> "I wish to be carved and hewn,
> To become a zither in your hall." (Chang 1986, 92)

Bao Zhao lived in an extremely chaotic period, with constant wars and the ruthless massacres of the common people by different emperors. Through the metaphor of a lonely tree, his poem reflects the harsh living conditions of the literati and conveys his sadness and discontent toward his society. Although Bao Zhao wanted to gain great achievements for his country, his desires were not fulfilled in his lifetime—he was killed in the frantic tumult of a rebellion (Chang 1986, 111).

Similar pain and grief are revealed in Qiao Guoliang's poem, although he is primarily concerned with his own mistreatment by people around him. Qiao suffered from humiliation and oppression, and he was enraged by the deconstruction of the old temples and the dismantlement of old traditions by locals—he could not stand the disrespect aimed at their own cultural roots. By drawing on the tradition of earlier literati lamenting the withered trees in the autumn, Qiao places himself within the lineage of traditional literati.

When Qiao Guoliang was diagnosed with cancer in 1996, he started to write "Biographies of Ehuang and Nüying." Qiao represented his own experience and his reasons for continuing local traditions in his manuscript:

> The class status of my family was not good, and I was labeled a counterrevolutionary, but I was never scared, because I had thoroughly thought over the basics of Ehuang and Nüying again and again. In general, it is not counterrevolutionary. Yao and Shun and the two aunties were real people during their time; their stories were true, not forged. Moreover, they were the ancestors of Chinese descendants, from ancient times up to the present; in China and abroad we all say "Yao Tian Shun Ri" (days of Yao and Shun), or the golden age of remote antiquity in Chinese history, times of peace and prosperity. This makes it clear that it is good, not bad. . . . Even I . . . was sent to prison, I did not feel ashamed, but felt honored and proud, because it is for the two aunties, and I had no complaints no matter how I had suffered. (Qiao 1997, section 9)

Qiao Guoliang believed that Yao and Shun were real ancient kings and regarded them as the ancient ancestors of the Chinese people. As a literatus, his goal was to transmit local knowledge of ancient Chinese history to his community and continue local practices of worship of Yao, Shun, and Ehuang and Nüying. He personally felt "honored and proud" of his insistence on observing and preserving these local beliefs and practices although he suffered for it. In his manuscript, he also drew on the local concept that "incense is kept burning" to articulate his responsibilities of

cultural transmission and production and his goal to keep cultural continuity without rupture in local communities.

"Biographies of Ehuang and Nüying"

Qiao Guoliang's family has preserved three versions of his "Biographies of
Ehuang and Nüying" (see fig. 2.3). The first version was finished on the third
day of the seventh lunar month (August 5) in 1997. It was written in classical
Chinese without any punctuation, and two of ten sections were missing from
it. The second version was completed on the twenty-first day of the eighth
lunar month (September 22) in 1997, written in combined traditional and
simplified Chinese with slight-pause marks between sentences. The third
was dated on the third day of the first lunar month (January 30) in 1998, not
long before Qiao Guoliang's death. The basic outline of these three versions
is almost the same, especially the second and third versions, and most of
my research here is based on the third version of his manuscript, from 1998.

Though Qiao Guoliang did not finish the manuscript, the extant text
can still be viewed as a complete work. The third version is fifty pages long,
divided into eleven sections, starting from Yao's age, "more than 4,800 years
ago," and ending in 1997. Qiao tried to present this long history of local traditions in his manuscript, but he primarily focused on the "days of Yao and
Shun" and the twentieth century. The first part is mainly based on historical
documents and local oral traditions and sometimes his own imagination;
the second part draws primarily from his personal experiences and from
accumulated knowledge in his communities. During my fieldwork, some of
his young friends told me that Qiao Guoliang liked to chat with sacred relatives in Lishan, Wan'an, and Xiqiao Zhuang when he went to receive aunties
on the third day of the third lunar month and when sacred relatives came
to Yangxie to celebrate Emperor Yao's birthday on the twenty-eighth day of
the fourth lunar month. He frequently communicated with shè executors
from other places to track how the old people practiced local traditions and
which stories they told. He wished to send his completed manuscript to Li
Xuezhi in Lishan for revisions and even eventual publication, and his ultimate goal was to unify local knowledge of and discourse on beliefs about
Ehuang and Nüying in Hongtong. However, he died before his goal could
be realized, and his manuscript was left in a friend's house in Yangxie for
several months before it was finally claimed by his third son. Later on, when
his oldest grandson, Qiao Longhai, took charge of temple affairs in Yangxie

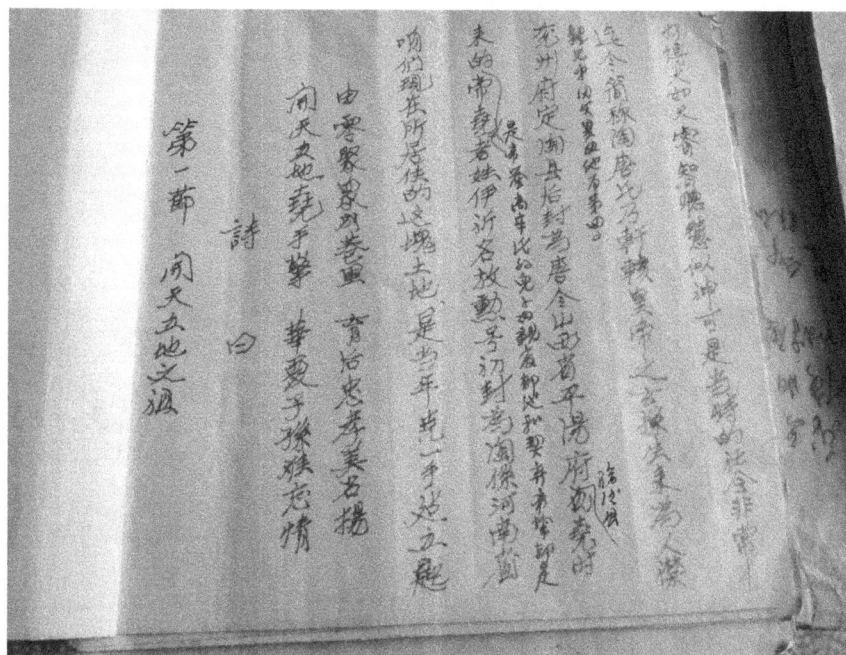

Fig. 2.3. The draft of Qiao Guoliang's *Biographies of Ehuang and Nüying*.

in the early 2000s, he got the manuscript back from his uncle, and he has preserved it up to the present.

After the flood in Yangxie on February 15, 2013, I was worried that Qiao Guoliang's original manuscript might have been destroyed, though a digital version would still survive, as I had scanned it during the summer of 2012. On the third day of the third lunar month (April 12) in 2013, I encountered Qiao Longhai in the annual ritual processions of receiving Ehuang and Nüying. As soon as he saw me, he told me that his grandfather's manuscript had survived the flood thanks to his son Qiao Ducheng (乔都丞) (b. 1994). Ducheng, whose two-year military service had given him extensive experience with natural disasters, stayed behind to protect his house and help with disaster response during the flood. He knew that his great-grandfather's invaluable work had been preserved in his family, so he found the manuscript and hung it in a bag high on a wall in the house. The document survived the flood, only needing to be carefully dried on the roof, and when Qiao Longhai came home, he was grateful to find that his son had saved the precious manuscript.

Qiao Longhai is the eldest son of Qiao Guoliang's eldest son. Qiao Guoliang trained Qiao Longhai to perform not only within the family but also at the village temple. Under Qiao Guoliang's influence, Qiao Longhai began to participate at a young age in the annual ritual processions of receiving aunties. Currently, Qiao Longhai is as influential in the area as his grandfather had been. When Qiao Longhai's son Ducheng was born in 1994, Qiao Guoliang was very happy, and he was given the honor of naming the boy. One of the meanings of *du* (都) is elegant or refined, and *cheng* (丞) is the same as *cheng* (承), "to continue," "to inherit." Thus the name *Ducheng* conveys Qiao Guoliang's concerns with the continuity of both family lineage and cultural heritage. Ducheng inherited not only the family bloodline but also local traditional culture, and from a young age, he would go to the village temple to burn incense for the aunties and participate with his father in the annual ritual processions of receiving aunties.

I interviewed Qiao Ducheng on April 23, 2013, and he still remembered how his great-grandfather wrote "Biographies of Ehuang and Nüying." At that time, Qiao Guoliang lived with his third son, and his room was in the western part of the house. He sat in a broken chair and wrote his manuscript on a worn-out table strewn with paper. He also practiced his calligraphy every day. Ducheng's father, Qiao Longhai, told me why Qiao Guoliang did not finish writing the manuscript during his final days: "When he wrote this manuscript, one day, when he was almost done with his work, he was writing some final lines. Suddenly the wind was blowing, and it blew one page away, which was never found. He wrote a few lines, it would be completed with a few lines, and his final page was not found. My third uncle told me this; I was not there when [my grandfather] wrote the manuscript. The final section was left unfinished; it was about whatever had happened. Eventually [he] did not finish the final manuscript."

Even though the last several lines are missing from the final manuscript, Qiao Guoliang's work chronicles local traditions coherently and represents local culture from the perspectives of the practitioners, making it an important source for understanding this local heritage.

Qiao Guoliang's Representations of Place and Space

In his book *The Production of Space* (1991), Henri Lefebvre shows that we cannot treat space simply as an inert and neutral container for people, events, and social institutions. He urges us to think of space as an ongoing social production of spatial structures and conceptions, as well as bodily incorporations of space, whose contours actively produce and transform social relations and whose historical development must be examined. Lefebvre is primarily preoccupied with the emergence of "abstract space," and his main concerns are not with the sense of place and space articulated and represented by local people. In my ethnographical research, I have found that village communities give spatial form to their common identities and community life by burning incense and making sacrificial offerings in temples and halls, by carrying the deities in annual ritual processions to mark out and negotiate community boundaries, and by celebrating the birthdays of deities and marking other festivals at temple fairs. These shared practices demarcate the land as a patchwork of community territories that often do not correspond to state administrative boundaries. Villagers' sense of place is intertwined with their sense of history, beliefs, and identities.

This sense of place, history, beliefs, and identities is mixed in with Qiao Guoliang's representations of local folklore and history. In "Biographies of Ehuang and Nüying," Qiao focuses on the history of the temples of Ehuang and Nüying in Yangxie, Lishan, Wan'an, and Xiqiao Zhuang. In the first two sections, Qiao introduces the stories of Emperor Yao and Ehuang and Nüying. In the third section he tells how the sacred goat *xie* was born in Yangxie Village during Yao's time, giving the village its name, and how local residents built the temple of Yao to memorialize him after his death, with the temple of Ehuang and Nüying being built on the eastern side of Yao's memorial hall. In the following two sections, Qiao relates the story of Shun, including how Emperor Yao tested Shun's ability to rule the country and, once finding him worthy, married him to his two daughters, Ehuang and Nüying. The story relates that, after moving to live with Shun in Lishan, the two women served the local people well and were honored by a temple to commemorate their good deeds and that later generations continued to worship Ehuang and Nüying on important occasions.

After introducing the origins of Ehuang and Nüying's temples in Yangxie and Lishan, Qiao Guoliang then illustrates how branch temples were built in Wan'an and Xiqiao Zhuang, helping to spread the beliefs in Ehuang and Nüying to a larger group of people dispersed over a greater area. In section 6, "Follow-Up in Wan'an," Qiao relates the story of a rich benefactor in Wan'an who began welcoming Yangxie villagers who participated in the annual ritual processions of receiving Ehuang and Nüying on the third day of third lunar month. According to Qiao, one year a serious drought led to famine throughout the local region. Even though most people were starving, the villagers from Yangxie still went to Lishan to receive their aunties, and there they were fed the best foods that their relatives could offer in the famine. When the villagers left Lishan the next day, they got very hungry on their way back home. One of them suggested going to Wan'an, a wealthy market center, to buy some food. What happened in Wan'an is described as follows:

> When they arrived at the Western Gate, it was closed, and they went to the Northern Gate. They entered the Northern Gate in the afternoon and got very tired and hungry. Then, they lay down near the road to have a rest. After a while, an old man came out of a house at the east of the road. He was in his sixties, with gray hair and bright, piercing eyes. The old man asked them: "Where did you come from? What are you doing here?" One of them came up and said to him: "We are from Yangxie, and we went to Yingshen Shan [Ying Sacred Mountain] to receive our two aunties." He then told everything to the old man. The old man was very happy to hear it, so he said immediately: "If this is the case, please stand up and come to my house. I will provide food and beds." After hearing it, everyone stood up and followed the old man into his house. They looked around and found that it was a spacious house. There were tall, large rooms with carved beams and painted rafters. The house was magnificent. The old man led them to sit in the living room, and after a while, four dishes and eight bowls of delicious foods, and many bottles of good alcohol, were put at the table. The old man asked all his family members to accompany and serve the guests. After the drinking had gone three rounds, [the host] served hot steamed buns and put them at the table. Everyone then got full with great satisfaction. They drank tea after meals, and after drinking tea, the old man said: "Let the guests have a rest." They entered a room; it was very clean. Everyone had a brand-new quilt-and-sheet set, and it was neatly laid. With the coming of dawn the next day, [the host] still treated them in the same way, and even bought some *bobo* [a special kind of local food, flat dry bread made of ground miscellaneous grains], made everyone take a dozen, in case they might get hungry on their way back home (this custom has been continued up to now), and did not ask for any money. However, Yangxie villagers did not feel comfortable about this; they insisted

on giving money to the old man. Right before leaving, the old man said: "Please make sure to come here again next year. Please keep your promise, and I will certainly make some preparations." Therefore, Yangxie villagers went there every year. Later, the old people said that the old man's family name was Qiao and that he was a rich man living inside the Northern Gate in Wan'an. Thousands of years passed; the family generously treated [Yangxie villagers]. Their economic conditions were not affected; instead, they became richer and richer. Over the years, other villagers also sent their invitations to the old man and asked to receive [Yangxie villagers], and the old man happily agreed, and more and more families got involved afterward. (Qiao 1998, section 6)

The reception of Yangxie residents in Wan'an persists both in story and in practice. The deities connect worshippers in different places, and the social interaction between Yangxie and Wan'an residents vividly represented in the story is quite common nowadays. This story is also represented as real history, though Qiao noted that "the exact date was untraceable." He assumes that the residents from Yangxie and Wan'an had been bonded together for "3,535 years" (by 1997), although he does not explain where this date came from. He makes it clear that the Yangxie villagers decided to pass Wan'an in the annual ritual processions primarily because Wan'an was a significant market center (it still is today) and they were desperate for food. It was believed that the rich man's benevolence in generously providing food and beds for the Yangxie villagers was rewarded by Ehuang and Nüying with wealth. This belief in reciprocity between deities and individuals inspired more residents in Wan'an to accommodate future Yangxie villagers who participated in the annual ritual processions of receiving deities. Later, a branch temple to the two goddesses was built in Wan'an.

In section 7, "Sought Asylum and Built Temple," Qiao Guoliang further records how the temple of Ehuang and Nüying was built in Xiqiao Zhuang in 1936. In the story, village heads were drinking tea in a local Buddhist temple on a hot afternoon, and suddenly they found two yellow snakes encircling each other in an incense burner on the altar. They burned incense, and then a local spiritual medium, or *mazi*, conveyed a message from Ehuang and Nüying, saying that their temple in Ying Sacred Mountain (present-day Lishan) would be burned soon and that they had to find another shelter in Xiqiao Zhuang. The villagers followed the words of the deities and built a new temple for them. The temple was completed within four months after the receipt of the message, thanks to the supplies and money provided by people from the village and other places. The consecration ceremony was held on the ninth day of the ninth lunar month in 1936, and villagers from Yangxie were invited to attend it.

After introducing the history of Ehuang and Nüying's temple in Xiqiao Zhuang, Qiao records many miraculous legends that he heard from Qiao Lide, the old shè accountant in Xiqiao Zhuang. One of these miraculous legends is the "silent toads" legend, which I also heard many times during my fieldwork in Xiqiao Zhuang. According to the legend, there used to be a pond outside the temple of Ehuang and Nüying, and the toads in it made ceaseless noise every night, keeping the two deities awake. The deities thus ordered a *mazi* to hold a whip and walk around the pond, snapping it as he went. After one round, the toads became silent, and they have kept silent right down to the present day.

With the stories recorded in his "Biographies of Ehuang and Nüying," Qiao Guoliang outlines four layers of social bonds in shared cultural space within local communities: (1) the sacred social bond between Yangxie and Lishan (also referred to as Shenli); (2) the sacred social bond between Yangxie and other villages along the route of the annual ritual processions of receiving Ehuang and Nüying; (3) the sacred social bond between Yangxie and Wan'an; and (4) the sacred social bond between Yangxie and Xiqiao Zhuang. These four layers of social relations in space are not a typology of different kinds of "spatial practices," which are physical and material constructions of space, nor are they representative of flows and interactions of people and things that both occur in space and impart social order to space (Lefebvre 1991, 33).[3] Rather, these social relations describe different aspects of the same spatial practices and are thought of as corresponding to the lived and imagined interactive sense of place, history, and beliefs within local communities.

The four layers of social bonds center on the shared spatial practices of worshipping Ehuang and Nüying in different places, and Qiao Guoliang also articulates a social hierarchy in the interactive process between the villages. The sacred social bond between Yangxie and Lishan is believed to be the longest and strongest, described as "one hundred times stronger than that of human relatives," and its history has been tracked to more than 4,800 years ago (Qiao 1998). This relationship was established and strengthened by Emperor Yao's marrying his two daughters off to Emperor Shun

in ancient times, and it is represented as the highest level of spatial practices within local communities. A lower-level sacred social bond connects
Yangxie and other villages along the route of the annual ritual processions
of receiving Ehuang and Nüying. In Qiao's accounts, believers from those
villages received Yangxie parades and saw them off, burned incense and
prayed to the deities in the holy sedan chair, and offered free tea and sacrificed food. They did not particularly treat Yangxie residents to meals or
accommodate them for a night. Yangxie parades passed through those villages without stopping for long. The social interaction between Yangxie and
these villages stood at the lowest level in terms of shared spatial practices
within local communities. The sacred social bond between Yangxie and
Wan'an is in the middle, between the two layers of social interactions discussed above. As Qiao records, Yangxie parades did not pass Wan'an in
older times, but in the year of the drought and famine, they went there to
buy cooked food. A rich benefactor initiated their social interaction and
established the social bond between Wan'an and Yangxie. Their social bond
was of a lower category than the one between Lishan and Yangxie, but
the status of Wan'an was much higher than that of the other villages that
Yangxie residents passed through. The fourth level of sacred social bonds
connects Yangxie and Xiqiao Zhuang. In older times, Yangxie parades
passed the village for *yaofan*, which would be any meals between breakfast
and lunch or between lunch and dinner. After the consecration ceremony
in the new temple of Ehuang and Nüying in Xiqiao Zhuang in 1936, villagers from Xiqiao Zhuang and Yangxie became relatives, and the latter stayed
in the village for one night on the first day of the third lunar month before
they left for Lishan the next day. In this way, the status of Xiqiao Zhuang
was changed from a relatively low-level social interaction to a middle-level
one, and it became another in-between village community in local traditions. Later, the Xiqiao Zhuang villagers found that their village was too
small to host the Yangxie villagers for one night, especially when the num-
bers of participants from Yangxie reached more than seven hundred in
1989 (there were about five hundred residents in Xiqiao Zhuang) (Xiqiao
Zhuang Miaoweihui 2006). Shè heads in Xiqiao Zhuang thus negotiated
with their counterparts from Yangxie, proposing to change the agenda and
host Yangxie participants only for lunch. Finally, a deal was made, and the
annual ritual processions of receiving Ehuang and Nüying from Yangxie
began on the second day of the third lunar month, with participants only
having lunch in Xiqiao Zhuang before they proceeded to Lishan. Because

of this changing process, Xiqiao Zhuang now holds a lower status than Wan'an in the annual ritual processions of receiving Ehuang and Nüying. Overall, Wan'an and Xiqiao Zhuang both changed their position and status in local traditions, but the different timing of their respective changes reflects a different importance of their in-between status. Qiao points out that by the end of 1997 the social bond between Wan'an and Yangxie had been maintained for "3,535 years," and the one between Xiqiao Zhuang and Yangxie had been continued for "61 years." The social hierarchy within the shared spatial practices is thus established and articulated in Qiao Guoliang's representations of local place and space.

Qiao Guoliang's Representations of Local History and Beliefs

In his "Biographies of Ehuang and Nüying," Qiao Guoliang outlines important events surrounding the beliefs of Ehuang and Nüying in Hongtong from the Second Sino-Japanese War (1937–45) up to 1997, and his chronicles are a mixture of history, legends, and beliefs. In the final four sections of his manuscript, Qiao records several of the times when the temples or rituals associated with Ehuang and Nüying were attacked or suppressed, and he details the interaction between these events and local belief systems.

The deconstruction and reconstruction of the temples of Ehuang and Nüying in Hongtong are closely intertwined with important events in modern Chinese history. According to Qiao Guoliang, Japanese soldiers burned the Temple of Ehuang and Nüying in present-day Lishan in 1938. This date is called into question by the records of some other folk literati in Hongtong, such as Wang Kaiyuan, a resident of Yangxie (Wang 2009b; Chen Yongchao 2015). According to Wang's accounts, the temple was burned after Japanese soldiers were defeated by Nationalist soldiers in Shi Family Village (Wang 2009b, 187), and the 2005 edition of *Hongtong County Annals* records this battle as happening in 1940. At that time, a small team of Japanese solders resided in two cave houses in Shi Family Village, and a group of Nationalist soldiers from Army 61 (under Yan Xishan's rule) unexpectedly attacked them at dawn on December 8, 1940, surprising the Japanese soldiers during their breakfast. When the Japanese soldiers refused to surrender, the Nationalist soldiers set fire to the cave houses, and all thirty-four Japanese soldiers were choked to death by the smoke (Zhang et al. 2005, 906). The story about this battle was also told to me by Wei Tianxing (b. 1936) in Lishan on June 20, 2012. He continued the tale, saying that other Japanese soldiers came to Shi Family Village the next day, only to find their fellow soldiers dead. Once the Nationalist soldiers were gone, the angry Japanese soldiers took revenge by setting fire to many houses in the neighborhood, along with the temples in Lishan.

Despite some contradictions in dates, Qiao Guoliang records how Japanese troops carried out the notorious "three-all policy" (*sanguang zhengce*) of killing, burning, and looting entire villages after they invaded Taiyuan, Shanxi, in 1937, provoking terror and destruction that is still recalled by local people. However, there are also stories about miracles in response to these atrocities. For instance, Qiao documents a miraculous legend told to him by Li Chunfu, an old shè head in Lishan. One day a young *mazi* went into a trance and conveyed a message from the two goddesses, asking the locals to fight Japanese troops at Miraculous Stone Mountain (*lingshi shan*). After hearing this message, Li went to see the county magistrate with the young *mazi* and explained everything to him. The magistrate contacted the head of the local troops the next day, they departed for Miraculous Stone Mountain, and on the third day, they defeated the Japanese troops there. Qiao particularly mentions that the two goddesses themselves appeared and used a grenade to kill thousands of Japanese soldiers. As the story goes, Ehuang and Nüying were punished by heaven for intervening in this way even though they saved local people's lives, and they were held down under Miraculous Stone Mountain for many years. After their release, they returned to Ying Sacred Mountain (present-day Lishan). This miraculous legend is different from traditional ones. Traditionally, the laity would ask the deities to cure illnesses, to enable them to conceive, or to bring fortunes; they then circulated the deities' miracles in response to their prayers by sharing their stories with others. However, in this legend, the two goddesses unexpectedly and directly participated in the war, expelling and killing Japanese troops. This unusual behavior violated the heavenly order, leading to their punishment. This story from Li Chunfu, written down by Qiao Guoliang, provided a significant source to sketch the social and cultural contexts of local beliefs during the Second Sino-Japanese War.

The Temple of Ehuang and Nüying in Yangxie was dismantled during the Civil War, which followed the end of the Second Sino-Japanese War. According to Qiao Guoliang, the Yangxie Village temple and many other local village temples were destroyed in the Battle of Linfen. This battle—fought between the Chinese Nationalist Party and the Chinese

Communist Party for seventy-two days from March 7 to May 17, 1948—was one of the bloodiest during the Civil War (Zhao 2008). At the time, about sixty thousand Communist troops from the People's Liberation Army (PLA) besieged about twenty-five thousand Nationalist soldiers in Linfen City, a strategically important site because of its defensibility. After failing to gain access to Linfen, PLA soldiers decided to dig tunnels under the city walls and dynamite the military fortresses from underground. The Communist Party mobilized masses in southern Shanxi to donate doors, rafters, and other supplies to make the tunnels for the assault. Eventually, 258,035 small door planks, 3,357 large door planks, and 102,137 rafters, along with other supplies, were donated and transported to the front (Zhao 2008, 12). The battle cost the lives of twenty-five thousand Nationalist soldiers and the lives of around fifteen thousand PLA soldiers; it also caused immeasurable damage to local culture. As Qiao records, the Temple of Ehuang and Nüying in Yangxie was dismantled during the battle, and all its wooden materials were sent to the front to support the PLA. Moreover, local traditions were officially stigmatized as "feudal superstitions" under the Communist regime. At the time, Qiao strongly believed in the miraculous message conveyed by a local ritual specialist—"One man, one horse, do not break my burning incense"—leading him to choose to continue local beliefs at all costs despite the official prohibitions against them.

In Qiao's manuscript, he notes that Ehuang and Nüying predicted the destruction of their temple, showed their power to local villagers, and motivated local people to continue in their beliefs:

> I remember that on the thirty-sixth year of the Republic of China [1947], eastern and western mountain areas were liberated, but the areas surrounding the railways were not yet. At the time, some troops were stationed in Yangxie, and they were a division of the Sixtieth Army, the Fifteenth Regiment [of Nationalist soldiers]. When the date of the temple fair was coming, temple executors automatically went to negotiate with the regiment in advance about the coming of relatives, and the head of the regiment consented without much deliberation. On the twenty-seventh day of the fourth lunar month, surely four gates were open, and people entered them freely. It was on the afternoon of the day when Yangxie residents received relatives to enter the village that Hong Wa fell into a trance. The old people said that Hong Wa became a spiritual medium of "General Fire-Dragon" when

he was twelve years old. He was known as an adolescent *Ma Tong*, and it was very efficacious every time he inquired of the deities when encountering something. It was on the afternoon of this day, when Yangxie residents received relatives to enter the village, that Hong Wa fell into trance. He said while crying: "One man, one horse, do not break my burning incense, even hide my tablet in your bosom. No matter what happens, you just run it, and I will become popular again in forty years." Unexpectedly, the regiment gave another order late at night. At dawn the next day, four gates were closed, and nobody was allowed to leave. It was said that there were spies in the village and that they must be combed out. When this order was given—it was not midnight yet—the head of the regiment suddenly had a painful stomachache. He asked doctors in the army to treat him, but it was in vain. Feeling helpless, they woke up the man in the host family, who then got up. The host knew the efficacy of the two [aunties], so he asked the head casually: "Did you say anything?" The head then told everything to the host. The host immediately responded: "Our aunties are very miraculous. You'd better find the temple executors and go with them to burn incense and ask for blessings in the temple. Also, you have to cancel the order, repeat your original order, and then you will be cured; otherwise, it would be in vain." The head of the regiment followed the instructions, and it was really efficacious, and his stomachache was cured immediately. If it was not in this way, Yangxie people would be really embarrassed. Afterward, the older generation of people said, it was not General Fire-Dragon who arrived here, but two [aunties] who arrived here. After breakfast the next day, when seeing relatives off, [two aunties] entered the gate of the temple three times and came out three times. [They] found it difficult to leave, and burst into tears. It was so moving that the viewers did not cry with them, because [they] knew not only that by the next year [1948] they could not be so imposing anymore but also that the old temple could not be preserved. [They] suffered heartbreaking pain and showed it to the people, thus making those righteous people understand what they thought, know their efficacy, and predict what would happen.

This time, Ehuang and Nüying did not participate directly in the war; instead, they appeared to the local people to tell them about the future dismantlement of their temple in Yangxie. However, despite their other miraculous actions, they seemed unable to protect their own temple, and the temple fairs were also soon canceled. Qiao continued with the story:

Soon the regiment was ordered to go to other places, and the village became half liberated. Because Linfen was not yet liberated, the remnant armies of World War II in the region all settled near Linfen, and they came to disturb [villagers] frequently, viciously asking for food and money, as if they viewed the people as their enemies. However, in the evening, it was the Eighth Route Army and the underground staffs [of the Communist Party] that entered the village and propagandized the party's policies; mass movements initiated by them were intense. On the twenty-ninth day of the fourth lunar month, Wan'an relatives were seen off just at noon, and then in the afternoon the head of temple executors, Zhang Zhongsu, was put in the prison located in Subu, and from then on, our village temple fairs were called "feudal superstitions." While the temple fairs were passed down by ancient people in our village, from generation to generation, from Tang Yao's age up to the present, it has been more than 4,800 years, and it is the event that people in this village care the most about and attach the most importance to. However, the staff from the Eighth Route Army all realized that the Aunties' Temple was the place that Yangxie residents valued the most; if it were not repressed, it would be difficult to carry out the [party's] work. At that time, the key policy was to replace the old with the new and to eliminate superstitions, and it was widely propagandized, made well-known to every household and clear to every individual. Therefore, the interaction among relatives came to an end. The Public Security Bureau posted notices everywhere, and it was said that the third day of the third lunar month [event] was illegitimate. Thus, everyone was scared and smitten with fear. In addition, a large number of troops besieged Linfen City; door planks were urgently needed at the front. Not only were the doors of every household, except the gates, all transported to the front in Linfen, but also the Aunties' Temple was dismantled and removed. At this crucial moment, when the road of the two [aunties] was about to be broken, the older generation of Yangxie Village, such as Yan Cai'er [an ordinary person], Wang Xiaowa [a temple gatekeeper], always kept in mind about what the two [aunties] said, and they did not forget it. Thus, in secret, one man, one horse, [they] hid the tablet in their bosom and still went back and forth on time without discontinuity. Especially during the time of the production team, the team leader supervised production tightly, and every day in the morning and in the early afternoon, when people went to the fields, he called the roll, and anyone who was absent once would be penalized with less grain rations. In order not to miss the roll call, old Yan Cai'er, during the busy time of the production team, when it was also the festival, after having dinner, old Yan Cai'er took a pouch worn at the girdle, put sacrificed foods inside, carried steamed corn buns to his bosom, went to the mountain to burn incense overnight, and then came back home to sleep. The next day, at dawn, [he] went to work without missing the roll call, and it was done this way for many years. While among relatives on the mountain, only Sun Yunliang and Guo Gen'er and other people came back and forth without discontinuity. After Yan Cai'er and Wang Xiaowa died, it was the author who took over, and I similarly went back and forth for more than ten years.

Despite political suppression, local people still believed in the deities, but they dared not worship them in public. Qiao Guoliang understood their dilemma and chose to continue the activities of receiving Ehuang and Nüying by himself. As he recalls, he revived the annual ritual processions of receiving the deities on the third day of the third lunar month in 1983, and more than sixty villagers in Yangxie joined the parades. After they came back, the deities "showed their efficacy, provided medicines in charity, and saved the common people" (Qiao 1998, section 9). Thousands of people came to the temple to burn incense and ask for medicines from the deities after the parades. However, their activities were soon suppressed by the local government, and worshippers from Yangxie, Lishan, Wan'an, and Han Family Village were sent to prison. Some even died during this suppression and detention, including Li Chunfu, the shè head from Lishan who told Qiao the legend about the intervention of Ehuang and Nüying on Miraculous Stone Mountain. Qiao relates the stories of these local people in his manuscript:

When it was almost the twenty-eighth day of the fourth lunar month, executors had arranged everything. Who would expect that the government sent some people to close the gates, destroy the tablets of deities, and forbid people to come and go?! Moreover, on the twenty-sixth day of the fourth lunar month, the Hongtong County government sent policemen to bind Yan Changhui and Zhang Yongxiang and ten other people and take them to Mamu prison and detain them there. During the detention, villagers went to visit them back and forth constantly, while these people did not feel ashamed but felt honored because it was for the two aunties; no matter how they had suffered, they had no complaints.

Relatives in the mountain such as Song Hesheng and Li Chunfu, Yang Baifu from Wan'an, Yan Yufu from Yangxie, and Guo Yanming [female] from Han Family Village were all labeled counterrevolutionaries, and they were sent to Hongtong prison, where Li Chunfu and Yang Baifu were detained and died. The rest of these people went through investigation; they did not do anything wrong, and things were all fabricated. As approved by the court, they were released and went back home. It is clear that this disaster not only made people suffer but also insulted the deities. (Qiao 1998, section 9)

Adam Yuet Chau sees a big rupture in the continuity of traditional Chinese folk beliefs and practices in contemporary China, and he notes that those beliefs and practices have reemerged and revived in the reform era (from the early 1980s onward) "all of a sudden" (Chau 2006, 1). However, on the basis of Qiao Guoliang's records, we can tell that the revival of folk beliefs and practices did not happen suddenly. The peasants wanted to keep their deities and managed to keep them underground. The incense was kept burning, not necessarily in temples and public shrines, but in temple ruins and at family altars. Meanwhile, the revival of folk beliefs and practices did not occur in China smoothly throughout the 1980s. Qiao records the government suppression of local temple activities in 1983, and later in 1987. Given what I know, the political control around folk beliefs was not relaxed until 1989. After the Tiananmen Square Incident of 1989, the Chinese government drew on tradition and history to reestablish its status as a legitimate regime and also adapted the concept of Western capitalism to their purposes to run the country (Oakes 2006). As an integrated part of traditional culture, folk beliefs—especially those related to the foundation of the Chinese nation-state—became a means to achieve economic success, which is an important signal and indicator for development, as well as a resource for the construction of local, regional, and national identities. The revival of folk beliefs did not happen suddenly or continue smoothly; rather it has been a dynamic process of construction, deconstruction, and reconstruction, and folk literati have played important roles in keeping the incense burning. Qiao's manuscript provides real proof of the hard work that folk literati have done behind the scenes, which has contributed to the contemporary cultural "revival" observed by scholars.

Folk Literati and Their Political Views

Shi or *wenren* (literati) is a socially constructed concept, and it was largely related to the self-perception of those who tried to maintain their status as cultural producers. It has never been a harmonious and fixed group, and its construction and identification has changed over time through Chinese history (Yu 1987; Huang 1995). In his book *The Last of China's Literati*, Bell Yung (2008) states that during the twentieth century, the literati tradition came to an end in the globalized world of marketing and entrepreneurship and deteriorating natural environments. However, from my fieldwork in southern Shanxi in 2012 and 2013, I have observed that the concept of literati still exists within some local community contexts, and it is closely related to the transmission and production of local traditions. Robert Hymes (1986) defines a similar social group as "local elite," and Adam Yuet Chau (2006) draws on this concept to study a local elite type like the temple boss Lao Wang in the Great Black Dragon King Temple in Shaanbei. Chau's accounts could also be used to describe local folk literati, who not only make local history but also represent local history in writing. However, unlike the powerful local elites like Lao Wang, folk literati like Qiao Guoliang did not have access to power, wealth, or prestige in local contexts, nor did they have control of local resources and local people's activities. Instead, they chose to be what they wanted to be and forged for themselves a social identity and sense of cultural responsibility. Sometimes, they were marginalized in the social hierarchy of power, but they chose to carry on their cultural responsibilities, to continue local traditions under intense social and political changes, and to draw on them to protest against the hegemonic power that oppressed them. But this should not be viewed as some kind of spiritual movement or a grassroots resistance against the Communist party-state (Chau 2006); in reality the process is much more complicated and interesting.

I have argued that the role of folk literati has shifted through history, illustrating that their main concerns were not with political agendas but with the concept that "incense is kept burning" within the dialectics of cultural continuity and rupture. However, one important area of inquiry opened up by Qiao Guoliang's story is the political standpoint of folk literati and their relationship to ordinary people in their communities. I got to know Qiao's political standpoint by accident during my fieldwork in Yangxie. On the afternoon of July 25, 2012, I was learning how to play gongs with two older musicians in the village. Bian Linping, the associate village party secretary in 2012 and the new village party secretary in 2013, came to visit me after hearing the music. He knew that I was digitizing Qiao's manuscript, so he casually talked about him with me. Qiao was much older than Bian, but they had become good friends despite the age difference. Qiao told Bian that he had never believed in socialism or Communism but strongly believed in the "Three People's Principles" (*Sanmin Zhuyi*), a political philosophy developed by Sun Yat-sen to help make China a free, prosperous, and powerful nation in the early twentieth century (Sun [1919] 1981–86; [1924a] 1981–86; [1924b] 1981–86). The three principles of *minzu*, *minquan*, and *minsheng* are often translated and summarized as nationalism, democracy, and the livelihood of the people. These three principles were the cornerstone of the Republic of China's policy as carried out by the Nationalists, and they remain an explicit part of the platform of the Nationalists in current-day Taiwan.

Qiao Guoliang's concept that incense is kept burning could be summarized as the view of cultural continuity "of the people, by the people, for the people." He fought against the repression of the opinions of common people and the threats to their livelihood. In his book *Representations of the Intellectual*, Edward Said characterizes the intellectual "as exile and marginal, as amateur, and as the author of a language that tries to speak truth to power." He further writes: "It is a spirit in opposition, rather than in accommodation, that grips me because the romance, the interest, the challenge of intellectual life is to be found in dissent against the status quo at a time when the struggle on behalf of underrepresented and disadvantaged groups seems so unfairly weighted against them" (Said 1994, xvi–xvii). As a folk literatus, Qiao shared such a spirit and fought for relative independence from political pressures. He scoured local sources, exhumed buried evidence, and revived abandoned history. He not only recorded local traditions in writing but spread them to audiences in his communities. His representations of local traditions did not win him official honors or benefits. Instead, he was lonely—as he expressed in his poem, like a lonely tree standing in the cold fall—but as Said notes, this position "is always a better one than a gregarious tolerance for the way things are" (1994, xviii).

Although folk literati like Qiao Guoliang have played an important role in remaking and representing local folklore in contemporary China, little attention has been paid to them in scholarship. Our view of intellectual life often focuses on famous scholars, prestigious writers, and influential thinkers. Some historians have begun to study ordinary intellectuals and local intellectual life, but their primary concerns are with the shaping of "Chinese modernity" (Cheek 2015, 92), not with the life of China's own traditions. Folk literati have always been active in their communities, but their role is easily missed in historical records since they are generally not influential at a metropolitan or national level. They attract the attention of the state only when they become "rebels" and "victims of purges or campaigns," or when they become "new members of the established system" (Cheek 2015, 207). In recent years, some folklorists have studied the role of folk intellectuals, folklore elites, local scholars, and writers in remaking and writing local legends by conducting direct interviews and gaining access to local records (Chen Yongchao 2010, 2015; Wang Yao 2010, 2011; Zhang 2012b); what is missed in their research, however, is a broader view of these individuals in remaking local traditions and engaging in rural life. When studying the role of "rural intellectuals," "local intellectuals," or "peasant intellectuals" in modern Chinese history, historians tend to focus on the Republican period (1912–49) and the Mao period (1949–76), when China experienced dramatic political changes. They show little interest in what is happening on the ground in the post-Mao period, especially in this new century. My fieldwork has enabled me to pick up what those folklorists and historians have left unexamined and to explore the way folk literati reconstruct the traditions of their communities and engage in rural life in contemporary times, and to do this from the viewpoint of villagers in Hongtong, connecting the social, cultural, political, and spiritual realms of their lives all together.

Notes

1. Mengzi (372–289 BC or 385–303 or 302 BC) was a Chinese philosopher who has frequently been known as the "second Sage" after Confucius.

2. The Four Books were selected by Zhu Xi in the Song dynasty to serve as a general introduction to Confucian thought; in the Ming and Qing dynasties, they were made the

core of the official curriculum for the civil service examinations. The Four Books include *Great Learning* (*Da Xue*, 大學), *The Doctrine of the Mean* (*Zhong Yong*, 中庸), *Analects* (*Lun Yu*, 論語), and *Mencius* (*Meng Zi*, 孟子). The Five Classics are pre-Qin Chinese books that form part of the traditional Confucian canon, and they include *Classic of Poetry* (*Shi Jing*, 詩經), *Book of Documents* (*Shang Shu*, 尚書), *Book of Rites* (*Li Ji*, 禮記), *I Ching* (*Yi Jing*, 易經), and *Spring and Autumn Annals* (*Chun Qiu*, 春秋) (Si shu wu jing 1985).

3. "Spatial practices" is a concept that I borrow from Lefebvre to analyze Qiao's assumptions.

3

CONTESTED MYTH, HISTORY, AND BELIEFS

Worshipping Yao and Shun at Village Temples in Hongtong

THE ERA OF YAO AND SHUN HAS BEEN constructed as the beginning of Chinese cultural history, and their stories have been recorded as an essential part of ancient history in China. This long-enduring construction was challenged and overturned by revisionist historians in the early twentieth century, however, and in the process, Yao and Shun's stories were transformed from "history" into "myths." This chapter challenges this process of deconstructing ancient history and reconstructing it into myth. Drawing on my ethnographic case study to explore the living traditions of the worship of Yao and Shun in Hongtong, Shanxi, I utilize locals' points of view to interpret written and oral narratives that some scholars reify as myths, and I explore the dynamics of constructing preliterate history in local contexts. It is particularly interesting to examine how Li Xuezhi (李学智), an influential folk literatus, has remade Yao and Shun's stories in Hongtong, how he has perceived himself through the reconstruction of contested ancient history, and how he has competed and negotiated with other local folk literati in the process of representing local myth, history, and beliefs.

My research on mythmaking in local communities echoes the paradigm shift from textual analysis to ethnographic research in Chinese folklore studies since the 1990s (Liu Xiaochun 2009) and the new trend to study myths "in contexts" (Yang 2015, 374), with a focus on the role of myth in local communities and individuals. Here I interpret myth as a metadiscourse on the basis of which social actors can construct social borders and also as "a discursive act" through which actors pursue certain cultural, political, and economic goals in practice within constructed communities (Lincoln 2014, 23).

Reification of Myth in Modern China

The Chinese term *shenhua* was borrowed from Japanese—it is the Chinese pronunciation of the Japanese word 神話 (しんわ), which was translated from the English term *myth* by Japanese scholar Takayama Chogyū (1871–1902) as early as 1899 (Ma 1992; Ye 2005; Liu 2006). Shortly after the *myth* term was introduced into Japanese culture, Chinese scholars studying in Japan rendered the concept into Chinese. Liang Qichao (1873–1929) was the first Chinese scholar to use the term *shenhua* in Chinese when he drew on the Japanese translation of myth while introducing Greek myths in his essay "The Relationship between History and Race" ("Lishi yu renzhong zhi guanxi") in 1902 (Liu 2006, 19). Nevertheless, Chinese scholars generally regard Jiang Guanyun (1866–1929) as the pioneer in the study of Chinese myth and see his essay "The People Cultivated through the Reading of Myth and History" ("Shenhua lishi yangcheng zhi renwu") (1903) as the first paper on Chinese myth studies in China (Ma 1992; Chen 1998; Ye 2005; Liu 2006; McNeal 2012).

The Chinese term *shenhua* was formulated within the tensions between Chinese tradition and Western culture, and the development of Chinese myth studies was itself stimulated by the cultural conflicts between East and West (Ma 1992; Wang 2005; Ye 2005). During this process, one of the challenges Chinese scholars faced was the perception that China had a dearth of myths or no myths at all. Realizing from the start of his career that Chinese mythology suffered acutely from the lack of a foundation of classical myth texts and of a research repertoire of edited and annotated myth narratives, Yuan Ke set about sifting through a vast number of little-known classical and traditional works to gather together the sources for a Chinese mythology. Over the years, he refined his research methodology so that today specialists have access to the most important narratives, some minor traditions, and a large number of myth variants, even though there is no agreement among scholars about what exactly myth is (Yuan 1984, 1987, 1991, 1993).

Since the introduction of the term in the early twentieth century, Chinese scholars have had differing definitions of *shenhua* (Yang et al. 1995; Wang 2005; Zhong 2006). Yuan Ke views the concept of myth in the broadest sense, and his corpus of Chinese mythology includes stories about gods or ancient ancestors, legends of historical figures, supernatural narratives, religious stories, and other kinds of tales (Yuan 1984, 1987, 1991, 1993). Basically, he does not separate myth from legend or history but blends them all together. Lü Wei disagrees with Yuan's approach and proposes to narrow the definition of myth to include only sacred prose narratives that employ symbols, such as images of gods, to explain the cosmos in exploration of the origins of the world, humans, and culture, the purpose being to provide sacred evidence to testify to the validity, rationality, and legitimacy of cultural and social institutions (Lü 1999). However, Yang Lihui and An Deming (2005) argue that myth is not necessarily sacred or always told in the form of prose.

In both discourse and practice, myth, legend, and history are seldom differentiated in China studies, although many scholars have attempted to do so. This confusion of myth, legend, and history is exposed in a preliminary way in the hypothesis of Cui Shu (1740–1816), whose proposition was that the lore presenting the most ancient kings and model emperors of the third millennium BC and before had been "built up in successive strata, so that the more remote from a given event, the more detailed becomes the information about that event" (Price 1946, 31). Cui Shu also pointed out that the writers of antiquity made a practice of substantiating their theories by illustrations drawn from folklore. After a long period of transmission, these illustrations, together with accretions and mistaken interpretations, were accepted as fact, thereby vitiating many histories, commentaries, and philosophical writings that appeared after the time of the Warring States period. This successive-strata hypothesis asserts that, for certain periods, later and later generations came to believe in earlier and earlier traditional figures.

The revisionist historian Gu Jiegang, known as "the founder of modern myth studies in China" (Birrell 1994b, 83), was devoted to disentangling the mythical era, differentiating myth from the historical period, and reestablishing the discipline of history in the context of ancient China. Gu and other scholars in the Doubting Antiquity School, such as Yang Kuan, tackled the problem of the traditional mode of historiography in China, subjecting what had previously been designated as "ancient history" to a fundamental and far-reaching scrutiny. Gu aroused considerable controversy when he published radical views on the demarcation between myth and history in a seven-volume collection of essays by himself and others between 1926 and 1941 (Gu [1926–41] 1982). Central to the authors' revisionist assessments of antiquity was the need to reclassify so-called ancient emperors into categories of deities and to eliminate spurious relationships and fallacious genealogies of the gods. In making that change, they challenged the authenticity of the oldest historical and canonical works of China, which for two millennia had symbolized textual and intellectual authority.

Was Gu Jiegang's reification of myth a process of "the mythologizing of history" or of "demythologizing" China's early history? In the article "Pioneers in Myth Studies" ("Shenhua yanjiu de kaituo zhe"), Wang Xiaolian summarizes the work of the Doubting Antiquity School and argues that the intertwined research of myths and ancient history that arose in Republican China deconstructed ancient history and reconstructed myths (Wang 2005). Wang uses the term *destruction* (*pohuai*) to describe the process of deconstruction of ancient history by Gu and other scholars, and he uses the term *restoration* (*huanyuan*) to summarize the process of reconstructing myths from history. If China did not have a vernacular concept of myth, what would be the goal of such restoration? And in the process of deconstructing history and reconstructing myth, did Chinese scholars create something new by creating a new category? Or did they adopt a new term to describe something already existing?

Shenhua is a term reified by Chinese scholars on the basis of a Western concept, and there is no vernacular conception exactly corresponding to it in Chinese culture. Chinese scholars used to draw on the Western conception of myth to track what myths are in ancient Chinese texts, but they have conflicting ideas about the definition of *myth*. In addition, they used textual analysis to rationalize the myths that they found in ancient texts and interpret their meaning based on their individual judgments or evaluations. In the process of creating Chinese mythology, they essentialized *myth* as a bounded category, even though they could not clearly define what it was, nor could they successfully demarcate myth from history. In other words, Chinese scholars objectified myth as something real and functional, and with a focus on the outcome and superficial dichotomy of myth and history, they did not reflect on how ordinary people understand what they reified as myth. In actuality, those stories that were classified as myths are still transmitted as living traditions in many regions in China.

To address that reality, since the 1990s Chinese folklorists have drawn on the methodology of ethnography to study the living myth traditions in contemporary China (Zhang 2009; Yang 1997, 1999, 2011, 2015; Yang et al. 2011; Liu 2008; Chen Yongchao 2015). Their focus has shifted from ancient texts to the dynamics of community and performance and to the local people's understanding and interpretation of "mythical" figures. Such an approach is crucial in de-essentializing the reification of *myth*, and it has been groundbreaking in contemporary Chinese folklore studies. Inspired by their work, I have applied this approach to my study of the living traditions about the ancient sage-kings Yao and Shun, understood both locally in Hongtong and in many places in China as among the most important of the early ancestors of the Chinese people. To do this, I have drawn on points of view communicated to me by local people to interpret stories that have been reified as myth by scholars and to explore how locals construct narratives of Chinese history and worship Yao and Shun as their ancestors in both bounded, formal rituals and in less formal expressive contexts in their daily lives. Moreover, I present how local people compete with each other over the representation of Yao and Shun. Before I fully illustrate the "competing discourses" of Yao and Shun in local texts (Epstein 2001), it is worth first introducing the Yao and Shun stories; the main sources for the stories; the ways the stories were constructed, deconstructed, and reconstructed through history; and the competing traditions about these stories.

Contested History and Competing Discourses: Yao and Shun's Stories

Yao and Shun's stories were canonized in the *Records of the Grand Historian* (*Shiji*), which recounted Chinese history from the time of the Yellow Emperor to the reign of Emperor Wu of Han (156–87 BC), written by Sima Qian (ca. 145 or 135–86 BC).[1] The first chapter, "The Basic Annals of the Five Emperors" (*wudi benji*), records Chinese prehistory from the Yellow Emperor to Yao and Shun. Sima Qian drew on both texts and oral traditions to write the stories of Yao and Shun, and one of his main sources is the *Book of Documents* (*Shangshu*), believed to be the earliest written work of Chinese history.[2] Despite controversies about the *Book of Documents*, many scholars agree that the stories of Yao and Shun in "The Basic Annals of the Five Emperors" are a compilation of all of the important sources that Sima Qian could reference, although some of these sources have long been lost; later stories about Yao and Shun have been based on the accounts in his chapter (Chen 2000).

Before Sima Qian wrote the *Shiji*, there were different versions of Yao and Shun's stories in ancient texts. Their stories were scattered in the philosophical texts *Analects* (*Lunyu*), *Mozi*, *Zhuangzi*, *Mengzi*, *Xunzi*, and *Hanfeizi*; in the historical texts *Discourses of the States* (*Guoyu*), *Commentary of Zuo* (*Zuo zhuan*), *Strategies of the Warring States* (*Zhanguo ce*), *Master Lü's Spring and Autumn Annals* (*Lüshi chunqiu*), *Huainanzi*, *The Records of the Grand Historian* (*Shiji*), and *Ancient Texts of Bamboo Tablet Annals* (*Guben zhushu jinian*), as well as in some sections of *Verses of Chu* or *Songs of Chu* (*Chuci*) (Allan 1981). In the pre-Qin philosophical texts, the authors did not recount full versions of Yao and Shun's stories. Instead, they primarily used short segments to support their own statements, and sometimes their interpretations of those stories contradict each other. Sarah Allan (1981) argues that the relationship between the predynastic rulers Yao and Shun could be expressed as an abdication, usurpation, or simply a matter of the changing allegiance of the population, depending on the viewpoint of the writer. Furthermore, she argues that historical legend functioned as myth used to mediate inherent social conflicts, such as the conflict between the hereditary right to rule and rule by virtue or between obligation to one's family and obligation to the larger social group.

Despite contradicting discourses and various theories about the relationship of Yao and Shun, different schools of philosophers in the pre-Qin era did treat Yao and Shun as real ancestral kings, and no scholars during that time doubted their existence in the way Gu Jiegang and other scholars in the Doubting Antiquity School have in modern China. Gu's study of the Yao and Shun stories focuses on Emperor Yao's abdication of his throne to Shun, an ordinary peasant, instead of to his own son, a golden-age event cherished by Confucians. Gu did not view Yao and Shun's age as the real beginning of Chinese cultural history; instead, he demonstrated that the abdication story was forged during the Warring States period, particularly by the Mozi school, and later was altered by the Confucian school.

Gu Jiegang's argument was subject to much debate and controversy during his time. In particular, he was criticized for not using all of the important sources on Yao and Shun and for his problematic method of "an argument from silence" (*mozheng*)—in other words, basing his conclusions on the absence of evidence (Zhang [1925] 1982; Qian 2008, 141). In this type of historical analysis, the absence of a reference to an event or a document is used to cast doubt on the event (Zhang [1925] 1982). For instance, Yao and Shun's stories appeared in a variety of philosophic texts, anthologies, historical texts, and literary works during the Warring States period. The stories of Yao and Shun were primarily used to convey particular arguments in these texts, and therefore the full details of the Yao and Shun stories were not always included. However, Gu did not find any records of Yao and Shun in earlier historical documents, such as in the early Zhou bronzes, so he concluded that the Yao and Shun stories were fabricated by the Moists and then altered by Confucianists. Zhang Yinlin criticized Gu for overusing this absence of evidence to arrive at invalid conclusions, and he further pointed out that any absence should not be relied on to prove the nonexistence of certain stories at certain times (Zhang [1925] 1982).

Since modern times, new archaeological discoveries and excavated texts have contributed to the study of ancient Chinese history, and Chinese scholars have developed three different approaches: "to doubt it, to believe it, and to interpret it" (Zhang 2012a, 35). Wang Guowei (1877–1927), an influential scholar in ancient Chinese history and culture, disagreed with the doubting approach and therefore established the famous method of "dual attestation" (*er'chong zhengju fa*), which draws on both textual materials and new archaeological finds to prove the legitimacy of various documents (1994). Since the 1990s, Li Xueqin (1933–2019), a prolific Chinese historian, archaeologist, and epigrapher, has called for scholars to "leave the 'Doubting Antiquity' period" and enter the "believing antiquity" era (1997). He argues that archaeological discoveries in recent decades have generally supported the historical documents about ancient Chinese history rather than contradicted them.

Through combined textual analysis and archaeological analysis, Chinese scholars have interpreted Yao and Shun's stories from different viewpoints. Moving away from this methodology, folklorists have turned to ethnography in order to study the living traditions of worshipping Yao and Shun in local communities (Chen et al. 2007; Chen 2010, 2015; Chen and Wang 2010; Cheng 2011; Zhou 2008). With this paradigm shift in Chinese folklore studies since the 1990s (Liu Xiaochun 2009), the focus has moved from the "conventionally dominant text-based research tradition" to the research on myths "in contexts" (Yang 2015, 374). This has brought a new focus on the interactive process of myth telling between narrators and audiences and the role of myth telling in certain groups and communities. When studying the dynamic process of mythmaking on the ground, Chinese folklorists are confronted with differences between textual research and contextual studies. In 2003 Chen Jianxian called for a "return to the text" in Chinese myth studies, emphasizing the stability of myth texts within changing contexts (5). Chen's argument stirred a heated debate on the relationship between textual analysis and fieldwork research among Chinese folklorists at the first annual conference of the Youth Forum of Folk Culture (*Minjian wenhua qingnian luntan*) in China in 2003 (Chen Jianxian 2004). Most folklorists agree that both textual analysis and fieldwork research are important in the creation of China's theories on myth, and therefore Yang Lihui has put forward a "synthetic approach" that integrates both "textual and contextual research" (2011, 2015).

The tension between textual analysis and fieldwork echoes the dilemma that Chinese folklorists have been confronted with since the discipline of folklore studies was shaped in modern China in 1918. Lydia H. Liu summarizes this dilemma with two key questions: "What to do with the pervasive impact of writing, literacy, and imperial bureaucracy on peoples and communities and their oral traditions, and what to do with the recorded histories of the past dynasties which have documented this impact continuously over the past 2,000-odd years" (2012, 193). Zhong Jingwen (1903–2002), known as the founding father of Chinese folklore studies, attempts to solve this dilemma by combining both written and oral sources in myth studies. He started to collect myths, legends, and folktales and edit them into volumes as early as the 1920s. In the 1930s, he wrote several articles about mythology in modern China, using both ancient written documents and the living myths collected from oral traditions to study Pangu myths, flood myths, and the myths of plant origins (Zhong 1982). Zhong's approach has been carried on by his student Yang Lihui in her study of living myth traditions in certain communities in contemporary China. I agree with Yang on the importance of combining history and ethnography (Yang 2011, 2015) but disagree on the theoretic framework that has been put forward to study living myth traditions.

Bruce Lincoln (2014) shows how myth and ritual have been and can be used in the construction and reconstruction of social groups and hierarchies. Robin McNeal (2015) studies the contemporary cultural revival of Shun at temples and monuments across China and shows how local elites have tried to construct cultural, historical, and moral identity in local communities while at the same time pursuing economic and political ends. McNeal further explores the role of myth in the construction of the Chinese nation-state and Chinese global identity in contemporary times, but he has paid little attention to the processes and conflicts that emerge in discourse and practice surrounding myth, history, and beliefs in local communities. My research not only demonstrates the profound entanglement of oral and written sources within the ethnographic case study itself but also highlights the individual construction of living myths within particular social, cultural, and political contexts. By combining history with ethnography in my studies, I have been able to explore how Yao and Shun are worshipped as ancient ancestors among ordinary villagers in Hongtong, Shanxi, and how their symbols and stories are constructed and negotiated within the local contexts through the eyes of local people.

Beliefs and Practices in the Old Temple of Tang Yao in Yangxie

According to the *Hongtong County Annals*, the Old Temple of Tang Yao in Yangxie was originally built in 1354 (Sun et al. 1917). The old temple was ruined and rebuilt many times during its long history, and it was dismantled in 1948 during the Chinese Civil War between the Communists and Nationalists and then rebuilt into a primary school in the 1950s (Yan 2012). The current temple was rebuilt in 1989 and renamed as the Old Temple of Tang Yao (*Tang Yao gu yuan*, 唐尧故园).[3] A commemorative stone stele was installed near the entrance to the temple complex; its text describes the history of the old temple, recording its long process of construction, destruction, and reconstruction:

> In Commemoration of the Reconstruction of the Old Temple of Tang Yao
> According to historical records, the Old Temple of Tang Yao was built by Emperor Yao with his people when Yao was the prince of Tang. When Yao came to the imperial throne, the Pingyang was flooded with a vast expanse of water, and the Old Temple of Tang Yao was ruined in the flood. During the Spring and Autumn period and Warring States period, the prince of the Yang State Gan and senior official of Yang County, Liao An, whose clan name is Yangshe, rebuilt the temple. . . . During the Song dynasty, a big earthquake occurred in Hongtong, 80 to 90 percent of buildings collapsed, and the old temple was ruined again. From the Yuan and Ming dynasties to the middle of Qing dynasty, villagers in Yangxie, in the name of royal relatives of Yao and Shun, in the hometowns of Yao and Shun, launched fund-raising for the reconstruction of the Old Temple of Tang Yao time after time. One after another, they built the Temple of Emperor

Yao, the Temple of Emperor Yao's Queen, the Temple of Imperial Aunties Ehuang and Nüying, and the Temple of Emperor Guan, the Temple of the Medicine King, Stage, Pavilion, the Long Corridor, and other grand buildings. After the Xinhai Revolution [1911], it was open as a school for villagers. During the Second Sino-Japanese War and the War of Liberation, some parts of the buildings were destroyed. After Liberation [1949], the underground water level rose year after year, and the village was relocated; furthermore, the old temple had fallen into disrepair for many years. Thus, the rest of the buildings in the old temple were dismantled and used for the construction of schools. In order to promote Emperor Yao's achievements and virtues of honesty, diligence, meritocracy, fondness for ordinary people, and strict law enforcement, in order to teach the descendants from Yao's hometown to improve their civilization, awareness, and quality, to revitalize various trades, and to strive for progress, to open a resting place for the people from Yao's hometown who come back home and visit relatives, and to provide a holy place for the descendants of the Yan Emperor and Yellow Emperor, who come to visit and pay their respects, following what the old temple used to be in history, with reference to the characteristics of the relics from primitive society, [we] make designs and arrangements and rebuild [the temple complex] by stages. Now that buildings in the early stage are completed, [we] write this essay and establish this stele, in commemoration of this event.

Summer 1989

(Wang et al. 2009, 738)

In the process of rebuilding the Yao temple, the Yangxie villagers named themselves the "royal relatives of Yao and Shun," and they called Yao's two daughters, Ehuang and Nüying, "imperial aunties." By calling Yao's two daughters "aunties," local people refer to themselves as if they were still living in Yao's time and their kinship relationships were completely stabilized and frozen in that distant past. In this way, the villagers have made a connection to Yao as their ancestor and linked Yao's old temple to the very foundation of their history and culture. When the Old Temple of Tang Yao was rebuilt in 1989, one of the main purposes was to provide a place for "the descendants from Yao's hometown" and "the descendants of the Yan Emperor and Yellow Emperor"—that is, all people of Chinese descent—to return to their roots and show high respect to their ancestors.

In the book *Records of Emperors and Kings* (*Diwang shiji,* 帝王世纪), Huangfu Mi (皇甫谧) (215–82 AD) states that Emperor Yao established the capital in Pingyang (平阳) (2000, 12), and historians have proved that the old capital of Pingyang is in the current Linfen City in Shanxi (Shi 1996, 41–42). Another stele text in the Old Temple of Tang Yao records how Juxian Lu, literally "Cottage of the Virtuous Gathering," was built in Yangxie during Yao's time:

> In Commemoration of the Reconstruction of the Cottage of the Virtuous Gathering
>
> Juxian Lu was the Hall of Diligence when Yao was the prince of Tang, and it was also used as the hall for ceremonies and sacrifices. Emperor Tang Yao invited Shun, who was well known for his filial piety; Houji or Prince Millet, who taught people how to plant grains; Gaoyao, who was honest and just; musician Kui; warrior Qie; and artisan Chui to gather, and they discussed important issues on how to serve and benefit ordinary people. The governors from the nine provinces and loyal and honest courtiers also came to the hall to visit Tang Yao. When Emperor Zhi died, officials from the four mountains got together in this hall and presented Yao as the emperor. Yao sat on the imperial throne and used the Old Temple of Tang Yao as the temporary palace. This thatched cottage was honored as Juxian Lu.
>
> Summer 1989
> (Wang et al. 2009, 737)

This stele text is primarily based on the biographies of Yao and Shun in *Records of the Grand Historian*. In "The Basic Annals of the Five Emperors," Houji or Prince Millet, Gaoyao, Kui, Qie, and Chui were presented as important officials of Shun, all from Yao's time. Yangxie is believed to be the place where the temporary palace of Yao was located. Naturally, local traditions focus on Yao, instead of Shun. This stele text is a short introduction to Yao's achievements in his career, with his important officials listed as his supporters. The main goal of reconstructing this local history is to convey the significance of the Cottage of the Virtuous Gathering and of Yangxie. Yao and those officials are represented as real historical figures in the text, and Yao in particular is reified as a real ancestor for local people in Yangxie.

When the Old Temple of Tang Yao was rebuilt in 1989, some shè heads and local residents were dissatisfied with the appearance and durability of the buildings (Yan 2012). After collecting sufficient incense money and hiring some professional construction teams, the shè mobilized the local people to reconstruct several of the main temple halls. The Temple of Ehuang and Nüying was renovated in 1990 and then again in 1993; it was eventually rebuilt in 2007. Yao's Resting Palace (*hougong*) was rebuilt first in 1993 and then again in 2009. The Cottage of the Virtuous Gathering was completely reconstructed in 2008, and its name was changed to the Great Hall of Emperor Yao (*yaowang dadian*). All of these new temple halls imitated the architectural style of the Imperial Palace, or the Forbidden City, in Beijing, which was constructed and renovated during the Ming and Qing dynasties.

A large temple fair is held in the Old Temple of Tang Yao in Yangxie around the twenty-eighth day of the fourth lunar month, which is believed to be Emperor Yao's birthday. Nowadays the temple fair usually lasts for ten days, from the twentieth day to the twenty-ninth day of the fourth lunar month. Recently, an official ceremony has been held to celebrate Emperor Yao's birthday on the morning of the twenty-eighth day of the fourth lunar month in the Old Temple of Tang Yao. I observed the ceremony first in 2007 and then again in 2013. A sacrifice is offered in front of Yao's Resting Palace behind the Great Hall of Emperor Yao, with the ceremony generally including the following elements: (1) local villagers set off firecrackers and set up the altar with Yao's tablet in front of the entrance door to Yao's Resting Palace; (2) local people place Shun's sacred picture and Ehuang and Nüying's sacred statues on the altar; (3) dressed-up local women offer five grains (*wugu*), fresh fruits, and birthday cakes at the altar; (4) the general shè head in Yangxie burns incense and genuflects toward the altar; (5) village heads and party secretaries sacrifice sacred alcohol and sacred water to Yao; (6) a local resident, allegedly Emperor Yao's descendant, gives the elegiac address in prose or in poetry, praising Yao's virtues and achievements and stiffening local residents' morale; (7) the shè head from Lishan holds Shun's picture while genuflecting toward Yao's tablet; (8) two girls from Yangxie hold the statues of their aunties while genuflecting toward Yao's tablet; (9) shè heads and shè members from Xiqiao Zhuang, Lishan, and Yangxie genuflect three times toward Yao's tablet, one after another; (10) a group of young girls from Yangxie perform classical dance to entertain Yao; (11) thirteen men from Yangxie play "the Awe-Inspiring Gongs and Drums" in memory of Yao; and (12) all participants genuflect toward the altar.

What follows this invented ceremony is the traditional ritual of receiving Ehuang and Nüying back to their temple in Lishan. In this traditional ceremony, the Yangxie villagers first put the statues of Ehuang and Nüying back in their temple in Yangxie, and then Yangxie and Lishan shè heads lead the ceremony of burning incenses, genuflecting, and asking for blessings from the deities. Afterward, they put the statues of Ehuang and Nüying in the divine sedan chair, which is carried by Lishan participants. After the ceremony in the Old Temple of Tang Yao, the Lishan participants carry their divine sedan chair in procession through Yangxie. The Yangxie residents accompany the Lishan parade along the procession route until they arrive at the small General's Temple at the entrance to Yangxie. After seeing Lishan relatives off at the Fen River, the Yangxie villagers welcome the Wan'an participants into the village and host them one night, the same as the Wan'an residents do for Yangxie villagers during the third day of the third lunar month.

The Temple of Shun in Lishan

The complex around the Temple of Shun in Lishan is one of the biggest reconstruction projects to have taken place in Hongtong. The project started in 1992 and ended in 2010 when the "debt crisis" broke out (see chap. 1). According to the *Hongtong County Annals*, the Temple of Shun was first built in Western Fence Village, about one mile away from the current Lishan, in 1029 (Sun et al. 1917). The old temple was burned by Japanese soldiers during the Second Sino-Japanese War and then destroyed during the Cultural Revolution. Reconstruction of the current Temple of Shun in Lishan began in 1995, and the project was completed in September 1996.

Lishan is traditionally known as Ying Mountain (Yingshan), or Ying Sacred Mountain, named after Nüying. The name of the mountain was changed from Yingshan to Lishan by folk literatus Li Xuezhi around 1992, when he mobilized local people to rebuild the ruined Temple of Shun in his hometown. The name change also reflects Li's assertion that the old Yingshan was the place where Shun plowed in ancient times (Li 2009). Li wanted to establish the place as Lishan because of the importance of Lishan in the stories and on the national stage. When the reconstruction of the Temple of Shun was completed in 1996, a commemorative stone stele was erected near the entrance to the temple. The stele's text was written by Li in classical Chinese, and it conveys the temple's official version of the story of Emperor Shun, Lishan, the temple, the temple's destruction, and its eventual reconstruction. This commemorative essay is a mixture of myth and history, and it has also been established as the authoritative version of Yao and Shun stories in local contexts (see appendix). The essay is primarily based on the biography of Shun in "The Basic Annals of the Five Emperors"; indeed, some passages from the biography are cited directly in the stele text. Other important sources used for the stele text include the "Wan Zhang" chapter in *Mengzi*, "the Canon of Yao" chapter in the *Book of Documents*, and the first chapter, "The Two Consorts of Youyu," in *The Biographies of Exemplary Women*. Like Sima Qian before him, Li mixes sources from both historical records and local folklore to create coherent stories of Yao and Shun. There are, of course, nuanced differences between the narratives.

Li Xuezhi and His Remaking of Lishan

I met Li Xuezhi (b. 1928) in Lishan for the first time on the evening of April 18 (the second day of the third lunar month), 2007, with a group of Chinese folklorists and graduate students from Beijing University. He told us the stories of Yao and Shun in detail in his office in the Temple of Shun (You 2015a). When I went back to Hongtong to conduct my dissertation fieldwork in 2012, I interviewed Li about his life and achievements (see fig. 3.1); I later returned to finish my fieldwork in Hongtong in 2013. After launching the reconstruction project in 1992, Li lived by himself in the Temple of Shun for many years, and I stayed there from July 8 to 21, 2012, with Li, five male guardians, one male custodian, and one female cook. Other people in the temple called him an "old man" (*lao han*), telling me that this old man had retired and was not in charge of temple affairs anymore.

The interview was an interesting process. I first told Li Xuezhi directly that I intended to interview him about his life history, especially about his personal experiences in rebuilding the Temple of Shun in Lishan; he then suggested that he would like to write a short introduction about himself. Thinking it would be a short autobiography and therefore very useful, I was excited to accept his suggestion. After several days, he gave me his manuscript "How Did I Make Lishan, Hongtong?" (Li 2012). With this text, he briefly traced the twenty-year history of rebuilding the Temple of Shun and reviving local temple fairs. However, his main goal was to draw on historical documents and local folklore to legitimatize the status of Lishan in Hongtong in response to that status being problematized and overturned by writers from Yuanqu, a county in the southern part of Shanxi where another Lishan is located.

Fig. 3.1. Interviewing the eighty-five-year-old Li Xuezhi at the Temple of Shun in Lishan, Hongtong, Shanxi, in summer 2012.

On the basis of historical records from a local gazetteer and some oral histories told by elderly men living around old Yingshan, Li Xuezhi argued that the current Lishan in Hongtong was where Shun plowed during ancient times. Proving this argument had been Li's goal for two decades. His agenda was first strongly supported by local residents around Lishan, who also sought legitimacy for their "illegal" beliefs toward Ehuang and Nüying and their annual ritual processions of receiving deities in the 1990s. Most of the residents were uneducated peasants who could not read historical books or tell Yao and Shun stories in a learned discourse. Because of his knowledge, Li obtained absolute power in changing the name of the mountain from Yingshan to Lishan and also in producing Yao and Shun stories within the local communities in the 1990s. By changing the name, Li successfully melded local history with the mainstream national history, which is well documented in written records. However, there are at least twenty-one places known as Lishan in China; Li's reinvention of local tradition thus made Lishan in Hongtong a contested place in the country. Confronted with challenges to his assertion, particularly from the old Lishan in Yuanqu, Li invited several archaeologists and historians to conduct research in Lishan in order to legitimatize the "authenticity" of Lishan in Hongtong (Li 2009). One of those scholars was Ma Zhizheng (1937–2013), a professor of geography at Shanxi Normal University, who published *A Collection of Research Articles on Yao-Shun and Old Lishan* (2011) to prove the relationship between Yao and Shun and old Lishan in Hongtong. Ma primarily drew on archaeological findings to prove that old Lishan was a part of the Taosi late Neolithic site about 4,000 to 4,700 years ago.

During my stay in the Temple of Shun in July 2012, Li Xuezhi was trying to plan an international conference called "Shun Plowed in Lishan, Hongtong"—an effort to compete with advocates from other Lishans in China—and was applying to the local government for two million yuan to fund the event. However, the local government did not promise him anything, and the local people did not support such a conference. During my interviews with the local people, some directly criticized the actions of Li and his old team and said that they "did it over, making local people suffer from it" (*zheteng de tai guohuo*). They said that he and his old team members originally cherished the "ordinary people" (*lao bai xing*) but abandoned them later on and only cared about their personal "honor, glory, wealth and high position" (*rong hua fu gui*).

Within the shifting power relations in Lishan primarily caused by the local debt crisis, Li Xuezhi's personal authority was eroded and his reconstruction of Shun stories temporarily discredited. The local people told me about how he changed the name Yingshan to Lishan, but when I asked Li directly when Yingshan was changed to Lishan, he answered: "On the seventh year of the Tiansheng period during the Song dynasty" (that is, 1029). He then asked me to refer to his manuscript and noted that he had made this point very clear in it.

Li Xuezhi's manuscript was not the autobiography I had hoped for. Rather, in the text he praises himself for the work he did for the Lishan people, especially his initiative in and dedication to rebuilding the Temple of Shun, without noting anything about his early life. I was able to get some information about his earlier years from the local people—for instance, the fact that he once worked as a secretary for Liang Huazhi (梁化之) (1905–49), a leading Nationalist official who served in the warlord Yan Xishan's Shanxi government in the 1940s. However, in order to learn more about him, I interviewed Li again on July 18, 2012, and he told me what had happened to him during the first half of his life. It soon became clear that talking about his earlier life brought painful memories for him.

Li Xuezhi was born into a very poor peasant family in Western Fence Village, one of the six villages around old Yingshan, on June 21, 1928. When he attended the elementary school, during the Second Sino-Japanese War, life was hard. After he finished the fourth grade, his father asked him to stay home to cultivate crops for a living—his family was too poor to support his education. Because he was an excellent student, his teachers took turns supporting him and helped him finish elementary school. After graduation, he was admitted to a public junior high school run by Yan Xishan (1883–1960), a warlord who effectively controlled the province of Shanxi from the 1911 Revolution to the 1949 Communist Revolution (Gillin 1967). The local government covered Li's tuition and living costs, and he received excellent training in classical Chinese. When Li was seventeen years old and still attending school, he married the daughter of one of his schoolteachers. His father passed away two months after his wedding. Li had to graduate as soon as possible in order to start earning a living, and so his school principal recommended him to Liang Huazhi, Yan's nephew. He then became a junior officer in one of Liang's spy organizations, and later he was promoted as a secretary in Taiyuan Suijing Gongshu Tezhong Jingxian Zhihui Chu, a high-level spy organization headquartered in Taiyuan. However, Li's career in Yan's Nationalist government ended when the Communists took control of most of Shanxi in 1949. Yan fled to Taiwan, and Liang was named the chairman of the government of Shanxi. For six months Liang led a savage resistance until the Communist troops finally entered Taiyuan. Liang killed himself after burning a prison filled with Communist soldiers captured during the Civil War (Gillin 1967, 288).

Li Xuezhi was only twenty-one years old when Yan Xishan fled to Taiwan. Li left for Beijing, wanting to follow Yan to Taiwan, but he could not get a ticket, even though he waited in the airport for half a month. He feared that the Communists might kill him after the Liberation. When Beijing was totally controlled by Communists in early 1949, Li saw posters about young people who were permitted to enter revolutionary colleges, and he signed up. However, he was sent to study in North China Military Area No. 2 Officers Training Group, a special training group for defeated Nationalists who fled to Beijing from all over China at the end of the Civil War. Li stayed in the training group for about seven months, his main task being to study Marxist theory and Mao Zedong thought with the other Nationalist officials. After Mao published his essay "On people's democratic dictatorship" (*Lun renmin minzu zhuanzheng*) on June 30, 1949, the defeated Nationalists were classified as "bourgeois" and forced to accept "reform through labor" (*laodong gaizao*). Li was then assigned to the Luozhen Ying reform-through-labor farm in Yanbei in the northern part of Shanxi. This site was a labor camp that taught political prisoners and people from the old ruling class how to farm. In the labor camp, the Communist officials kept saying that Li and other Nationalists would be released "in the near future" if they reformed themselves adequately through labor, but "the near future" never came.

In 1955 Mao Zedong launched a second wave of anti-counterrevolution campaigns, and many political opponents and capitalists were sent to prison or killed. Li Xuezhi was frightened again. He knew that he did not have any future—his wife was still waiting for him at home, but he forced her to divorce him. In the anti-counterrevolution campaigns, Li was sent to a prison in Taiyuan, where he stayed with Japanese soldiers, Nationalist officials, and Yan Xishan's senior officers. Li was accused of killing a Communist when he served in Liang Huazhi's spy organization. Since Liang had committed suicide after the fall of Taiyuan in 1949, Li became a scapegoat for the murder, and he was sentenced to twelve years in prison. He was then sent to another labor camp and finally was released in 1966.

When Li Xuezhi came out of prison, the Socialist Education Movement (1963–66) had just ended and the Cultural Revolution (1966–76) was launched. He was given a counterrevolutionary hat (*fan geming maozi*) before he was released, and he had to wear this hat when he went back home to Western Fence Village. Li described himself as "a prisoner out of prison" during the ten years of the Cultural Revolution. In the village, he was assigned to do some dirty and hard labor, such as cleaning up excrement. After suffering for twenty-seven years, Li eventually got his freedom when Deng Xiaoping started the reform era in 1978. Li was almost fifty years old by then, and he married a widow who had four children. Since Li did not have any children, he treated his second wife's children as his own. When he talked about what motivated his devotion to rebuilding the Temple of Shun in Lishan and remaking Shun's stories in his hometown, he said: "I was unjustly treated in my life, wrongfully treated. During the golden age of my life, I was in prison. . . . I feel that the first half of my life was not worthwhile, I did nothing. Because this place [Lishan] has bright prospects, I am willing to do something here to benefit people, contribute to our society, and compensate for the hardships during the first half of my life. This is what I think."

Locally, Li Xuezhi is well known as "a pen holder or a powerful writer" (*bi gan zi*) or "literatus" (*wenren*) owing to his training in classical Chinese. He wrote many stele texts for Lishan—*In Commemoration of the Reconstruction of the Shun Temple* is one splendid example. In addition to stele texts, Li published essays in various journals and newspapers, released his booklet *Records of Connections between Yangxie and Lishan through Sacred Marriage* in 1997, and published his edited book *Lishan Where Shun Plowed Was in Hongtong* in 2009.

Adam Yuet Chau points out that a variety of genres and texts can coexist in one social space centered on a temple and that it is difficult to determine which are dominant voices and which are subordinate ones (2006, 96). However, in my fieldwork, I have found that such texts are produced within a specific cultural hierarchy in local contexts. Texts written by local literati can overshadow unofficial and low-level texts, especially when the literati draw on significant historical sources to create their texts and when they inscribe them on stone. From local perspectives, stele texts have a high-level status; their power derives from their potential longevity and sense of monumentality. However, it does not necessarily follow that all stele texts are equally powerful. The individuals who produce stele texts for certain audiences can shape the texts to express their will and to prioritize certain voices over others.

After establishing the authority of his stele text about Shun, Li Xuezhi attempted to produce some simple texts for ordinary audiences. The basic outlines of Yao and Shun stories in his 1997 booklet are the same as those in the stele text; they are also in accord with the "Basic Annals" of Yao and Shun in the *Shiji*. However, the former is written in colloquial language, and the latter is written in classical Chinese. Like Sima Qian, Li drew on a mixture of sources from both written historical documents and living oral tradition to reconstruct Yao and Shun's stories. When Sima composed the "Basic Annals" of Yao and Shun in the *Shiji*, he found some problems in ancient texts, and so he traveled to many places to collect data. He noticed that people in different places had "different discourses and teachings" about the ancient emperors but that they all followed "the basic keys recorded in ancient historical documents" (Sima [91 BC] 1959, 46). When composing his authoritative version of Yao and Shun stories in Hongtong, Li followed Sima's method. Meanwhile, Li made his own contributions to representing Yao and Shun, the most important being to situate the place Shun plowed in Lishan, Hongtong, although this contribution aroused more problems and controversies than it solved.

Li Xuezhi represented Shun's stories not only in stele text and his booklet but also in his oral storytelling, which followed the same story line as his written work (You 2015a). His oral stories were connected with his interpretation of local annual ritual processions and temple fairs. Noticing the competing discourses on Yao and Shun in classical works of Confucianism and Daoism, Li mixed them together and used them to illustrate the importance of his hometown, the present-day Lishan, in history.

Because of Li Xuezhi's intelligence, his coherent narration, and his personal devotion to the reconstruction of the Shun temple complex, his oral stories of Yao and Shun were very well received in Lishan. He also successfully invented some rituals during the annual procession. For instance, he identified the particular location where Shun plowed during Yao's time, and today Lishan residents receive their Yangxie relatives at that site on the early evening of the second day of the third lunar month. On April 11, 2013, I participated in the annual ritual procession and observed the reception at the place where Shun plowed. It was on the top of a hill, close to the mountain where the Temple of Shun was built. After the villagers from Yangxie arrived around 7:30 p.m., the shè heads and executors from Lishan led the people who were carrying the divine sedan chair to the place where Shun plowed so that they could burn incense and genuflect. The participants carrying the divine sedan chair stopped in this place for a while, indicating the importance of the location—in general, the divine sedan chair only stops at local temples during the annual ritual procession. However, Li added this event to the procession and instructed the shè heads to practice this invented ritual. Then the processions from Yangxie joined those from Lishan to proceed toward the Temple of Shun.

From Yingshan to Lishan

When the name of Yingshan changed to Lishan, the focus of local traditions was shifted from Ehuang and Nüying to Yao and Shun. At the same time, the oral legends of Ehuang and Nüying also became less dominant, giving way to the stories of Yao and Shun in local contexts. This shifting discourse has contributed to the revival of local traditions in public space since the 1990s, but it has also caused problems. Because Li Xuezhi played such a crucial role in shifting the focus of the local traditions in Lishan, he obtained authority to represent those traditions. The villagers there did not really know these stories in the way Li did, perhaps because most of them had never been trained in classical Chinese and they were not familiar with such works as *Shiji*. Therefore a gap developed between Li's reconstruction of Yao and Shun's stories in Lishan and ordinary villagers' understanding of their own traditions.

In the local oral tradition, Nüying is believed to have been born in Hongtong, and many frequently told stories also center on Ehuang and Nüying in Lishan. One of those stories is about the origin of the name of the Memorial Temple of Ehuang and Nüying on Yingshan (present-day Lishan), traditionally known as Shenli Temple (神立庙), or "Deities-Built Temple." The name of Shenli Temple comes from a legend widely known in the local area: A long time ago the old temple collapsed, and local people decided to build a new temple for Ehuang and Nüying. Someone suggested building the new temple in Wu'er Geda, about two *li* away from the original temple site, for some people believed that the collapse of the old temple had been caused by the bad feng shui of its original location. Therefore, the villagers moved all the construction materials to Wu'er Geda and chose the date for the foundation-laying ceremony. Early on the day of the ceremony, people went to the new site, but they couldn't find any construction materials there. They became scared and frustrated at this unexpected event, but suddenly they saw footprints of various animals, such as bulls, horses, and mules. They tracked the footprints and finally found all the construction materials at the original temple site. The villagers then realized that Ehuang and Nüying did not want to change the old temple site but preferred it to stay in its original location. The local people believed that it was Ehuang and Nüying who moved all the construction materials and thus came the name of Shenli Temple, or "Deities-Built Temple." Although the mountain's name changed from Yingshan to Lishan, local people still call the temple Shenli Temple and call the place Shenli.

The story about Shenli Temple is closely related to a local landmark—*niangniang jiao* (娘娘脚)—which is believed to contain the footprints of Nüying and her horse near present-day Lishan (see fig. 3.2). As the stories go, Ehuang and Nüying were visiting their parents in Yangxie when they found out that the local villagers intended to build their new temple in Wu'er Geda. They then rode their horses back to Yingshan in the moonlight. As they climbed the mountain, Nüying got down from her horse and urinated, and when she mounted her horse on a big bluestone, she and her horse left their footprints there. The place became a famous sacred site, with many local people visiting it. During my stay in the Lishan temple complex in the summer of 2012, the custodian Yang Jianli made a point of showing me the footprints, explaining that *niangniang jiao* had been preserved up to the present because the local residents believed in their miraculous power and they dared not destroy them, even though the stones near the site had been quarried in recent years.

The popular stories about the origin of the Shenli Temple and the *niangniang jiao* were recorded in Li Xuezhi's booklet (1997), but often he did not discuss them when he introduced local traditions to outsiders. Instead the focus of his oral storytelling was always on the themes of Emperor Yao seeking talents and Shun plowing in Lishan, which are mainly drawn from national historical records instead of local legends. While Li's background in classical Chinese and his Nationalist political connections caused him to suffer tremendously during the Mao era, he eventually took advantage of this background, using it to gain status in present-day Lishan during the reform era. Through the rebuilding of the temple and the reconstruction of local rituals and narratives, sometimes outside the bounds of locals' understanding of these beliefs, he reasserted his authority as a local cultural and moral leader, roles that had been denied to him in the previous era.

Fig. 3.2. *Niangniang jiao* (娘娘脚), the footprints of Nüying, near present-day Lishan, Hong-tong, Shanxi, seen on July 16, 2012.

Li Xuezhi's reconstruction of Yao and Shun stories has contributed to the reestablishment of the legitimacy of local traditions, especially after local activities were stigmatized as "feudal superstitions" during the Cultural Revolution. Although the annual ritual procession was continued in secret during the Mao era, Li helped local people get official approval for it from the county-level government in 1992. In his application, one of his significant arguments was that Yao and Shun, as well as Ehuang and Nüying, were the ancestors of Chinese descendants and that the local residents worshipped them to repay their favor, which could not be regarded as "feudal superstitions" (Li 2012). By promoting the historical elements and downplaying religious content, Li successfully helped the people strengthen the legitimacy of their local traditions.

Li also drew on Yao and Shun stories to mobilize local people to donate money and raise funds for the temple reconstruction projects and eventually to develop tourism in the area (Li 2012). With support from local residents, more than twenty-one temple halls for a variety of deities from Confucianism, Buddhism, Daoism, and folk beliefs have been built in present-day Lishan, and the temple complex there has become the biggest one in Hongtong. Unfortunately, with the debt crisis in 2010, the temple reconstruction projects came to an end. This change in circumstance also affected Li, who was accused of appropriating the private loans for temple reconstruction and was viewed as partially responsible for the debt crisis. Therefore, support for Li waned, much of his authority was lost, and his interpretations of local history and beliefs were dismissed to an extent.

Competing Narratives and Competing Agency

Although Li Xuezhi attempted to reconstruct the hegemonic narratives on Yao and Shun, there were competing discourses on the local tradition within interconnected local communities. In his oral storytelling, Li said that Ehuang had a fiancé who died soon after Emperor Yao married Nüying off to Shun, and so later Yao also married Ehuang off to Shun. A few learned villagers from Yangxie questioned his construction and completely disagreed with him about this story line, drawing on the first chapter of *Shiji* to argue that Emperor Yao married his two daughters off to Shun at the same time, not one after another.

Other villagers in Hongtong also offer competing narratives about Shun, and the contradictions have never been fully resolved. The key issue centers on the birthplace of Shun, and the debates between local folk literati have exerted immeasurable impact on the relationships and interactions between different village communities. In particular, the different stories from Li Xuezhi in Lishan and Liu Baoshan in Wan'an about the birthplace of Shun illustrate how these competing narratives have exacerbated local tensions and conflicts between Lishan and Wan'an.

Liu Baoshan (刘宝山) (1927–2008) was an important local cultural figure devoted to reconstructing Shun's historical sites and narratives in Wan'an Village. Liu used to be the director of the cultural center in Pu County, adjoining Hongtong County. He returned home after his retirement, devoting the rest of his life to cultural preservation in his hometown. From 1989 to 2002, Liu wrote a series of manuscripts, including *The Landscape of Shun's Birthplace, Love of Yao and Shun's Hometown*, and *Stories of Yao and Shun's Hometown*. In these manuscripts, Liu represents Wan'an as the birthplace of Shun; indeed, he named Wan'an "Shun's Birthplace" (*Shun di*) or "Yao and Shun's Hometown" (*Yao Shun guxiang*). This reconstruction is controversial in the local area, and Li Xuezhi strongly took issue with Liu.

In the 1996 stele text "In Commemoration of the Reconstruction of the Shun Temple," Li Xuezhi points out that Shun was born in Zhufeng, Hongtong. This statement is from the chapter "Li Lou II" in *Mengzi*, in which Mencius said: "Shun was born in Zhufeng." Li wrote: "Zhufeng Village is the current Sage King Village (*Shengwang cun*). It is known as Sage King Village because Shun was a sage king, with loyalty, filial piety, benevolence, and love all embodied in him. Later generations changed the name of Zhufeng where Shun was born into Sage King; nowadays there is still the place named Zhufeng Geda in current Sage King Village" (1997, 6).

Li Xuezhi primarily drew on the traditional methodology of textual research (*kaoju*) to support his argument; he introduces this process in detail in his essay "Textual Criticism That Shun Was Born in Zhufeng" (*Shun sheng Zhufeng kao*) (Li 2009, 103–5). His main sources include *Mengzi, Zhushu Jinian, Kao Jing Yuan Shen Qi, Fengtu Ji, Fangyu Jiyao, Kuaiji Jiuji, Shiji, Kuodi Zhi*, and *Hongtong County Annals*. When referring to these texts, Li's main purpose is not to distinguish authentic sources from fake ones but to prove that the birthplace of Shun is Sage King Village, Hongtong. Aware of the controversial implications, Li mixes all these sources together to forge a coherent argument. For instance, *Mengzi* records that Shun was born in Zhufeng; *Zhushu Jinian* and *Kao Jing Yuan Shen Qi* state that Shun was born in Yaoxu; and *Feng Tu Ji* states that Shun was born in

Yaoqiu. Li Xuezhi does not intend to find out which statement is correct; rather, his main goal is to find one place where these different names are situated together, and he has found Sage King Village. In his essay, Li further records how, in conducting research in Sage King Village in 1991, he discovered that Zhufeng Geda and Yaoxu, which adjoin, are connected. He then drew the conclusion that these places in Sage King Village were the very Zhufeng and Yaoxu recorded in the textual sources, leading him to determine that Shun's birthplace is the place with these two different names (Li 2009, 104–5).

In addition to textual evidence, Li Xuezhi also draws on local folklore to prove his argument. He says that villagers from Sage King Village made an annual ritual procession to the Temple of Shun in Lishan to celebrate Shun's birthday on the Double Fifth Festival, which further proves that the birthplace of Shun was in Sage King Village (Li 2009, 104–5). In my opinion, Li's usage of both textual evidence and local folklore are not methodologically grounded. The textual evidence Li references does not support his argument directly; moreover, I have not found any substantial evidence in the current temple dedicated to Shun in Sage King Village to support his hypothesis, since the temple was rebuilt in 1998 and no older evidence has survived. Furthermore, the local customs that Li drew on are also controversial and not frequently practiced by villagers. When I went to observe Shun's birthday celebration at the Temple of Shun in Lishan on the Double Fifth Festival on June 23, 2012, I did not see any villager from Sage King Village coming to celebrate Shun's birthday. I asked Li what had happened, and he explained that the head of Sage King Village's temple was sick and could not coordinate any ritual procession that day. On July 22, 2012, I went to Sage King Village and visited the temple there. To my surprise, the temple was locked, and there were no other visitors besides me. One villager told me that they had only recently initiated their ritual procession to the Temple of Shun in Lishan; most villagers had no strong interest in participating in it, and in fact, nobody had proceeded to Lishan in the past few years. Only the temple head could tell Shun's stories and introduce the temple history, and it seemed as if he was running temple affairs all by himself.

The name of the temple in Sage King Village is also controversial. According to the stele texts inscribed on the stone tablets in front of the current Temple of Shun there, the temple was originally built on the eighth year (1464) of the Tianshun period during the Ming dynasty, and it was known as Sage King Temple. The old temple was destroyed during a period of political chaos, and it was completely rebuilt only in 1998. The new name—Sage King Shun Temple—was established at the time of the temple reconstruction. The birthplace of Shun may therefore be invented tradition in this area.

In contrast to Li Xuezhi's reconstruction, Liu Baoshan attempted to prove that Shun was born in the current Wan'an Village, his own hometown. His textual evidence is from one stele installed near the old Sage King Temple in Wan'an. The stele was inscribed on the fifteenth year of the Chongzhen reign (1642) during the Ming dynasty; it commemorates the installment, to the left of the Sage King Temple, of a public mill for grinding rice and wheat. The Sage King Temple and the mill no longer exist; only the stele has survived. Liu argued that the Sage King Temple was the Shun Temple and that it was built in memory of Shun's birth in Wan'an (Liu 1990).

Liu Baoshan and Li Xuezhi, local influential folk literati, were both devoted to rebuilding local temples and preserving local traditions; however, they disagreed on the stories of these traditions, and they frequently published materials to argue against each other. Both are known as "a pen holder" or "a powerful writer" in their local communities, and their debates are known as "fighting with each other with pens or debating with each other in writing" (*da bi zhang*). In 1985 Liu founded the Wan'an Cultural Relics Maintenance Station (*Wan'an Wenwu Baoyang Zhan*), a local folk institution aimed at protecting local cultural relics and traditions, and in the early 1990s, he published a series of manuscripts to promote local traditions. After Liu published his materials, Li immediately responded with his own set of materials. Liu in turn wrote a new set to argue against Li, and so it continued. In short, both were occupied with continually debating the reconstruction of local history and traditions, especially the birthplace of Shun.

The debates between Liu and Li ended in 2008 when Liu passed away, but they have had a far-reaching influence on local communities. This can be seen, for instance, in the conflicts between Lishan and Wan'an. When the Wan'an villagers built their own temple dedicated to Shun near the old Temple of Ehuang and Nüying, the conflicts, not only between Lishan and Wan'an but also between Yangxie and Wan'an, intensified. In practice, people in Yangxie and Lishan are bonded together through their annual temple fairs and ritual parades, and they strongly support each other in their reconstructions and representations of the life histories of Yao and Shun. Therefore, when people from Lishan and Wan'an are involved in debates and conflicts, people from Yangxie often side with the Lishan people—for instance, because Yangxie shè heads state that there is only one main Temple of Shun in Hongtong and that it is in Lishan, they therefore view any Temple of Shun in Wan'an as unauthentic. This taking of sides in turn leads to tension between Yangxie and Wan'an.

During my fieldwork on the Double Fifth Festival on June 12, 2013, I observed that the Wan'an shè heads tried to induce the Yangxie shè heads to burn incense in their Shun Temple by saying that the one whose birthday was celebrated should be the first to be worshipped. The Yangxie shè heads were clearly aware of this trap, and they did not follow the rules set by their Wan'an relatives. The Wan'an shè heads then led their own residents to burn incense and genuflect in the Shun Temple and then in the Temple of Ehuang and Nüying. The Yangxie shè heads eventually decided to burn incense and genuflect to their aunties without the company of their Wan'an relatives. North Yangxie shè head Qiao Bao told me that there should not have been any Shun Temple in Wan'an and that the Shun Temple should have been the key landmark that differentiated Lishan from Wan'an. In other words, the only legitimate Temple of Shun in Hongtong was in Lishan, not Wan'an, and Lishan played a much more important role in the local traditions than Wan'an did. Despite the friction between the two sides, the shè heads from Yangxie and Wan'an did get together to burn incense and genuflect to Ehuang and Nüying after they had lunch in the temple and before the Yangxie participants went back to the Old Temple of Tang Yao in their native village.

The profound conflicts between Lishan and Wan'an and between Yangxie and Wan'an are beyond the scope of this chapter. What I want to emphasize is how the debates between local folk literati illustrate competing agency in remaking local traditions and how their conflicts have reflected and shaped local tensions on the ground. However, it does not necessarily follow that local folk literati completely disagreed with each other and created their own set of mutually exclusive discourses on local traditions. Indeed, they often shared perspectives and adhered to similar narrative lines. After reading manuscripts and publications from both Liu Baoshan and Li Xuezhi, I noticed that both borrowed from each other, and they agreed on the general outline of Yao and Shun narratives, such as the notion that Yao married his two daughters to Shun, that Shun's parents tried to kill him three times but failed, and that Yao passed his throne over to Shun. In addition, despite the difference in their writing styles and in their use of sources, both are deeply concerned with the reconstruction of

Yao and Shun's stories in local contexts and with the intertwining relationship between the past and the present. In my opinion, both of them have
contributed greatly to the reconstruction of local traditions and the protection of local cultural heritage, and it is through their competing agency that
the local traditions have been continuously remade, contested, negotiated,
and refreshed.

Conclusion

Yao and Shun's age has been established as the early beginning of Chinese
cultural history, and both of them have been represented as morally perfect
sage-kings (Sima [91 BC] 1959). Yao's benevolence and diligence and Shun's
filial piety and modesty were highly extolled by Confucian philosophers in
later centuries, and they served as a model for Chinese kings and emperors.
However, this construction was problematized by revisionist historians in
the Doubting Antiquity School in the 1920s, and their stories were reified as
myth instead of history. Since the 1990s, historians have drawn on archaeological discoveries to prove the legitimacy of Yao and Shun's age. Archaeological findings in the ruins of Taosi in Linfen suggest that it stands a good
chance of being the location of the capital of the Yao period around 4,200
years ago. In spite of controversy and debates about Yao and Shun, local
villagers in Hongtong believe in them and worship them as their ancient
ancestors. They build temples for them, hold annual ritual processions, and
celebrate their birthdays at temple fairs. Despite their disagreements on the
details, some of the local folk literati reconstruct their stories by drawing
on both written historical documents and local folklore. Myth is important
not only for the construction of the nation-state but also for bonding in
social communities and the identification of active individuals. Therefore,
myth can be interpreted as a metadiscourse, on the basis of which social
actors can construct social borders, and also as "a discursive act" through
which actors pursue certain cultural, political, and economic goals in practice within constructed communities (Lincoln 2014, 23).

Possessing both credibility and authority, myth is used by ordinary
people to make their sense of place in the social-cultural world. Sometimes
their main concerns are not with authenticity but with the contested meanings and functions of myths. In my ethnographic case study, the folk literati involved in constructing myth and local history employ a diversity of
historical and cultural resources, and they reorganize local knowledge and

discourse in response to a specific place and a certain time. Such construction makes it impossible to establish a canon of myth, and the meanings of existing stories are contested and negotiated in a dynamic process.

When myth is interpreted as a metadiscourse and discursive act, it is open to the continuing contestations of meaning and function. The cultural reproduction of myth is driven not only by different actors but by different motivations among competing agents. This process leaves space for new actors to move myth into new places in new settings and to make new stories meaningful for new audiences. It also allows new actors to remake their own claims and creations. Therefore, myth is forged on the ground through a dialectic process of both continuity and contestation.

Notes

1. Sima Qian was a Chinese historian of the Han dynasty (206 BC–220 AD). He is considered the father of Chinese historiography for his *Records of the Grand Historian*, a *Jizhuanti*-style (history presented in a series of biographies) general history of China. This work was influential on history writing for centuries afterward, not only in China but also in other Asian countries, such as Korea, Japan, and Vietnam (Jay 1999).

2. There have been controversies about the texts of the *Book of Documents* and its dating. Later tradition has ascribed the compilation of this book to Confucius (551–479 BC), but its early history is obscure. The first chapter of the *Book of Documents* is known as the "Canon of Yao" ("*Yaodian*"). Its date is uncertain, but most scholars place it sometime in the Zhou dynasty, with estimates ranging from the beginning of the dynasty to the fourth or third century BC (Allan 1981, 58).

3. Yao's ancestral family name (姓) is Yi Qi (伊祁) or Qi (祁), his clan name (氏) is Taotang (陶唐), his given name is Fangxun (放勳), and his name is also known as Tang Yao (唐堯) (Sima [91 BC] 1959, 15–48). Thus, the temple complex is named after Tang Yao.

4

TRADITION ECOLOGY

The Debating and Remaking of Ehuang and Nüying's Conflict Legends by Folk Literati

IN MY RESEARCH, I DRAW ON LAURI HONKO's term *tradition ecology* to interpret both cultural changes and continuity in the remaking of local legends in Hongtong. I propose it as a framework to study the dynamic process of tradition making in contemporary China. This framework provides us with an approach to look at the interrelations between different social actors remaking local traditions and at the complicated relationship between history and place, between discourse and practice, and between individuals and local beliefs. In this process, the components and boundaries of cultural landscape are constantly contested. The ecology I speak of refers to a process of interactive change, adaptation, refreshment, and innovation. It implies neither a nostalgia for a romantic and harmonious past nor a call to protect the past as it is frozen at a particular time.

Honko suggests combining both diachronic and synchronic approaches to construct "a three-dimensional model" in which comparisons are made from the perspectives of "tradition phenomenology," "tradition ecology," and "tradition history" (Honko 1986, 111). He adds one more level of complexity by bringing the problems of interpretation into the theory, asking, "What kind of meaning or whose meaning can we elicit and analyze in the context of phenomenological, tradition-ecological, and historical comparison?" (Honko 1986, 111). Honko's main concerns are with cross-cultural comparisons, and he holds an essentialist viewpoint to interpret the substance of tradition as an organic given. Although I use his term, in my study's context *tradition ecology* mainly refers to a complex process of balance in cultural continuity and change on the ground, and it is used to interpret the dynamic process of debating and remaking Ehuang and Nüying's conflict legends by folk literati and ordinary people in Hongtong. It is a conceptual tool to understand the interactions between the written and the oral, between legends and rituals, between history and place, and between individuals and folklore. The interrelationships of individuals, legends, beliefs, practice, history, and place shape and reflect the cultural landscape within local contexts and encompass the sustainable future of local communities.

Folklorists used to define a legend as "an objectively untrue story that is believed to be true," but this formulation has been problematized by Linda Dégh. Dégh stresses that "the truth of a story neither qualifies nor disqualifies it as a legend . . . we will call extranormal stories legends, whether they are objectively true or not" (Dégh 2001, 4). Carl Lindahl further summarizes the definition of a legend as "by nature a debate about belief, an expression of our warring convictions concerning what is possible, what is probable, and what is right" (Lindahl 2012, 140). By drawing on his research on legends of Hurricane Katrina, Lindahl makes it clear that disaster legends might not "report the facts" but that "they are an essential vernacular tool for expressing how the tellers feel about the prevailing social order and for helping their communities seek explanations that square with their convictions" (Lindahl 2012, 143). Similarly, the legends of Yao and Shun and of Ehuang and Nüying are not necessarily believed to be true by storytellers and scholars, but they are significant vernacular expressions for folk literati and ordinary people to conceptualize their local traditions and to help them gain communicative competence in articulating their beliefs. These legends are not only a debate about beliefs but also a debate about their places and identities.

In addition to Qiao Guoliang, Li Xuezhi, and Liu Baoshan, there are others who are viewed as literati by ordinary peasants in village communities in Hongtong. This cultural group is not homogeneous, and its members do not always agree with one another, but they have played an important role in transmitting, reproducing, and representing local traditions. In my study, these folk literati often debate and negotiate with one another in the process of cultural reproduction and representation, and their remaking of legends about conflicts between Ehuang and Nüying is a good example. In this chapter, I address the warring relationships among folk literati in Hongtong and explore their contradictory representations and negotiations of Ehuang and Nüying's conflict legends within a community context. Finally,

I analyze how common people view the roles of these folk literati in the remaking of the different legends and how they receive the changing stories about Ehuang and Nüying in their local communities.

Usually, the term *lao baixing* (老百姓) is used in Chinese when people speak of "common people" or "ordinary people." *Baixing* literally means "hundreds of surnames," and the word *lao* is added before *baixing* to indicate an affectionate meaning. Since the beginning of Chinese civilization, surnames have been used to represent the origin of families and clans, and they have played an important role in the Chinese kinship system. Although the exact number of Chinese surnames is unknown, *The Book of Family Names* (*Baijiaxing* 百家姓), a popular children's textbook written in 960, listed 408 single-character surnames and 30 double-character ones. In general, the most commonly used surnames are in the hundreds, and *baixing* thus refers to ordinary people with hundreds of surnames in the Chinese nation-state. Folk literati often see themselves as members of the common people, and they view their role as builders of bridges between the local and the national.

Ehuang and Nüying's Conflict Legends

Ehuang and Nüying's conflict legends are well known as "*zheng da xiao* (争大小)" in Yangxie, Lishan, Wan'an, and many other villages in Hongtong. *Zheng* means to fight for, to win over; *da* means big, great, old; and *xiao* means small, little, young. In premodern China, when a man is married to more than one wife at a time, *da* refers to the legal wife or the "first lady," whereas *xiao* refers to the concubine(s). Ehuang and Nüying's *zheng da xiao* legends are those narratives that recount Ehuang and Nüying's competitions to earn the status of queen after both were married to Shun by their father, Emperor Yao. These stories are not only the most frequently told narratives among ordinary villagers in Hongtong but also the most contentious ones within local interconnected communities. Since I first conducted my fieldwork in Hongtong in 2007, I have paid special attention to the different tellings of these stories within different contexts, and the versions that I analyze here are based on twenty interviews with local people in 2007, 2012, and 2013. The informants include folk literati and ordinary peasants in Yangxie, Lishan, Wan'an, and other villages who participated in the annual ritual processions of receiving Ehuang and Nüying in Hongtong. From 2007 to 2013, various actors have changed these stories, though ordinary peasants do not necessarily take the changes as settled, and the negotiation of these stories is an ongoing process.

Although Ehuang and Nüying's conflict legends have never been fixed or stable across time and space and they vary in different contexts, the basic narrative outline can be neatly summarized. After Emperor Yao married his two daughters, Ehuang and Nüying, to his successor, Shun, Nüying asked Shun to choose one as the first lady or queen. This was a difficult problem for Shun. Although Ehuang was older than Nüying and might naturally be regarded as the first lady, Nüying was much more capable and smarter than her older sister. In order to solve his problem, Shun asked the two sisters to compete with each other. The first competition was to cook beans. Shun gave each sister seven dry sticks and seven yellow beans and said that the one who got the beans cooked first would be the first lady. Ehuang burned all the sticks at once, and the water hadn't even boiled. Nüying burned the sticks one by one, so the beans were cooked by the time the sticks were burned up. Therefore, Nüying won the first competition. However, Ehuang was dissatisfied with the result, and she asked for another competition. Shun prepared a wagon and a horse and asked Ehuang and Nüying to choose one and take it to visit their father in Yangxie; the one who arrived at Yangxie first would be the first lady. Ehuang chose to ride a horse, and Nüying chose to take a wagon. Unexpectedly, the horse gave birth to a colt on the way, and the wagon broke down; therefore both sisters were delayed, and they arrived at Yangxie at about the same time. No one won the second round, so they had to do a third competition. In this final contest, the two sisters were asked to sew the soles of a pair of cloth shoes with a long thread. Ehuang used the entire thread directly to sew the soles, while Nüying cut the long thread into several short ones and saved a lot of time. Nüying won the third competition and thus became the first lady of Shun and the queen.[1] In the variants of these legends, the competition order changes in different contexts, and the winner of each competition also varies.

Overall, the competition involving traveling from present-day Lishan to Yangxie (or sometimes from Yangxie to present-day Lishan) is the most important one in the stories, and it is used to interpret the annual ritual processions of receiving the deities between Lishan and Yangxie and explain the origins of some places in Hongtong. The colt's birthplace is named Maju (马驹, Colt) Village, and the place where the wheel spokes on the wagon broke is named Chefu (车辐, Wagon Spokes) Village. As the stories go, after the horse recovered from the delivery, it started to run again. After running for about two miles, the horse became very thirsty and stopped. It dug with one of its hooves, and water came out from the hole; thus the place became known as Ma Pao Quan (马刨泉, Spring Dug by the Horse). Today the spring is in Chijing (赤荆) Village, where villagers are also traditionally involved in the annual ritual processions of receiving Ehuang and Nüying.

The three villages marked in local legends are related to the annual ritual processions of receiving Ehuang and Nüying in Hongtong, although the status of Chefu Village is a bit controversial. Maju Village was later divided into South Maju and North Maju, separated by a river, and both villages have been involved in the annual ritual processions of receiving deities on both the third day of the third lunar month and the twenty-eighth day of the fourth lunar month, as has Chijing Village. Nowadays, Yangxie participants pass South Maju, North Maju, and Chijing before proceeding to Lishan to receive their aunties on the second day of the third lunar month. On the twenty-eighth day of the fourth lunar month, villagers from Xiqiao Zhuang pass these villages before they go back to the Temple of Ehuang and Nüying in their village after they receive the two deities from Yangxie. According to Wang Kaiyuan (1951–2009), one of the folk literati from Yangxie, before Wan'an joined the annual ritual processions of receiving deities, Yangxie residents used to pass Chefu Village before proceeding to Yingshan (present-day Lishan) in older times (Wang 2008). During interviews in Chefu on May 19, 2013, some people in their seventies told me that their village was the place where one of the two sisters repaired the broken spokes of the wagon during Emperor Yao's time, but villagers there had never participated in the annual ritual processions of Yangxie's receiving aunties. There used to be a Temple of Ehuang and Nüying in the village, but only a few old women worshipped the two deities, and belief in them is not very strong there.

I discussed the tense relationships between Yangxie, Lishan, and Wan'an in chapter 3; in practice, folk literati's remakings of Ehuang and Nüying's conflict legends have shaped and taken shape from such local tensions. Folk literati have exerted agency in remaking Ehuang and Nüying's conflict legends within local communities, and their warring reconstruction has been intertwined with their sense of place, history, beliefs, and themselves. Overall, some folk literati from Yangxie regard their aunties as highly virtuous and do not believe that Ehuang and Nüying really competed with each other for the status of queen during Emperor Yao's time. Some have tried to remake or even delete these stories from local traditions. Folk literati from

Wan'an emphasize these conflict legends to support their belief that one of the sisters was living in Wan'an after the competition. Folk literati from Lishan, especially Li Xuezhi, tend to tell these stories as they were, though Li also had to negotiate with other folk literati when remaking the legends.

The Debating of Ehuang and Nüying's Conflict Legends by Folk Literati

During the interview with Li Xuezhi on April 18, 2007, he told me the details of the Ehuang and Nüying conflict legends, and the story line was very similar to the one that he reported in *Records of Connections between Yangxie and Lishan through Sacred Marriage* (1997). However, the competition rounds between Ehuang and Nüying came in a different order in his oral retelling of this story. Li Xuezhi recounted the following order: (1) sewing the soles of a pair of cloth shoes; (2) cooking beans; and (3) riding a horse or taking a wagon from Lishan to Yangxie. In his oral version, Nüying won the first and second rounds. Though neither of the two sisters won the third round, Ehuang finally gave up and let her younger sister become the queen. Li emphasized that this was the old legend, and on that basis, in the old temples of these two sisters, the statue of Nüying, looking happy, was on the left, in an honorific position, while the statue of Ehuang, looking slightly unhappy, was on the right, subordinate to her younger sister.

It's interesting to note that the historical record contradicts the local legends as to which sister was recognized as Emperor Shun's queen. "Two Consorts of Youyu," the first chapter in *The Biographies of Exemplary Women*, states: "When Shun succeeded Yao, he was raised to the rank of Son of Heaven. Ehuang became queen and Nüying his secondary royal consort" (Liu [18 BC] 2007, 31). Both sisters were highly praised for being "pure in virtue and magnanimous in conduct" (Liu [18 BC] 2007, 31), and there is no historical record of their fighting for the status of first lady. However, local legends highlight the story of their conflict—one where it is often asserted that the younger sister, Nüying, won the competitions and became queen—primarily because Nüying is believed to have been born in Hongtong. Naturally she had a higher status in the local area than her older sister, Ehuang, whose birthplace was not in Hongtong.[2]

When the temples to the two deities in Hongtong were rebuilt in the second half of the 1990s, some authorities suggested that Li Xuezhi and other temple heads should follow the record in historical documents (especially

Fig. 4.1. The statues of Ehuang and Nüying at their temple in Yangxie, Hongtong, Shanxi. Photo taken on May 27, 2013.

Liu Xiang's *The Biographies of Exemplary Women*) and establish Ehuang, the older sister, as the queen. Li and the other temple heads accepted the suggestion, but they did not follow it completely. Instead, they worshipped the two deities equally as queens and placed the statues of the two sisters side by side in the newly built temples. The statue of Ehuang is now on the left and the statue of Nüying on the right in their temples, but the statues themselves are exactly the same, and any differences between them are difficult to discern (see fig. 4.1). In reality, ordinary people worship the two deities equally, as expressed in one couplet posted outside the Temple of Ehuang and Nüying in Yangxie:

> Their father was king, their husband was king, their father and husband were both kings.
> The older sister was queen, the younger sister was queen, the older and younger sisters were both queens.

父帝王夫帝王父夫帝王
姐皇后妹皇后姐妹皇后

Confronted with the contradiction between the historical records and local legends, Li did not draw on the records to completely change the legends; instead, he told the stories as they were and also recounted what occurred after local legends had been challenged by some authorities.

Although both sisters are worshipped equally as queens, their status is still differentiated in a variety of the conflict legends. In old legends, although Ehuang was older than Nüying, after the competition "the older sister became the concubine, while the younger sister became queen" (*da de cheng le xiao de, xiao de cheng le da de* 大的成了小的, 小的成了大的). Many local people still told these old legends during the time I did my fieldwork in Hongtong. Meanwhile, some people followed Li Xuezhi's correction and changed the ending of the stories to say: "the older sister was still queen, while the younger sister was the concubine" (*da de hai shi da de, xiao de hai shi xiao de* 大的还是大的, 小的还是小的). Variants of these stories coexist within the same village community as well as in interconnected village communities.

In his "Biographies of Ehuang and Nüying," Qiao Guoliang does not mention the conflict legends of the two sisters at all. During my interview with Qiao's friend Wang Zhizhong on June 9, 2013, he stated:

> When Qiao Guoliang was alive, he stayed with them [those who participated in the annual ritual processions and who told Ehuang and Nüying's conflict legends], and said, These two aunties were sisters; they got along with each other harmoniously, didn't they? Otherwise, how could it [local tradition] be passed down up to the present? Why? You see, the older sister was the older sister, the younger sister was the younger sister, and how could they fight for the status of queen? It was impossible. . . . If they were not sisters, it is said that they fought for the queen status, some people would have believed it. But they were sisters in a family, harmoniously as the "harmonious society."

From Wang's explanation it is clear that Qiao Guoliang did not believe that the conflict stories of Ehuang and Nüying were real, and therefore he deleted them from his manuscript. The folk literati who accepted his influence include Wang Kaiyuan and Yan Zhenghong, who later sought to resolve the contradictory discourses on Ehuang and Nüying's conflict legends when they began to write down local legends. Neither of them chose to delete these important local legends; instead, they changed the reasons for the competition between the two sisters. Where the old legends tell of the two sisters fighting for queen status after Yao married them both off to Shun, the new stories focus on Emperor Yao's use of the three-round competition to test his two daughters' capabilities before their wedding (Wang and Yan 2006). Neither the old nor the new legends explicitly mention who won the competitions at the end.

Like Qiao Guoliang, Wang Kaiyuan and Yan Zhenghong intended to highlight Ehuang's and Nüying's virtues and their harmonious relations, and so they also changed some details of the conflict legends to reflect that emphasis. In addition to the change in the motivation for the competitions, Wang and Yan altered the time of the third competition, making it take place on the wedding day. They highlighted that the competition was also an opportunity to investigate the ideas and lives of ordinary people:

> Then Ehuang and Nüying asked their queen-mother to let them go through two different routes on their wedding day, in order to understand folklore and the conditions of ordinary people in different places and to investigate mountains, rivers, and geography, thus gaining important data and a basis for Shun's governing the country and benefiting the people. In addition, they would use that as their dowry given by their king-father and queen-mother. Emperor Yao and his wife felt very happy to hear this; they thought that the country would flourish and that people would be happy and prosperous when Shun had these two sisters' assistance. (Wang and Yan 2006, 186)

In the story, Nüying rode a horse while Ehuang took the wagon, and their experiences while traveling in the countryside became their special and meaningful "dowry." These details illustrate the two sisters' great virtues, but they contradict the customs of local weddings. I observed several weddings in Hongtong during my fieldwork, and for these contemporary weddings, the groom is supposed to receive the bride in her parents' house early on the wedding day, and then both the bride and groom proceed to the groom's house, where the wedding is held. The dowry from the bride and her parents must comprise material objects, such as the bride's belongings, quilts, furniture, jewelry, and so on. Wang and Yan's creation is too far from reality, and so both of them later deleted the dowry plot and left the third competition as it had been originally recorded (Wang 2009b; Yan 2012).

When writing down local legends, folk literati attach great importance to their respective native areas and temples. For instance, folk literati from Yangxie followed their annual ritual processions of receiving deities from Yangxie to Lishan on the third day of the third lunar month and named the Temple of Shun in Lishan as the destination of the third competition. Folk literati from Lishan, especially Li Xuezhi, followed their annual ritual procession of receiving deities from Lishan to Yangxie on the twenty-eighth day of the fourth lunar month and made the Temple of Tang Yao in Yangxie the destination of Ehuang and Nüying's competing trips. And some folk literati from Wan'an, introduced later in this chapter, even made Wan'an the destination of Ehuang and Nüying's competing trips. In short, these folk literati told Ehuang and Nüying's conflict legends from different perspectives and positions, and their sense of native place was intertwined with their beliefs and their self-identification.

Competing Folk Literati in Lishan: Li Xuezhi and Li Chunwen

Two folk literati from Lishan—Li Xuezhi and Li Chunwen—present competing stories. Local residents call the former Lao Li, Li Lao, or Old Li, whereas the latter is called Xiao Li or Little Li because of a difference of twenty years in their ages. Both men excel at poetry, calligraphy, classical Chinese language, and literature, and local residents view both as literati. However, they have different political standpoints, and they have promoted different sets of knowledge about and discourses on local traditions.

Li Chunwen is a retired Chinese Communist Party (CCP) member from Three Religions Village who served as party secretary in his village for twelve years. He joined the Lishan temple reconstruction association in 2000 and has served as its accountant since then (see fig. 4.2). With his devotion to reviving local traditions, Li Xuezhi has obtained a certain power in representing local traditions to wider audiences, whereas Li Chunwen has had little chance to make his voice heard in public. In Lishan, Li Xuezhi wrote all the important stele texts for different temple halls at the complex. Even though Li Chunwen prepared some stele texts, Li Xuezhi rejected them. During my stay in Lishan in summer 2012, Li Chunwen told me that Li Xuezhi's biggest problem was "to reject good advice and gloss over faults" (*ju jian shi fei*, 拒谏饰非). Other people who lived in the Temple of Shun and oversaw temple affairs in Lishan also said that Old Li was very stubborn and that he did not like to accept good advice from other people.

Fig. 4.2. Li Chunwen in his office in Lishan, Hongtong, Shanxi. Photo taken on July 12, 2012.

Old Li and Little Li have competing opinions on local legends and the status of Lishan in Hongtong. I have discussed how Old Li shifted the focus of local traditions from Ehuang and Nüying to Emperor Shun and intended to prove that Lishan in Hongtong was the place where Shun plowed and Emperor Yao visited Shun (Li Xuezhi 2009). By contrast, though Little Li recognized Lishan as a mountain that Shun passed by, he thought that Lishan was not necessarily the only place where Shun plowed (Li Chunwen 2012).

Li Chunwen followed the style of local gazetteers and wrote *Gazetteer of Lishan, Hongtong, China* (*Huaxia Hongtong Lishan Zhi,* 華夏洪洞歷山誌) to record the local history of Lishan (2012) (see fig. 4.3), but he did not intend to publish it in his lifetime. Instead, he wanted to leave the manuscript to his offspring, who may make it public after his death. Li Chunwen kindly showed me his manuscript and allowed me to make a digital copy of it. This manuscript is written in classical Chinese with beautiful calligraphy. It is an ongoing work, and he is still updating it with new events and materials. Local legends are a very small part of the work, and he is including only those centered on Lishan, such as the legends of the origin of the Shenli Temple, the magic birth of Nüying, and the sacred bond between Lishan and Yangxie.

Li Chunwen does not include Ehuang and Nüying's conflict legends in his manuscript because they are not centered on Lishan; however, he told me these stories in my interview with him on June 11, 2013, and commented on their content: "They competed through some kinds of contests, for instance, whoever finished a thing first became queen, whoever completed it late became the concubine. . . . Later, the older sister became the concubine, and the younger sister became queen. In our modern words, the older sister did not have high IQ; she lost every contest." Li Chunwen's version of Ehuang and Nüying's conflict legends is similar to the old version of local legends, and he personally used the modern concept of low IQ to explain why Ehuang had lost the competitions. His representation is from the perspective of a local historian, whose purpose is to record local history and folklore as it was.

From what I have observed, Li Chunwen always aligns himself with his conception of ordinary people in local politics, and his representation is produced from that political perspective. He expresses his political goal thus: "Power is used for ordinary people, emotion is bonded for ordinary people, and benefits are earned for ordinary people" (*quan wei min suo yong, qing wei min suo xi, li wei min suo mou*). This ideal seems glaringly at odds with the harsh reality of the intense power struggles between local

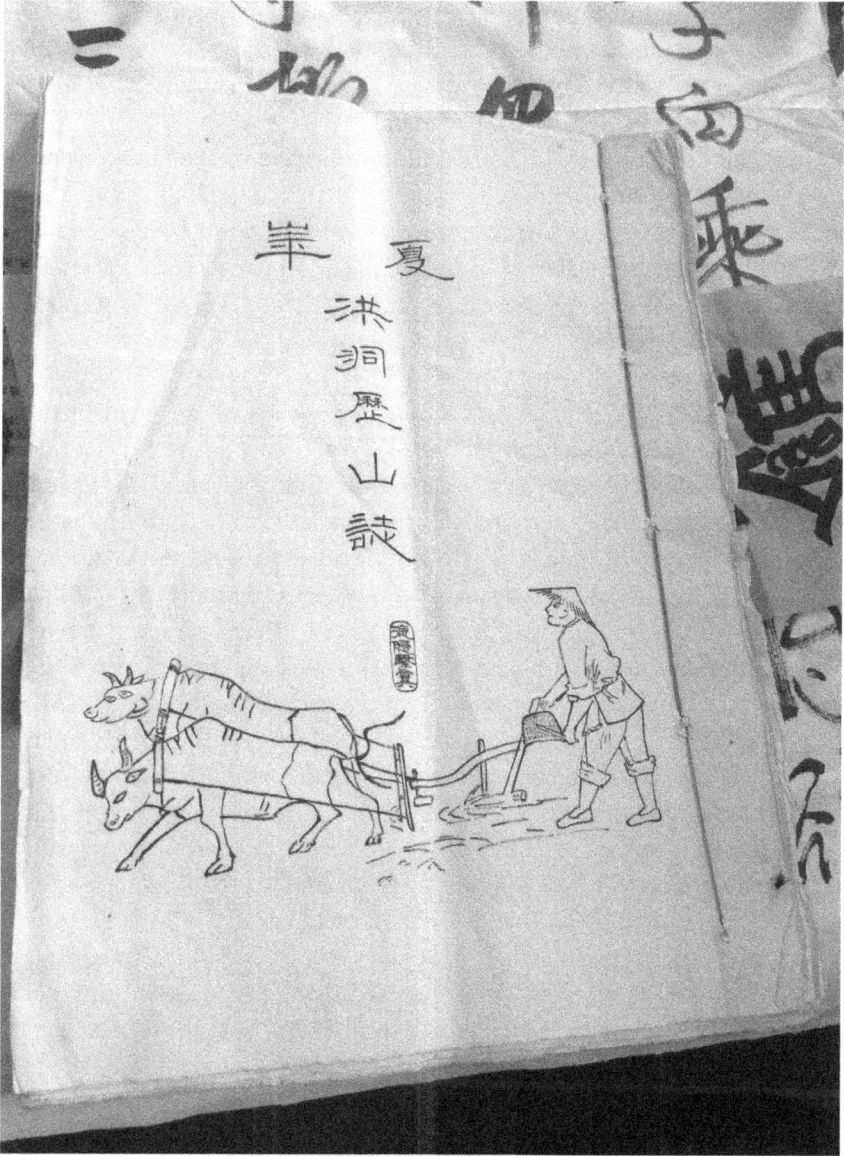

Fig. 4.3. The cover of *Gazetteer of Lishan, Hongtong, China*, written by Li Chunwen. Photo taken on July 11, 2012.

governments and ordinary people in the region (and around China). In reality, corrupt officials abuse power, the commonweal is sacrificed for personal interests, and the bonds between official elites and ordinary people have been weakened.

Unlike Li Chunwen, Li Xuezhi did not believe in the power of ordinary people. Instead, he believed in his personal capabilities and ambitions, and in our interviews he always emphasized his important role in remaking local traditions (Li 2012). On June 12, 2013, I interviewed Li Xuezhi in Lishan about Ehuang and Nüying's conflict legends. He reflected on the changes of these legends:

As for the conflict [*zheng da xiao*], there was such a legend in the past. How was this legend produced? [We] do not know. Now, we do not talk about the conflict, because we think the conflict has some negative effects on the virtues of the two ladies. *Da* is *da* [the older sister was queen], *xiao* is *xiao* [the younger sister was the concubine]; why should [they] fight against each other? Originally, the conflict emerged when both sisters married Shun. [Emperor Yao's] younger daughter married Shun first, and [his] older daughter married Shun later. Thus, after the younger daughter married, she thought that she married Shun first and so she should be the queen; the older daughter married later, so she should be the concubine. Now, we do not talk about this issue. We corrected it. Here it was Shun's testing his two wives. Because of the conflict, they [the two ladies] were criticized by Emperor Yao, and ordinary people had the same response. In other words, the two ladies' conflict had negative effects on their virtues, and eventually no, [we] do not spread this in words, it became a test of the two ladies. Why were the two ladies tested? [Emperor Yao] married his two daughters to him [Shun], but their intelligence could not be as even as chopsticks; there is a difference. In order to appoint them to their respective positions on the basis of their talents and capabilities, Shun tested the two sisters and saw who was more intelligent. Thus, he tested them, and what followed were the conflict legends. That is, cooking beans with hay, sewing soles of shoes, and riding. They are the same. That was changed to the test of the two ladies. In the past, there was such a conflict legend, there was such a legend, and it was very popular among ordinary people. The conflict had such an influence, very popular. Now, we have changed it.

Overall, I think Li Xuezhi has balanced the opinions from different perspectives and made the storytelling of Ehuang and Nüying's conflict into a dynamic interactive process. This process is socially and culturally reflexive, and such dimensions of consciousness are crucial in illuminating folk literati's creative agency in debating local legends.

Competing Folk Literati in Yangxie: Wang Kaiyuan and Pei Beiji

In Yangxie, Wang Kaiyuan and Pei Beiji have both been influenced by Qiao Guoliang, and both regard him as a role model. Despite their mutual connection to Qiao, Wang and Pei composed competing renditions of the legends of Ehuang and Nüying in the late 2000s. Given this conflictive relationship, the life stories of Wang and Pei and their literary representations will shed light on folk literati's competing agency in the remaking of local legends within local communities.

Wang Kaiyuan was born in Yangxie Village on November 2, 1951; he died in an accident on June 10, 2009.[3] He was the main electrician in Yangxie from 1968 to 1985 and later ran his own restaurant—the Kaiyuan Restaurant—from 1986 to 2008. He was the associate head of the Southern shè in Yangxie from 1982 to 1988, actively participating in the official revival of local traditions in the 1980s. In 1982, Wang, Qiao Guoliang, and other shè executors were sent to prison in Mamu (马牧) because they revived the annual ritual processions of receiving deities on the third day of the third lunar month in public; they were kept there for fifteen days. In 1985 Wang was again detained in the local police station with other shè executors in Yangxie because they had remade the divine sedan chair for their aunties; this time they were imprisoned for seven days. During the annual ritual processions, Wang's main responsibilities were to contact shè executors or temple heads from other villages that were involved in the processions and coordinate with them to arrange accommodations. When promoting the local traditions as China's national intangible cultural heritage from 2006 to 2008, he extended his hospitality to folklorists who conducted fieldwork in the local communities and actively contributed to the collection of sources on local traditions. From 2006 to 2009, he collected some local legends and published several articles on local traditions (Wang and Yan 2006; Wang 2008, 2009a, 2009b).

Even though Wang Kaiyuan was not formally well educated, he trained and educated himself while promoting local traditions in the late 2000s.

He accompanied folklorists conducting fieldwork in Hongtong, and as a result, he got to know many local legends and written classics on local traditions. However, because of his limited education, it was not easy for him to compile these important historical sources, and so he invited Wang Quansuo, a retired teacher from Yangxie, to collaborate with him to write the manuscript "Legends and Anecdotes of the Two Sages Ehuang and Nüying" (Ehuang Nüying erwei shengxian chuanwen yishi) or "Legends and Anecdotes of Ehuang and Nüying" (Ehuang Nüying yishi chuanwen) (Wang and Wang 2007–9). Unfortunately, Wang Kaiyuan fell off the roof of his two-story house on June 10, 2009, and died soon afterward. Many officials, temple heads, and folklorists attended his funeral to show their gratitude and respect to him and his family. Meanwhile, publication of the manuscript was halted because of conflict between Wang Quansuo and Wang Kaiyuan's family. After Wang Kaiyuan's sudden death, Wang Quansuo wanted all the materials and sources collected by Wang Kaiyuan, intending to make himself the sole author of the manuscript. In order to prevent this, Wang Kaiyuan's two sons eventually decided to donate all the materials and sources to the general shè in the Old Temple of Emperor Yao in Yangxie.

I interviewed Pei Beiji in 2013 (see fig. 4.4). Pei was born in Yangxie in 1960; he reached middle school, but because of his family's poverty, he left after only half a year. He then cut grass to feed the livestock for his production team and earned work points (*gong fen*) for his family. Afterward he worked in a local brick kiln, molding raw clay bricks. He got married in the early 1980s and then returned home, where he helped other people build houses to earn his living; however, he did not like the heavy labor, so later he became a veterinarian. After he lost his job on a pig farm, he went back to the building trade, working part-time on a variety of local construction sites. He has two sons; his first son has a granddaughter, and at the time of our interview, Pei was trying to find a daughter-in-law for his younger son.

Pei Beiji became a local spiritual medium in 2005, and he claimed that Ehuang and Nüying told him many stories in his dreams, asking him to write them down; if he did not do so when he woke up the next day, he would have painful headaches and wouldn't be able to function. Pei said that his aunties appointed him as the new literary *mazi* because Qiao Guoliang did not complete his obligations; therefore, Pei could now help his two aunties spread their legends in local communities. His manuscript is entitled "Discovering the Mysteries of the Deities with the Glorious History of Thousands of Years: Biographies of Ehuang and Nüying" (Qiannian

Fig. 4.4. Pei Beiji (*left*) drinking tea with his village fellows at the temple in Baishi Village during the annual ritual procession of receiving aunties on the third day of the third lunar month, 2013. Photo taken on April 13, 2013.

rongxian shenmi jie: E Ying zhuan) (Pei 2005–12). Although he said the manuscript was based on his dreams of Ehuang and Nüying, he admitted that he also collected oral legends from many people, listened to other *mazi* to learn about messages from the deities, and used a variety of written sources. In addition, he asked for advice from many scholars when he finished the first draft around 2006, and he continued to revise his manuscript until 2012, when I first met him.

Pei Beiji's manuscript is roughly divided into thirty chapters, chronicling Chinese society from the Yellow Emperor to the present day, but his emphasis is primarily on Yao and Shun's time. Based on his account, Yao's era started in 2290 BC, and Shun's era started in 2211 BC. He refers to their time as "primitive society" (*yuanshi shehui*). He also claims that Ehuang was born around 2253 BC, that Nüying was born around 2250 BC, and that both died in 2170 BC. In his writing, the history of primitive society is intertwined with myths, legends, and a variety of supernatural stories.

Like Qiao Guoliang, Pei Beiji did not believe that Ehuang and Nüying fought against each other for queen status; instead, he asserts that the two sisters competed with each other to see who was more intelligent. In his manuscript, he keeps the plots of the boiling of beans and sewing of shoe soles and states that Nüying won both competitions and that she was smarter than her older sister. The riding competition took place on their wedding day in 2230 BC, and it is used to explain the origins of the names of Maju Village and Chefu Village (Pei 2005–12, chap. 8). Pei also told how the two women taught ordinary people to rear silkworms, make silk, and make clothes and how they became healers to help local people cure their illnesses. He writes the stories as if he, as a *mazi*, is conveying a message from Ehuang and Nüying. Usually, *mazi* sing songs with seven-character lines when they practice rituals and speak for the deities. Pei imitates this style of verse in his manuscript, making it difficult for ordinary villagers to read; instead, his main audiences are scholars who are interested in local history and legends.

The conflicting accounts of Wang Kaiyuan and Pei Beiji are revealed in their writings about the origin of the Temple of the Second Aunt (*er gugu miao*) outside Yangxie Village. This small temple located near the Fen River is believed to be the place where Nüying stays overnight on the fourth day of the third lunar month when she comes back from Lishan to visit her parents in Yangxie. There are different interpretations about the origin of this temple among villagers, and these interpretations are intertwined with the two deities' conflict legends. Some villagers said that their two "aunties" did not get along with each other after the competitions, and they did not want to go back to visit their parents at the same time. Nüying therefore stayed outside the village for one night and arrived on the following day after Ehuang went back. Some said that Nüying was criticized by Emperor Yao after the competitions, and therefore she felt ashamed of herself and let her older sister go first. Wang offered a different interpretation of the origin of this temple, a vividly told story of Nüying fighting a water dragon who was responsible for a flood of the Fen River (Wang 2009a). In this version of the legend, Nüying was depicted as a brave heroine, using her sword to stab the dragon through its abdomen. As she drove the dragon away, the river became calm again. Wang stated that local residents commemorated Nüying for her good deeds by building a temple in the place where she fell asleep after she drove the dragon away. Wang's story also records that afterward Nüying stayed there every year when she came back in order to "investigate the conditions of ordinary people" (Wang 2009a, 303), and that later

Nüying and Ehuang helped local people build ferries and bridges along the Fen River. With this story, Wang represented Nüying as a responsible and powerful deity, instead of just a capable human being.

Wang Kaiyuan was aware of various local origin legends of Nüyng's temple, ones that were different from his own version, and he noted at the end of his essay: "But because a long time has passed and the story has been rarely handed down orally, it is not surprising that nowadays people make strained interpretations to produce a variety of versions (of the legends)" (Wang 2009a, 303). Wang therefore tried to standardize these local legends and make his version the accepted one. Similar to Wang Kaiyuan, Pei Beiji thought that his own version of the origin of the Temple of the Second Aunt was the correct one, despite the many variants of this local legend. In his telling of the story, Nüying could not go home overnight because she stopped to help the local people deal with a flood in the Fen River and to help build bridges along the river. He viewed himself as speaking for the two deities and asked people not to make irresponsible remarks and talk nonsense when their version of the legend disagreed with his own.

Both Wang Kaiyuan and Pei Beiji intended their versions of stories to become standard among local people, and thus they competed with each other when remaking local legends. However, the question arises, Who are their real audiences? In the end, their main audiences are outsiders, those who visit the local region or conduct research on local traditions (Chen 2010, 66). Although they tried to debate with local residents who told different versions of the legends, the latter did not necessarily accept their opinions. During my fieldwork, I still heard different versions of the stories from locals. From my observation, in the locals' everyday lives, these stories are of minor importance; what matters to them most are the beliefs and practices surrounding the two sisters. Most local believers ask for blessings from the deities and seek "safety and soundness" (*ping'an*) for their whole family. Not all local residents could tell the stories about Ehuang and Nüying clearly, and their interest is not necessarily attached to the details of these stories. Instead, it is the folk literati who attach great importance to the local legends and who debate with one another about the often-contradictory details of those stories.

Folk Literati in Wan'an: Liu Baoshan and Han Xiaomao

In Hongtong, Liu Baoshan was the first person to collect Ehuang and Nüying's conflict legends and include them in his booklet (Liu 1990). In Liu's stories, in order to decide which of the sisters would be the first lady, their father, Emperor Yao, asked them to boil beans, and their mother asked them to sew shoes, with Nüying winning both competitions. For the third competition, which was settled on the wedding day, the two sisters took the route from Yangxie to Wan'an, Emperor Shun's "hometown," which was known as Yaoqiu during his time (Liu 1990, 102). Ehuang was riding a horse, which gave birth to a colt in the current Maju Village and dug out a spring at Ma Pao Quan, while Nüying took a wagon and its spokes broke in the current Chefu Village. Both arrived at Yaoqiu after darkness on the same day, and Shun held a wedding ceremony with them that evening. The basic outlines of this story are similar to those recounted by folk literati from Lishan and Yangxie, but Liu Baoshan changed the destination of Ehuang and Nüying's third competition to Yaoqiu, present-day Wan'an.

Liu Baoshan's contribution was not only in collecting Ehuang and Nüying's conflict legends but also in reinterpreting local rituals drawn from those stories. In his booklet, Liu's version of the story notes that the two women realized their own shortcomings and decided to get along with each other after the competitions. Ehuang admitted that Nüying was smarter than she was, and she decided to live in Lishan, farming with Shun and providing grains for the family, while Nüying lived in Yaoqiu, serving Emperor Shun's parents and doing housework (Liu 1990). Given this arrangement, Liu reinterpreted the annual ritual processions of receiving Ehuang and Nüying as follows:

> When Yangxie [residents] receive [their] aunties, they receive their first aunt [Ehuang] on the second day [of the third lunar month] [from Lishan]. "The two ladies called each other sister," the old sister was *da*, who should be received first, and this reflected benevolence, righteousness, and virtue. Although Nüying was young, smart, and clever, and she earned the queen status, [Yangxie residents] arrive at Wan'an on the right day [that is, the third day of the third lunar month] to receive her, the second aunt. Therefore, when Yangxie [residents] go back on the fourth day [of the third lunar month], they first receive their first aunt to enter the temple. The next day, that is, on the fifth day [of the third lunar month], dumplings are made [by housewives] in every household. [Yangxie residents] go to the Temple of the Second Aunt, also known as the Little Temple of Emperor Shun, outside the village and receive the second aunt to enter the temple. It is more exciting

than the first day. This is the tradition left by Tang Yao and Yu Shun, and it has been passed down for more than 4,700 years. (Liu 1990, 35)

Liu Baoshan promoted the Temple of Ehuang and Nüying in Wan'an as the place where Nüying resided, and the Temple of Ehuang and Nüying in Lishan as the place where Ehuang resided, even though in both temples the statues of Ehuang and Nüying stood side by side. In doing so, Liu asserted Wan'an's place in local traditions and advocated for Wan'an to be considered as important as Lishan in the annual ritual processions.

Liu Baoshan's interpretations contradicted the existing discourses about local traditions and subsequently aroused conflict and tension among folk literati from different communities. Liu published his booklet *Love of Yao and Shun's Hometown* (*Yao Shun guxiang qing*) (1990) at his own expense. When he tried to sell some copies at the temple fairs in Yangxie in 1990, he was rebuffed by Yan Zhenghong and other temple executors from Yangxie. Folk literati from Lishan and Yangxie also published new materials to refute Liu's representations. For example, when Li Xuezhi from Lishan published his influential booklet in 1997 highlighting Lishan's and Yangxie's high status in local traditions, he completely excluded Wan'an's role. Moreover, Qiao Guoliang from Yangxie wrote his manuscript "Biographies of Ehuang and Nüying" from 1997 to 1998, and his friend Wang Zhizhong told me that Qiao intended to correct Liu's misinterpretations of local traditions. Qiao observed how Liu used Ehuang and Nüying's conflict legends to promote his own native area and temple, and because he did not believe that the competitions had really taken place, he deleted the conflict legends from his manuscript.

Another important folk literatus from Wan'an Town is Han Xiaomao (韩小毛) (b. 1965), a native of Dongliang Village, which is about three kilometers away from Wan'an Village. He is a local *mazi*, and I got to know him through the recommendation of the temple head Chen Baozi (陈保子) (b. 1948) from Anle Temple (安乐庙). Chen was Liu Baoshan's old neighbor, and Liu persuaded him to participate in the temple reconstruction of Anle Temple and to run temple affairs beginning in 2007. Before Liu passed away, he left some of his manuscripts and materials to Chen. During my fieldwork in Wan'an in the summer of 2012, Chen was one of my main tour guides. He strongly recommended Han to me, calling him "Liu Baoshan's disciple." He did not mean that Han had really studied with Liu; instead, he meant that Han had inherited Liu's thoughts and ideas.

On August 7, 2012, Chen Baozi and his friend Chen Zhongwei accompanied me to visit Han Xiaomao in his newly opened restaurant in Dongliang Village (see fig. 4.5). At the time, Han was forty-eight years old. Chen Baozi told me that Han had believed in deities and served them wholeheartedly because he wished to have a son; his wish eventually came true, and his son was now eight years old. Han told me that he had become a *mazi* when he was sixteen years old, after he graduated from a local junior high school, and he started to speak for deities and heal people when he was twenty-six years old. Meanwhile, he became a cook to earn a living. He was a *mazi* who would speak not for Ehuang and Nüying but for the Jade Emperor, a central figure in popular Daoism. In his early years, he worked with his town fellows to rebuild Qianyuan Shan, an important Daoist center in Hongtong, and to revive religious festivals there. In his thirties, he went back to Dongliang, his home village, and started to rebuild the village temple. During the annual ritual processions, he convened villagers to play drums and gongs, make preparations at the village temple, and receive Yangxie relatives when they passed by on the morning of the fourth day of the third lunar month.

Han Xiaomao drew on his personal experience in serving deities and on a variety of written sources to complete a manuscript titled "Textual Research of Inscriptions on Metal Utensils and Stone Tablets in Wan'an, the Hometown of Shun, Hongtong County, during Tang Yao and Yu Shun's Time" (Tang Yao Yu Shun Hongtong xian Shun xiang Wan'an jinshi ming kao) in September 2007. He cited a variety of stele inscriptions and other written sources from Liu Baoshan's work, and his manuscript can be seen as an up-to-date version of the latter with more detailed textual sources. In addition to promoting the same ideas and materials as Liu, Han critiqued some of the interpretations of Li Xuezhi, Liu's main rival. First, whereas Li interpreted *niangniang* as "grandmothers," Han pointed out that Lishan and Wan'an residents called Ehuang and Nüying *niangniang* because the two women were both queens and queens were referred to as *niangniang* in Chinese. Second, Li stated that the Yangxie residents were senior to the Lishan residents in the royal family hierarchy because the former called Ehuang and Nüying aunties and the latter called them grandmothers (Li 1997). In contrast, Han explained that people from Yangxie, Lishan, and Wan'an called each other relatives and that there was no difference in their position in the family hierarchy (Han 2007, 41). Furthermore, unlike Li, Han did not intend to compose coherent narratives of Yao and Shun in Hongtong,

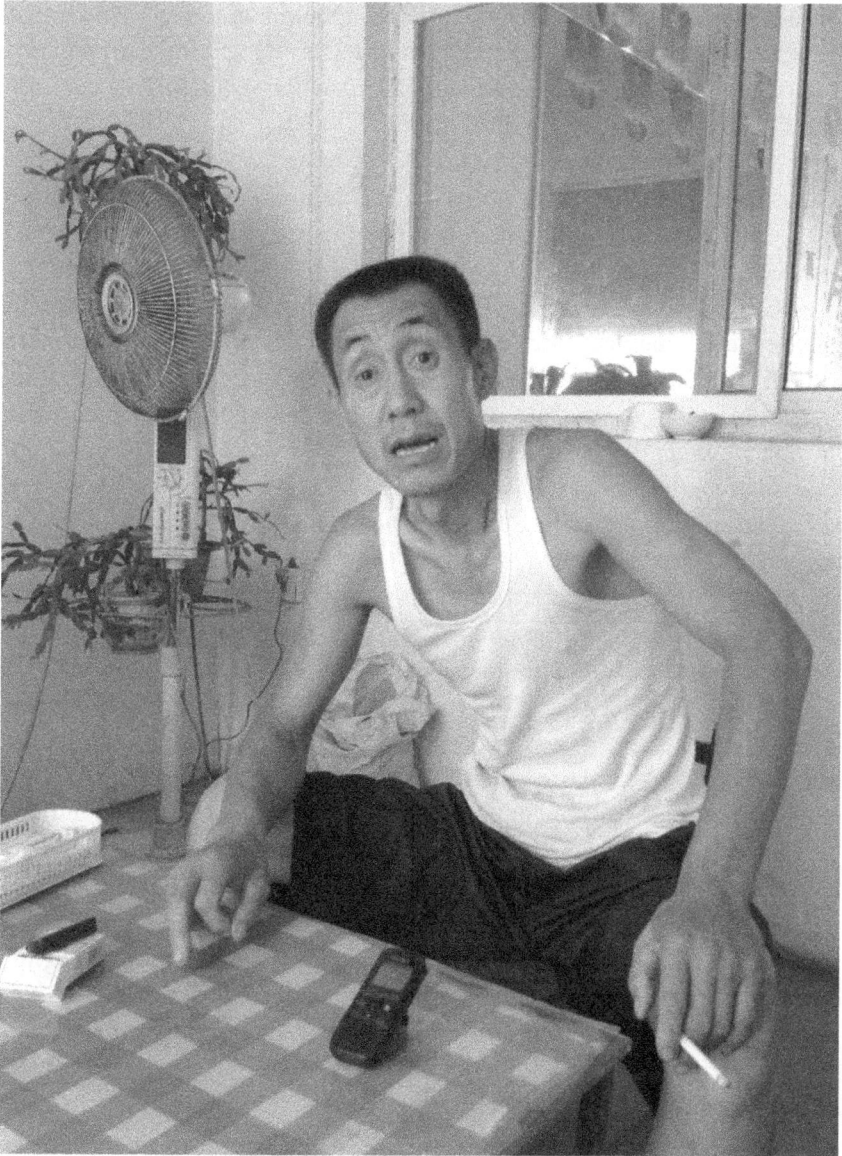

Fig. 4.5. Han Xiaomao was interviewed in his restaurant in Dongliang Village, Wan'an Town, Hongtong, Shanxi. Photo taken on August 7, 2012.

but instead he worked to compile different chapters of the local history of Hongtong from the time of Pangu, the creator of all in Chinese mythology, to the time of Yao and Shun, although his manuscript is actually a mixture of history, myths, legends, and beliefs.

Han Xiaomao included Ehuang and Nüying's conflict legends in his manuscript, and the basic narrative outline is similar to the one recorded in Li Xuezhi's booklet (1997). Han said that Nüying won two rounds of the competition and became the queen, and in our interview he also emphasized that one of the two sisters lived in Wan'an. Liu Baoshan intended to prove that Nüying had lived in Wan'an, and I think Han tried to promote the same idea, though during our interview, Han's interpretations contradicted Liu's. The contradictions centered on different concepts about who the *da niangniang*, "the first queen," was. Both Liu and Han legitimized the idea that *da niangniang* had lived in Wan'an; however, Liu regarded Nüying as the *da niangniang* because she won the competitions with her older sister, whereas Han considered Ehuang as the *da niangniang* because she was older than Nüying. The contradictions revealed the contentious status of Ehuang and Nüying's stories and these stories' reflections of the conflictive relationship between Wan'an, Lishan, and Yangxie.

Although Liu Baoshan's interpretations are not well received by residents of Lishan and Yangxie, they reveal some contradictions in locals' interpretations of the annual ritual processions of receiving Ehuang and Nüying. The key issues include why Nüying is received in the Old Temple of Tang Yao by Yangxie participants on the fifth day of the third lunar month, after her older sister, Ehuang, is taken back on the fourth day, and why Wan'an participants come to Yangxie to receive Ehuang and Nüying after the two are taken back by Lishan participants on the twenty-eighth day of the fourth lunar month. I have elaborated on the first issue, for it is closely integrated with locals' interpretations of the origin of the Second Aunt Temple in Yangxie, and in the following sections, I discuss the second key issue about Wan'an's participation in detail.

Intersection of Narrative, Beliefs, and Rituals

Despite the contradictory versions of the Ehuang and Nüying stories found in different locations, the stories are still frequently told among ordinary people in Hongtong. Two of the competitions in particular—cooking beans and sewing shoe soles—are popular plot points in local people's storytelling because the contests reveal the basic skills that local women have to master in their everyday lives. Local married women are expected to cook three meals a day for their household and sew shoes and prepare clothes for the whole family; these skills are often passed down through the generations. I encountered a woman sewing a shoe sole when I was conducting fieldwork in the Temple of Ehuang and Nüying in Yangxie in the summer of 2012. She told me that she had learned how to sew the soles of cloth shoes from her mother when she was fifteen years old; she had also learned how to cook when she was very young. Her experience is shared by most local women in their forties and older. It is also notable that when sewing shoe soles, these women have to cut the long thread into several short pieces so that they can save time in stitching, a detail included in some of the competition stories. As for cooking, families in Yangxie are still using *tu guotai*, a local stove made of soft wet earth. Their main fuels are firewood and straw. The plots of Ehuang and Nüying's conflict legends are closely intertwined with the daily practices of the local people.

The conflict legends are also intertwined with living beliefs and the annual ritual processions. Yangxie participants called the annual ritual processions that occur around the third day of the third lunar month "receiving aunties" and those around the twenty-eighth day of the fourth lunar month "seeing aunties off." Lishan participants called the annual ritual processions from the twenty-seventh day to the twenty-ninth day of the fourth lunar month "welcoming or receiving niangniang" (*ying niangniang*). Despite the different names, the annual ritual processions that occur around the twenty-eighth day of the fourth lunar month are similar to those around the third day of the third lunar month, although participants from Lishan and Wan'an may return via different routes.

Both the Lishan and Wan'an processions go to Yangxie around Emperor Yao's birthday, and they both carry their respective divine sedan chairs with them. Liu Baoshan, from Wan'an, claimed that Lishan participants went to Yangxie to bring Ehuang back to Lishan on the twenty-eighth day while Wan'an participants went to bring Nüying back to Wan'an on the twenty-ninth day of the fourth lunar month. Folk literati and temple executors from Yangxie and Lishan disagreed with Liu's interpretation. They stated that Lishan participants took the two sisters back to Lishan on the twenty-eighth day after celebrating Emperor Yao's birthday and that Wan'an participants came later to do some cleaning at the temple. In rituals, the participants from Lishan received the mini statues of Ehuang and

Fig. 4.6. Mini statues of Ehuang and Nüying (*in front*) were brought back by Yangxie devotees from Lishan on the third day of the third lunar month. Photo taken on April 20, 2013.

Nüying on Lishan's divine sedan chair at the two deities' temple in Yangxie and carried the divine sedan chair back to Lishan along the procession routes on the twenty-eighth day of the fourth lunar month (see fig. 4.6). Wan'an participants did not receive any mini statues from the temple in Yangxie on the next day; instead they carried their own statues of Ehuang and Nüying in their divine sedan chair back and forth along the procession routes.

Along the returning procession routes, Lishan and Wan'an parades both pass Tunli, Hongbu, Dushu, Baishi, Longzhang, East Longma, West Longma, and Shubu, although on different days, a fact that has exacerbated conflicts and confusion among local communities. I interviewed some devotees in these villages when I followed the Wan'an returning parade on the twenty-ninth day of the fourth lunar month (June 7) in 2013, and they briefly introduced various local legends and rituals to me, though some of their descriptions contradicted others. In the following sections, I organize the local responses according to the name of their native village, presenting them in full detail before I turn to an analysis of their different standpoints in representing local traditions to an outsider like me.

Local Response from Hongbu

I met Zhang Xiumiao (seventy-three years old) and Tai Haifeng (sixty-two years old) in Hongbu on the afternoon of June 7, 2013, and they told Ehuang and Nüying's conflict legends in the traditional way. Both women called Ehuang and Nüying aunties because they felt that the deities were very close to Yangxie, and they said that those stories were passed down by old people. On the fourth day of the third lunar month, they received their aunties so they could "visit their own parents," and around the twenty-eighth day of the fourth lunar month, they saw their aunties off so they could "go back to their husband's house." They regarded Hongbu as "a way station for resting horses and eating meals" or "a halfway resting place." Around the twenty-eighth day of the fourth lunar month, they used to receive only the younger aunt, not the older aunt, noting: "Previously the two aunties could not meet each other. If they met, the wind blew and it rained. This is what the old people said. Nowadays, people have changed. Deities are united together.... In the past two to three years, we received both [aunties]. Previously, we did not do so; we only received one aunt, only received the younger aunt. The older aunt came and then went away on the other side; she did not come here."

Zhang and Tai further noted that formerly they only received the Wan'an processions but now they also received the processions from Lishan. They also believed that Lishan received the older aunt back on the twenty-eighth day and that Wan'an received the younger aunt back on the following day. Their interpretations corresponded to Liu Baoshan's construction, for Hongbu was once tied with Wan'an instead of Lishan in the annual ritual processions. I did not ask the two women who "the younger aunt" was and who "the older aunt" was. When I interviewed them, some other women also said that the older aunt lived in Wan'an, while the younger aunt lived in Lishan. There were contradictions in their interpretations, and these contradictions also existed in Liu Baoshan's and Han Xiaomao's interpretations. I have discussed how Liu promoted the idea that the younger sister, Nüying, lived in Wan'an while Han thought that the older sister, Ehuang, lived there; both sets of discourses were accepted among some devotees in Hongbu, and the contradictions among local women's interpretations reveal the changing process of local traditions.

Local Response from Dushu

In 2013 when the Wan'an procession arrived at the village temple in Dushu on the afternoon of the twenty-ninth day of the fourth lunar month, I interviewed an old woman at random in the temple, and she then introduced me to Wang Dongjiao (fifty-six years old), a local *mazi*. Wang told me legends of Ehuang and Nüying's conflicts that were very similar to Li Xuezhi's versions. Wang concluded that "the younger sister became the first wife, and the older sister became the second." However, another old woman interrupted her, saying that "now it is said that the older sister was the first wife and the younger sister was the second." Wang noted that she had learned these stories from older residents of Dushu, who had been passing them down to others.

I asked Wang Dongjiao why Dushu devotees received the Lishan parade on the twenty-eighth day of the fourth lunar month and then received the Wan'an parade on the following day. At first, she was not sure of the order in which the two sisters were received in Dushu, but an old woman told us that "the older sister was received first, and the younger one was received later." Wang continued: "The two sisters did not get along with each other, and they did not return home on the same day. If one returned on the first day, the other returned on the second day. Lishan received the older one, and Wan'an received the younger one. It is like this."

The old woman whom I interviewed first in the temple did not tell me the stories; instead she simply said: "*Da niangniang* is Ehuang, *xiao niangniang* is Nüying. They carried out good deeds in the past, just as Chairman Mao, they obtained great achievements, thus they have been memorialized here." With her comparison of Ehuang and Nüying to Chairman Mao, it seems that this old woman regarded them as real historical figures. Her ideas are shared among many ordinary people in Hongtong; they accept that the two sisters fought with each other like ordinary human beings because they were human.

Local Response from Baishi

Baishi is a village in Xincun Town, and its Chinese name literally means "white stone." According to local legends, when Nüwa sealed the broken sky using stones of seven different colors in ancient China, she left a white stone in the village, and the village was thus named White Stone. In the annual ritual processions, Baishi is an important resting place for the Yangxie participants on the fourth day of the third lunar month, for the

Fig. 4.7. Steamed buns and four dishes were served to treat the Yangxie relatives in Baishi on April 13, 2013, the fourth day of the third lunar month. The dishes seen here are *dou ya* (*upper left*), *fen tiao* (*upper right*), *kuku cai* (*below left*), and *huizi bai* (*below right*).

Lishan participants on the twenty-eighth day of the fourth lunar month, and for the Wan'an participants on the twenty-ninth day of the fourth lunar month. Through an introduction from a shè executor from Yangxie, I got to know Duan Yuan'er (eighty years old) in the village temple on April 13, 2013, the fourth day of the third lunar month, when she was leading local devotees to receive Yangxie relatives. Most of the participants from Yangxie know Duan, since she has participated in the local activities of receiving the two sisters for more than forty years.

In 2013 Duan Yuan'er and Baishi devotees of Ehuang and Nüying served the Yangxie relatives steam buns and four dishes, including Herba Taraxaci (*kuku cai*, 苦苦菜), bean sprouts (*dou ya*, 豆芽), potato noodles (*fen tiao*, 粉条), and cabbage (*huizi bai*, 茴子白) (see fig. 4.7). Duan explained these four dishes to me: "That is *kuku cai* [*ku* means bitterness]; it symbolized that our *niang-niang* suffered from bitterness, and they ate it when they stopped at Hetan [during ancient times]. The dish of *kuku cai* is only served here every year.

You see, *dou ya* symbolized the prospects of being developed. *Fen tiao* symbolized smooth and good luck. The *huizi bai* sounds like *hui mian*, meeting."[4]

Duan Yuan'er said that during the forty years she served Ehuang and Nüying, she also suffered from bitterness during politically chaotic periods. Starting in the early 1970s, she collected incense money from villagers to receive the two deities and sacred relatives during the annual ritual processions, and she was once sent to prison because of her activities. Despite her personal suffering, she did not give up her beliefs and practices. Over the past twenty years, the activities of receiving Ehuang and Nüying have been officially revived and supported, and she led local devotees to build the village temple for the sisters and other deities in Baishi. She cried several times when she recalled the bitterness of her past life. She said: "[I] endured hardships, tortures, and pains, when serving *niangniang*." In our interview, Duan did not regret what she had suffered because of her devotion to the two sisters, and she also said that everything had improved and that life was much better now than before (see fig. 4.8).

On June 7, 2013, the twenty-ninth day of the fourth lunar month, I met Duan Yuan'er in the village temple in Baishi again when I followed the Wan'an parade from Yangxie back to Wan'an. This time she explained to me how Wan'an got involved in the local activities of receiving *niangniang* and why Wan'an participants passed Baishi just as Lishan participants did:

> If we talk about the legends of *niangniang*, here they are. You see, on the third year of Guangxu, there was a famine, and life was very miserable and painful. [Yangxie participants] went to the mountain, waited to eat; our relatives waited to eat. Yangxie called [the two ladies] aunties; they went to receive aunties and waited to eat. Aiya! They could not help crying [because of the famine]; they could not eat anything and could not swallow anything. [Someone] said that Wan'an was an important town, Wan'an was a city, and foods were sold there, they'd better buy some foods there. They then went to Wan'an. They went to the Southern Gate; the door was locked. They went to the Western Gate; the door was locked. They went to the Northern Gate; the door was open. The northern door was open; they were very happy about that. At that moment, an old man came out of the door. He came out and said, "Oh, well, what are you doing here?"
>
> "Oh, what am I doing? I am receiving aunties, I called aunties to go back."

Fig. 4.8. Duan Yuan'er standing in front of the village temple in Baishi on April 13, 2013, the fourth day of the third lunar month. She led local people to build the village temple twenty years ago.

"What happened when you called aunties to go back?"

"Oh, there are no foods, and no drinks. I am here buying some foods to eat; otherwise, I could not walk back." At that time, [they] all walked. They wanted to buy some foods to eat.

That old man then said, "Let's go, go, go! Please tell me if you have any problems. Please come to have some meals in my house." He thus treated them to meals.

After treating them to meals, the old man followed them and said, "Please stay here for one night." [They] thus stayed for one night. They stayed for one night and went back on the following day.

Afterward, the old man's business was very prosperous. He earned lots of money in his business. In the following year, he wanted to establish the sacred bond [between Wan'an and Yangxie] as relatives, and he did so. In the following year, when receiving relatives, the man from Wan'an said that it was good to be relatives, and yes, Lishan was the lead actor; here was a way station for resting horses and eating meals. According to legends, Wan'an is a way station for resting horses and eating meals.

Why did the Wan'an parade arrive here one day after the Lishan parade passed by? The stories went as follows. [Wan'an] is a way station for resting horses and eating meals, and relatives were bonded. This old man went back to ask for help from residents who lived near the Northern Gate; this was their business. They built the Niangniang Temple next to the Northern Gate. This is how the bond between relatives was established. These are legends passed down by old people.

When I was very young, Wan'an devotees did not carry the divine sedan chair [during the parade]; instead they carried stacks of food containers. . . . After [Lishan relatives] left [Yangxie], [Wan'an devotees] went to put everything in order and do some cleaning. These are legends about Wan'an. What is said by them now is not correct. Why is it not correct? I still remember what happened. My parents lived in Shubu, which is ten *li* away from Wan'an. My third uncle used to receive *niangniang* there. . . . We could not say that *da niangniang* left on the first day, and *xiao niangniang* left on the second day. There is nothing like this at all. I can guarantee that there is nothing like this.

With her narrative, Duan Yuan'er basically criticized what Liu Baoshan had stated and what the women that I interviewed in Hongbu and Dushu had said about receiving the two deities on two different days. She made it clear that this local discourse was made up and was not correct. She believed that Wan'an was always "a way station for resting horses and eating meals" and Lishan was the real "lead actor" (*zhujue*) during the annual ritual processions.

Interestingly, Duan Yuan'er stated that Wan'an devotees began to participate in local traditions in "the third year of Guangxu" (1877). I think she agreed with Wang Kaiyuan and probably meant to say "the third year of Shunzhi" (1646). The stele inscribed in the Niangniang Temple in Wan'an in 1674 dated the existence of the temple at least back to 1648, and Wang drew on this stele text and some written records from *Hongtong County Annals* about the famine in "the third year of Shunzhi" (1646) to date local legends and argue that Wan'an started to participate in receiving *niangniang* in 1646 (Wang 2008, 1). In so dating the precise moment when Wan'an began to be involved in local traditions, both Wang and Duan intended to legitimatize the leading role of Lishan and reiterate the status of Wan'an as a way station. For me, the exact dates do not matter; what matters is the hierarchy of involved village communities.

I asked Duan Yuan'er if she had heard of Ehuang and Nüying's conflict legends, and she did not respond directly. Instead, she told me that both women were not Emperor Yao's biological daughters but his adopted daughters. She said that Yao's older daughter was a shepherdess, his younger daughter a fairy maiden, and that Emperor Yao encountered them by chance and then adopted them as his daughters. The two first served Emperor Yao and his wife and later served Emperor Shun as his two wives. Duan's stories are similar to those documented by Qiao Guoliang, and like him, she also avoided talking about Ehuang and Nüying's conflict legends. In this way, she maintained a detached standpoint, which is similar to that of some folk literati from Yangxie but different from those from Wan'an. Her opinion corresponded to the view generally held by temple heads and shè executors from both Yangxie and Lishan, who believed that Lishan devotees took both deities back to Lishan on the twenty-eighth day of the fourth lunar month and that Wan'an devotees went to Yangxie to do some cleaning afterward.

Local Response from Longzhang, Longma, and Shubu

Despite the generally held view on Lishan's and Wan'an's different roles in receiving Ehuang and Nüying, local devotees from Longzhang, Longma, and Shubu provided different interpretations of these local traditions. The village temple head Han Jinxiang (seventy-eight years old) from Longzhang believed that the older sister was received back by the Lishan parade on the twenty-eighth day while the younger sister was received back by the Wan'an parade on the twenty-ninth day. However, some devotees from East Longma said that Lishan devotees went to Yangxie to receive *niangniang* back, while Wan'an devotees went to "put everything in order" and "clean up" after the two deities left. When I interviewed an old man in Shubu about Lishan's and Wan'an's different roles in receiving the two sisters, he did not want to express an opinion. He said: "Oh, for this situation, [I] can't say for sure; I do not know it." He said that people from Shubu treated Lishan and Wan'an participants in the same way along the processions, providing the same foods and dishes to them. On the basis of his response, I think that the man from Shubu indicates that some local people did not want to get involved in local conflicts related to the roles of the various villages in the ritual ceremonies and therefore avoided expressing their opinions in public. In this case, Shubu devotees were receiving participants from Wan'an in the village temple during our interview, and the old man was wise enough not to want to offend the Wan'an participants by offering a different interpretation of the rituals.

As for the conflict legends about Ehuang and Nüying, most of the people I interviewed along the procession routes could tell me the stories clearly. Most vividly described how the two sisters competed with each other in cooking beans and sewing shoe soles, and most of them believed that the younger sister, Nüying, won the competitions and became the queen. Some of them commented on Nüying's personality and said that she was "very easygoing" (*tebie kailang*), "smart" (*cong ming*), "clever" (*ji ling*), and "sharp" (*jing*), and therefore she naturally won the competitions and became the queen. At the end of their storytelling, some of the local people also commented that interpretations had changed recently: "In the past, *xiao de* [the younger sister] became the queen; now it is said that *da de* [the older sister] became the queen." Some attributed this change in the stories to the idea that "the society has changed" (*shehui bian le*) or "times have changed" (*shidai bian le*).

Tradition Ecology and Folk Literati

Ehuang and Nüying's conflict legends have changed over time and across space, and there is no fixed version or single meaning to the legends. These legends have been transformed and reconstructed according to the needs of narrators and audiences, and they reflect social changes in local society. Meanwhile, the basic plots remain unchanged and still resonate the same way with different people. Folk literati in Hongtong have attached great importance to these legends, and they have debated and negotiated with one another in remaking them. Their competing discourses reflect and shape conflictive interactions between local communities. Ordinary local people have received these changes in different ways, and no single voice dominates on the ground, even though some folk literati have tried to standardize the legends and make a definitive version. This dynamic process could be interpreted under the framework of tradition ecology.

In this context, *tradition ecology* is interpreted as a dynamic process of balance between cultural continuity and changes, and any disturbance in the system can lead to complex changes with unforeseen consequences. In oral traditions, Nüying's queen status is intertwined with local beliefs, rituals, and other legends. By debating her queen status and balancing the relationship between her and her older sister in the process of competition, folk literati unexpectedly cause confusion and contradictions within their interconnected communities. Although they have negotiated with one another to homogenize Ehuang and Nüying's conflict legends to an extent, these legends have never been homogeneous among ordinary peasants. Folk literati could be viewed as an inescapable part of tradition ecology; they are both objects of and factors in the cultural changes on the ground. In this interactive process, folk literati have recorded their discourses and interpretations in writing, offering a meaningful way of understanding local tradition.

Tradition ecology's complex process of cultural balance is similar to but distinct from another productive term in folklore studies: *traditionalization* (Hymes 1975; Mould 2005). Dell Hymes argues that traditionalization is a process in which individuals and groups make efforts to ground themselves in the past rather than become bulldozed by the present, and thus the past is *traditionalized* to serve the present (Hymes 1975, 353). Contrary to Hymes, Richard Bauman and Donald Braid argue that traditionalization is "the creation in the present of ties to a meaningful past that is itself constructed in the act of performance" (1998, 112). Drawing from Hymes (1975), Bauman and Braid (1998), Hobsbawm and Ranger (1983), and Handler and Linnekin (1984), Tom Mould suggests that traditionalization can be understood "as a symbolic quality granted to elements of culture in an ongoing interpretive process that establishes continuity with the past by standing in opposition to modernity" (2005, 259). However, some folklorists object to the binary division between tradition and modernity and argue that "just as the traditional is modern, so the modern is traditional" (Noyes 2009, 244). Like Dorothy Noyes, I adopt a dialectical understanding of the relationship between these two apparently contrasting concepts and add historical and spatial dimensions into the theory of tradition ecology, interpreting it as a dynamic process in which different social actors construct, deconstruct, and reconstruct the past to serve the present and to face the future. The framework of tradition ecology helps us to interpret the dynamic interactions between various elements such as the written and the oral. The interrelationships we observe among individuals, beliefs, legends, history, and place reflect and affect the changing cultural landscape on the ground and sustain local communities' future in modern society.

As discussed, folk literati are not a bounded, fixed, static, and natural class but a dynamic group of individuals who are viewed as knowledgeable and capable in writing by insiders. They often disagree with one another, and their innovations both shape and reflect conflicts in local communities. Their process of creation is a kind of reification similar to that of some scholars: they first construct something new, apply it as real, and then continue their analysis as if it really exists in the minds of local villagers. In reality, this reification is problematized by some of my interviewees—they know how local legends have changed, but they still prefer to tell these stories as they have known them because the tales are integrated not only with their beliefs and practices but also with their history and place. This complicated process of balancing both cultural changes and continuities among competing actors and communities unfolds the theory of tradition ecology, which provides us with a powerful way to understand the reconstruction and reception of local tradition in a changing world.

Notes

1. This basic narrative outline is based on Li Xuezhi's collection of local legends, which is included in his booklet *Records of Connections between Yangxie and Lishan through Sacred Marriage* (Li 1997).

2. Ehuang was believed to have been born in Yicun (伊村), Linfen, where the Temple of Yao was located (information based on my interview with my host Wang Wei).

3. Wang Kaiyuan's biography is based on my interviews with his oldest son, Wang Wei, in 2012 and 2013, along with some records that he left for his son.

4. Local people use the above-ground parts and roots of *kuku cai* to make food and medicine. As food it is used as greens in various dishes or soup; as medicine it is used to improve digestion, treat infection, increase urine production, and increase bowel movements. *Kuku cai* is also used in rituals to connect the distant past during Ehuang and Nüying's time with the present, and even with the future. Based on her narrative, Duan Yuan'er believed that Ehuang and Nüying ate *kuku cai* during their time, and its name indicates that the two sisters did not forget that they had suffered from bitterness.

5

REPRODUCING TRADITION

Folk Literati, Sociocultural Differentiation, and
Their Interaction with Other Social Actors

S EVERAL FOLKLORISTS REPRESENTED IN THE EDITED VOLUME *The Indi-*
vidual and Tradition: Folkloristic Perspectives (2011) examine the interrelationship between the individual and tradition. The individual they focus
on is "the star," no matter whether he or she is "the star informant," "the star
performer," or both (Cashman, Mould, and Shukla 2011, 11). However, these
folklorists do not focus on the role of competing individuals in the remaking of tradition. In chapters 3 and 4, I discussed the competing agency of
folk literati in the transmitting and reproducing of tradition within local
communities. In this chapter, I examine the sociocultural differentiation
of folk literati and the interrelationship between them and tradition, illustrating how folk literati are formed as a social group within local contexts;
how they are differentiated from and connected to their native hometown
fellows; what roles they have played in continuing, changing, representing,
and reproducing local legends and beliefs; and how their roles have been
received in local communities. I also analyze how folk literati interact with
other social actors, including shè, temple reconstruction associations, ritual
specialists, and ordinary people when remaking local traditions.

I propose that tradition can be conceptualized as a dynamic process of
the transfer of appreciation, an ability to understand the meaning or importance of a valued practice or cultural process. In this chapter, I explore how
acceptance of the role of folk literati in their communities depends on
how much these literati appreciate local beliefs, history, and legends and
how well they represent their knowledge in writing. Folk literati are active
agents in the remaking of local traditions, but they have to respect existing

knowledge and practice within their communities. They may draw on their personal imagination to create something new, but their fellow villagers will resist this invention and authority if the change is too arbitrary and ungrounded. In this interactive process of transmitting and reproducing local traditions, folk literati and ordinary peasants are both inventors and participants.

The Dialectics of the Making and Differentiation of Folk Literati

Dorothy Noyes points out that the hyphen commonly placed between *folk* and *lore* indicates some key questions in the field of folklore studies, one of which is "What commonsense relationships exist between bodies of knowledge and groups of people?" (Noyes 2012, 13). When examining the puzzle of "the social bond," "the dialectics of group-making and differentiation" become the main concerns for many folklorists (Noyes 2012, 22). My key interests here are with the dialectics of the making and differentiation of folk literati within local communities. As mentioned, insiders generally view folk literati as talented writers, but the identity of this dynamic social group has been interpreted differently within different contexts. Some folk literati call themselves "ordinary peasants" or "ordinary people," and in doing so they identify with their native hometown residents. Even if other villagers and their friends refer to them as *literati* (*wenren*), that term has no fixed definition in local communities. Moreover, the term is sometimes used interchangeably with others, such as *talented scholars* (*caizi*), *men of culture* (*wenhua ren*), or *scholars* (*dushu ren*). The variety of designations for folk literati indicates that their role in local communities is flexible. The making and representation of their identification as folk literati entails the forging of a social bond within local communities, sometimes among themselves, sometimes between them and their audience.

The modern Chinese folk literature movement began in 1918, and since then a high/low dichotomy has been crucial in defining folk literature in Chinese folklore scholarship (Hung 1985, 163). The "low-class literati" were excluded from the social group of the folk in the early twentieth century (Hung 1985, 163), and their status in folklore studies was never fully resolved. Should folk literati be classified as "high-class literati" or "low-class folk"? Should their work be categorized as folk literature or elite literature? In practice, this group crosses the boundary between high and low in social class, especially in light of the dramatic political changes in China in the twentieth century, as expressed in Qiao Guoliang's couplet about the rise and fall of literati and their changing role in revolutionary China (see chap. 2). Furthermore, their work exemplifies the interaction between high and low literature as well as between written and oral literature. For these reasons, folk literati should not be excluded from the purview of folklore studies and cultural studies.

Despite its problematic hypothesis, the high and low dichotomy had an important afterlife in Chinese folklore studies, and some folklorists saw folklore as the "little tradition" coexisting with a shared "great tradition" (Huang 2005). The model of little and great traditions was proposed by Robert Redfield (1956). Basically, Redfield views peasants "as the rural dimension of old civilization" and emphasizes the constant relationship between the peasant and the elite. He regards peasant society as a "half-society," just as he regards peasant culture as a "half-culture." He conceptualizes the relations between the unreflective mass of peasants and the reflective few of urban or aristocratic elites as the interaction between a "little tradition" and a "great tradition" (Redfield 1956, 67–70). By doing so, Redfield reifies his model as real and functional, and with a focus on the outcome and superficial dichotomy of two traditions, he ignores what people actually do in their daily lives. Furthermore, he does not allow enough room for social actors and the assertion of agency in the practice of local traditions.

Pierre Bourdieu ([1980] 1990) warns us not to reify objectifications that are not real. According to him, culture provides the very grounds for human communication and interaction; it is also a source of power and domination. When scholars reify distinctions of the high and the low or of the great tradition and the little tradition, they do not consider that traditions mediate practices by connecting individuals and groups to institutionalized hierarchies, which embody power relations. In other words, traditions are constructed, deconstructed, and reconstructed continuously through power struggles. The key question is how traditional resources, processes, and institutions hold individuals and groups in competitive and self-perpetuating hierarchies of domination.

Noyes expresses her dissatisfaction with the split between "folklore as a project of domination" and "folklore as a trajectory of resistance." She argues that "compromise and accommodation" form the zone that the folk or folklorists normally inhabit (Noyes 2016, 6). In my research, folklore is conceptualized sometimes as a form of resistance and sometimes as a form of compromise and accommodation. Its meaning and form are mediated by the active people who have produced and reproduced it. As local intellectuals, some folk literati use folklore to resist the dominating ideology, especially during politically disastrous periods, and some make compromises and accommodations to cater to a broader audience with different needs when remaking local traditions as heritage. The understanding and interpretation of the creative cultural expressions of folk literati should therefore be situated and scrutinized within particular social, cultural, historical, political, and economic contexts. No matter whether folklore is constructed as a form of resistance or as a form of compromise and accommodation, folk literati mediate between their village fellows and provincial or metropolitan intellectuals, and they connect their village with the nation-state and even the global world.

Folk Literati and Culture

The definition of *literati* is not homogeneous or stable in local communities, but *culture* (*wenhua*) is a key term often used to define who literati are in local contexts. For example, Wang Wei, Wang Kaiyuan's son and a resident in South Yangxie Village, defines literati as "men of culture, capable of writing and speaking, and knowledgeable in local knowledge" (*you wenhua, hui xie hui shuo, dongde defang de zhishi de ren*).[1] The local interpretation of culture is different from the one in the nation-state discourse. Regarding the nation-state context, Tim Oakes (2006) points out that culture is used as a means to gain economic achievements as well as a resource for national identity and pride that is necessary for the consolidation of the Chinese Communist Party (CCP) regime and governance mechanism in contemporary China. However, local people's concept of culture is articulated at the individual level, intertwined with the concept of "reading books or studying" (*dushu*, 读书) or "educational background" (*xueli*, 学历). When folk literati evaluated their peers and themselves during interviews, they often mentioned their education first. The educational background of folk literati and their interest in literature could be counted among the resources that allow them to perform socially within a system of cultural exchange that includes accumulated cultural knowledge. Folk literati's cultural resources include not only the forms of their knowledge and education but also those of their language abilities and writing or literary skills, especially their skills in classical Chinese. Many folk literati can refer to classical books (such as

Shiji and *Mengzi*), local gazetteers (such as *Hongtong County Annals*), and stele texts as important sources to represent local legends and history in their work. These language and literary skills in classical Chinese give them an advantaged position in cultural production.

The educational background of folk literati could be scrutinized within nuanced contexts and could be connected with their linguistic and literary skills. Some villagers are aware of the difference in the quality of education during various periods in the Republic of China and in the People's Republic of China (PRC). In an interview on May 19, 2013, Zhang Zhizhong, an old man from Chefu Village, said that those who graduated from elementary school in the Republic of China could teach in elementary school, whereas those who graduated from high school in more recent times could not necessarily teach in elementary school. When defining *literati*, Zhang emphasized that they were educated and knowledgeable and knew how to write essays that could be understood easily by them and by others. Zhang highlighted in particular the literati's skills in composing couplets for different purposes and within different contexts. In addition, noticing the dramatic changes in modern society, he commented: "Now people all pay attention to money, being ignorant of the history of their own, or counting the records but forgetting the ancestors, [they] do not pay attention to . . . ancient culture . . . culture is drying up in our society today."

In his interview, Zhang Zhizhong criticized the decline in the quality of education in classical Chinese in today's China and the consequent deterioration of cultural production in the countryside. His also emphasized the marginalized status of folk literati. Zhang was known as a literatus in Chefu Village, and he tried to record local history and preserve local traditional culture in the village. He was in the same generation as Li Xuezhi, Qiao Guoliang, and Liu Baoshan, although he was not as influential as they were in their respective native areas. They all received their education in the Republican era and knew how to read and write in classical Chinese. Even though they did not have outstanding educational backgrounds or high-level degrees, they kept learning on their own and tried their best to protect local culture. They carried on the cultural responsibility of traditional literati, choosing to continue local traditions and even to represent them in writing. Not all their efforts were well received by their fellow villagers, and not all their essays were appreciated by ordinary people. Sometimes they were caught in the gap between their ideals and messy reality, and it was not easy for them to effect any social or cultural change based on these ideals. Their cultural resources gave them a good position from which they could represent local traditions but did not necessarily give them a higher status in their communities, especially in today's "economic society" when "people all pay attention to money" instead of culture. Unlike many literati in premodern China, who had high social status, folk literati are a marginalized social group in contemporary China, even though they have played important roles in continuing and reproducing local traditions.

Self-Evaluation and Peer Review of Folk Literati

The designation of literati is fluid within local contexts, and the self-evaluation of folk literati and their views vary from case to case. On June 5, 2013, when I interviewed Li Xuezhi and asked him if he viewed himself as a literatus, he responded: "Those who receive a certain level of education and have a certain cultural awareness can be regarded as literati; my education level is low, and I only graduated from junior high school, and I do not deserve to be a literatus." He then commented that nobody working in the local temples could be viewed as a literatus either, adding: "People from a variety of classes all view me as a literatus, which is their misconception. In fact, I do not deserve to be a literatus. . . . My knowledge is very limited, and I am not good enough to be a literatus at all. I am just an ordinary man."

There is a paradox at the heart of Li Xuezhi's comments: on the one hand, he wants to be very humble in evaluating himself; on the other hand, he needs to establish his credentials and assert himself as an important local cultural figure in remaking Yao and Shun's stories and marking the significance of Hongtong's Lishan (as seen in chap. 3). Li regarded himself as "an ordinary man," thus underlining his modesty. At the same time, he thought nobody else in the local temples deserved to be honored as a literatus. His comments indicate that if he did not deserve to be a literatus, nobody else did either. Actually, many old people in Lishan regarded Li as an outstanding literatus, and they told me that nobody could really compete with him in writing.

The definition of *literati* has never been fixed within local communities, and everyone seems to have a unique interpretation. I interviewed Li Xuezhi's rival Li Chunwen in Lishan on June 11, 2013, and asked him if he and Li Xuezhi could be considered literati. Li Chunwen responded by saying that none of them deserved to be a literatus. His definition of *literati* was as follows: "Literati (*wenren*), first, must be very knowledgeable, but it does not follow that they have to know everything in our society, nobody can do that . . . in our society, the knowledge is very broad; what everyone knows is just a drop in an ocean." Li Chunwen's definition of *literati* was followed by an explanation, delivered in a very straightforward fashion, of why he did not think of Li Xuezhi as a literatus:

> First, his own education, he just finished elementary school. . . . If you do not give up but continue to study and accumulate knowledge through endless practice, it would be fine. But his attitudes of learning are problematic. I have been his colleague for thirteen years. We have known each other for thirteen years, and we did not get along . . . why did we not get along with each other? I am not willing to be hypocritical. Here is my opinion. I am a human being; you are a human being. If you accept that you are a human being, "to err is human." Everyone makes mistakes in life, doesn't he? The question is how you deal with mistakes. For instance, if I have black spots on my face, other people do not point it out, but if I find it out when I see myself in the mirror, I will wash it. If other people point it out, you still refuse to accept it, which is . . .
>
> Why do I not accept that he is a literatus? I summarize his life, ah, what is his biggest strength in life? For the temple [reconstruction], he does whatever he can; this is his biggest strength. What is his biggest weakness in life? He likes to reject good advice and gloss over faults; this is his biggest weakness . . . he does not accept his own mistakes. It is not a shame to make a mistake; the question is how you deal with it. It is not a mistake if you accept your mistake and correct it. You know you make a mistake, but you do not accept it when other people point it out, you still think that you are a number one knowledgeable person in the world, alas!

Overall, Li Chunwen's evaluation of Li Xuezhi emphasizes his low level of formal education and his problematic attitude of not accepting other people's suggestions. Li Chunwen also did not think of himself as a literatus; he told me that he only completed elementary school and had always lived in the countryside, so he was not knowledgeable enough to be a literatus. However, he showed a strong interest in lifelong learning. Some of his friends told me that his grandfather was an old *xiucai* (秀才), one who passed the imperial examination at the county level during the late Qing dynasty, that his father was a local literatus, and that both influenced him greatly. Li

Chunwen trained himself to be a scholar even though he did not receive a high level of formal education. When I stayed in Lishan in the summer of 2012, I found that he practiced calligraphy every day and copied by hand classical books, such as *Commentary on the Classic of Waterways (Shui jing zhu)*. In addition to his "Gazetteer of Lishan, Hongtong, China" (2012), Li Chunwen also wrote a personal collection of classical poems "Lü lu chu yiwen lu" (呂麓樗逸文錄). Most people in Lishan viewed Li Chunwen as a literatus, although some commented that he was not as talented as Li Xuezhi.

As detailed in chapter 3, Li Xuezhi has worked hard to prove that Lishan in Hongtong was the place where Shun plowed and where Yao visited Shun, with the larger intention of asserting the primacy of his hometown on the national stage, particularly competing with the claims by Lishan in Yuanqu, Shanxi, concerning Shun culture. None of the other folk literati in Hongtong or the local residents in Lishan really support his argument; instead, they believe that Lishan, Hongtong, is as important as other Lishans in China but that it does not necessarily have higher status.

However, Li Xuezhi has continually insisted on his assertion, leading to other people questioning him. For instance, his representation of Shun's stories in Lishan, Hongtong, was interpreted as "reversing history" (*niuzhuan lishi*) by Han Xiaomao.[2] Li was also blamed by some temple heads in Wan'an for contributing to local conflicts. I was told that Li did not like to negotiate with others when representing local traditions, and his personal construction was viewed as "nonsense" by some locals. During an interview on August 8, 2012, Hu Zhikan (胡志侃), a devotee of the temple from Yangjia Zhuang, commented on Li and his work: "He is very capable, very well educated, but his writings are not well grounded . . . historical legends are both reliable and not reliable . . . based on what happened, he inevitably exaggerates or reduces something." It seems from these reactions that Li, as a representative literatus, often fails to persuade others with his interpretations in the ongoing process of remaking local traditions.

This leads to the question: To what extent can folk literati exert their creative agency in cultural production? Li Genwa, one resident in the Lishan temple complex, provided his own interpretation during my interview with him on June 11, 2012: "Originally they [Li Xuezhi and his colleagues] cared about ordinary people very much, but later they threw them away, only seeking their own fame and wealth. It got bad when they tossed aside [these people]." According to Li Genwa, the viewpoints of folk literati are essential, and they are more likely to succeed if they stand with, for, and by ordinary people. In Li Xuezhi's case, there is a dramatic contrast between his work in the 1990s and his more recent work. When compiling local legends in the 1990s, Li talked with many local people and recorded what they told him. His 1997 booklet was a coherent representation of local legends and beliefs, widely circulated in the area, although Wan'an residents felt that they were excluded. In the 2000s, by contrast, Li made up many stories that had never circulated in Lishan before and that were sometimes beyond the understanding of local residents, such as the stories about the Wei and Rui Rivers where Nüying and Ehuang were wed to Shun (Li 2009). Tradition is an ongoing process of cultural production, but it does not necessarily follow that tradition came from nowhere and could therefore be invented and remade freely. When catering to local audiences, folk literati have to respect the accumulation of local knowledge and discourse about local folklore. Otherwise, they might isolate themselves from ordinary people, conceptualize their ideas irrespective of external circumstances, and indulge in self-admiration, thus losing their authority and also the respect of their peers and fellow villagers.

The Interplay of Folk Literati's Agency and Local Traditions

Folk literati's cultural production is not a direct, unmediated response to external forces or a simple outgrowth from internal factors. The literati are active agents by themselves, but their cultural production is dictated by local traditions. They may draw on their own imagination to narrate local legends and enjoy certain freedom in their literary representations, but they have to respect what has been shared among ordinary people in local communities and to acknowledge the traditional practices on the ground. There are some boundaries that they cannot cross when remaking local traditions; completely challenging preexisting knowledge and practice would put them in a difficult position.

An example of such a violation is seen in a widely circulated legend in Hongtong. The legend highlights the hail disaster that occurred one year after the date was changed for receiving Ehuang and Nüying in the fourth lunar month. Li Xuezhi recounted the emergence and circulation of this local legend as follows:

> When talking about making a documentary on TV [about local rituals], there is a miraculous event that I have to mention: the TV

documentary [on the rituals] on the twenty-eighth day of the fourth month in the lunar calendar [the lunar April 28 for short hereafter] should have been made on the exact day based on customs. Because I thought that, on the lunar April 28, it was during a busy summer season of harvests this year, which might affect film shooting, I discussed it with my Yangxie relatives and changed the date to ten days earlier.

On the day of film shooting, the sky was first blue and clear when the Lishan parade departed from Yangxie. In the middle of their trip, it suddenly became very cloudy, and a storm soon brought rarely seen large hail, which immediately hit people and made them flee in all directions.

The storm and hail stopped after about ten minutes; people then got together again from all directions. They played drums and gongs again, and in a great state they followed the original route to go back to Lishan.

The next day, a legend spread everywhere. People said that the wheat from the twelve villages on the route of receiving the goddesses was flattened in the fields, while those villages adjacent to these villages were not affected by the hail, and no wheat was hit there, even though their fields were adjacent to those hailed fields. Only those villages related to the custom of visiting sacred relatives were damaged. Why? Here is the reason. The lunar April 28 is the birthday of Emperor Yao. Why did not the two goddesses return from their parents' family to their husband's family until the lunar April 28? Because they had to wait till the lunar April 28 to celebrate their father Emperor Yao's birthday, and they returned to Lishan after that. This year, the returning date was changed to ten days earlier, and they were received back to their husband's family on the lunar April 18, which hurt their filial piety for celebrating their father's birthday. Therefore, the two goddesses got very angry, and they punished the people of Lishan with hail. Why did the villages on the route of receiving the goddesses all suffer from the hail disaster? Because no people from these villages refused to change the date when [we] discussed it with them, all were punished.

This thing spread everywhere, from the officials to the folk; everyone knows it, and they even talk about it now. Yangxie and Lishan people accepted the lessons, and they dare not violate the transmitted customs anymore. (Li 2012, 10)

This legend is widely known in Hongtong, and the hail disaster is seen as a punishment from the deities for those who dared to "violate the transmitted customs" and change the date of the ritual processions; as Li Xuezhi noted, nobody dared to do it again after this incident. When I interviewed many local residents in Yangxie, Lishan, and Wan'an, everyone knew the story, and like Li, they said those villages that agreed to change the date were all affected by the hail. For instance, some local people talked about the different situation in North Yangxie Village and South Yangxie Village. North Yangxie was on duty that year, and South Yangxie assisted in receiving relatives, and while the North Yangxie villagers agreed to change the date, the South Yangxie villagers objected to it. As a result, the wheat fields in North Yangxie were all damaged by hail, whereas those in South Yangxie were not affected at all, even though their fields were separated only by a narrow path.

Although many people remember the hail disaster, the date of its occurrence is open to question. Li Xuezhi recalled that it happened in 1989, but he was not sure about the exact date. Yan Zhenghong from Yangxie recorded that it occurred in 1991, and he said that he had proposed to change the date first (Yan 2007a). The documentary series that Li refers to is *Nei lu jiu san* (*Inland China in 1993*), produced by Zhao Yu (赵瑜) and Shanxi Television Station in 1993; therefore the hail disaster might have happened in 1993.

This contemporary legend of the hail disaster is similar to another legend that I heard, about the Ox King Temple (*Niuwang miao*) in Beiyang Village, adjacent to South Yangxie. This temple is one of the most popular in Hongtong, and its annual temple fairs on the lunar April 10 (which is believed to be the birthday of Ox King) attract tens of thousands of people from several provinces. On June 27, 2012, I went to Beiyang to meet an official who attended the laying foundation (*dianji*) ceremony for a new temple there. According to the stele texts, the old temple was originally built in 1014 and was destroyed in 1940 during the Second Sino-Japanese War. The temple was rebuilt in 2000 and then renovated in 2004. Because of the popularity of its annual temple fairs, the local government decided to protect and promote this temple as a part of local cultural heritage. A rich businessman donated millions of yuan (the Chinese currency) to build a new temple, and he requested that the old temple be dismantled. Several weeks later after the lay foundation ceremony, my host Wang Wei told me that Beiyang and Yangxie suffered from a drought that summer, even though it rained heavily in the adjacent neighborhood. Some villagers said that the god in the

Ox King Temple was angry about the destruction of his old temple so he brought the drought as a penalty for this desecration.

People worldwide often view disasters as punishment from gods across time and space (Horigan 2010), and in China disasters are often tied to deities' miraculous powers by those interpreting the acts of the deities. During the Song dynasty (960–1279), Hong Mai (1123–1202) recorded several disaster legends in *Yijian Zhi* (*The Records of the Listener*).[3] In one story, a local magistrate in Jing County (Anhui) refused to follow the head clerk's advice to visit a local temple within three days after he took office. Soon his office was flooded in a terrible storm, soaking all his documents, and the local people concluded that the god was punishing the official. In another story, a different official refused to make the requisite offering of a pig to a Suzhou dragon deity although a boatman repeatedly urged him to do so. A resulting sea squall drowned many people. Valerie Hansen summarizes the interpretation of these legends thus: "The official who ignored the counsel of a local person to worship a local god brought disaster upon themselves" (1990, 71). She suggests that these legends illustrate "a common pool of interpretative mechanisms" based on "the principle of reciprocity" between humans and deities (1990, 71).

I view contemporary legends of disasters as not only revealing the interpreters' understandings of the reciprocity between humans and deities but also conveying their resistance to cultural and political authority. In other words, these legends are remarkable inventions of ordinary people who express their resistance to cultural and political control in local communities. In the hail disaster legend, ordinary villagers express their resistance to the abrupt date change made by folk literati—especially when that change is made only for the convenience of the documentary filmmakers at the cost of the local communities—and those who proposed or agreed to the change are blamed for bringing the hailstorm and for its consequent destruction of the crops. Within this story, the deities seem to also act fairly toward those who objected to or refused to make the change, and they reward them by sparing those communities from the effects of the storm. The people then learn from this manifestation of the miraculous power of the deities, as indicated by the fact that they do not dare to change the dates of the annual ritual processions again. In the miraculous legend of the drought, storytellers express their resistance to the political authority of the local government and their use of that authority to dismantle the old temple site. However, this legend is not as well known and influential as the hail disaster legend, since a new magnificent temple was eventually built on the original site of the old Ox King Temple, despite the negative effects outlined in the legend. No matter the consequences, these contemporary legends about disasters can be understood as everyday forms of resistance (Scott 1985, 1990, 2013) and as a means of empowerment for the local people.

The disaster legends convey the creative agency of ordinary peasants who are faced with cultural and political authority in their local region. It is unclear who created these legends in the first place, but whoever the creators might be, they use these stories as an important expressive weapon to resist the changes made to local practice and as a way to articulate their own beliefs about local traditions and themselves. Through these daily forms of resistance, local traditions are transmitted continuously and consistently, and a balance of cultural continuities and change is maintained in local communities.

Given the story of the hail disaster, it also seems that the cultural authority of folk literati can be easily resisted within local communities and that this resistance is often accepted—indeed, those who proposed the change to the ritual processions' date readily accepted the penalty from the deities and thereafter chose to keep local customs as they originally were. The folk literati are from these local communities, and they receive their authority from their village fellows. Therefore, while folk literati are active agents in the remaking of local traditions, their creativity is balanced with continuities and consistencies espoused by local communities, where existing discourse and practice circumscribe the agency and action of the folk literati. In this interactive process of transmitting and reproducing local traditions, folk literati and ordinary people are both creators and participants. Living legends are a significant vernacular tool allowing them to interact with one another and empower themselves.

Folk Literati and Their Social Networks

When folk literati transmit and reproduce local beliefs, rituals, and legends from their native villages and temples, their individual agency shapes and is shaped not only by existing knowledge and practice but also by social networks. They interact not only with local shè and the temple reconstruction associations but also with other important local social actors as well as the local government and outsiders. Not all folk literati have successfully built extensive social networks within their communities and beyond, but those who have succeeded in doing so have obtained authority and power in representing local traditions. Of the people I interviewed, Li Xuezhi from Lishan is probably the most well-known and authoritative literatus in the local communities, and he has mainly drawn on his cultural resources and political background to establish his reputation and authority in Lishan. In contrast, Pei Beiji from Yangxie is probably the least influential or recognized literatus in the region, and some local residents commented on him by saying "his brand is not solid" (*ta paizi bu ying*). Other folk literati fall somewhere in the middle, and their fame is spread by word of mouth. In the following sections, I illustrate how folk literati have interacted with other actors in building social networks within and beyond their local communities.

Folk Literati, Shè, and the Temple Reconstruction Associations

Folk literati are often active participants in local ritual processions and annual temple fairs in their native areas and temples, and they are usually active members of local shè or temple reconstruction associations too. Most folk literati are devotees of Ehuang and Nüying, and some of them, such as Qiao Guoliang and Wang Kaiyuan from Yangxie, once served as the shè head or associate head in their village temple. After the temple reconstruction associations were founded in the 1990s and the 2000s, most folk literati served as important members in these institutions. For instance, Li Xuezhi was a cofounder of the Lishan temple reconstruction association, and he has served as its associate director for many years. In Yangxie, Yan Zhenghong is the consultant, archivist, and receptionist for official visitors in the temple reconstruction association. In Wan'an, Liu Baoshan founded the Wan'an Cultural Relics Maintenance Station in the spring of 1985 and used this organization to revive the local shè and its activities. These connections make sense because folk literati often made use of shè to mobilize local people to rebuild temples, to revive traditional activities, and to negotiate with the local government for the legitimization of their local traditions.

Despite the temple reconstruction association's change of leadership in Lishan, Li Xuezhi's status has not dramatically changed. He is still the most productive and influential literatus in Lishan, which has made him special in local communities. In addition to books and essays, he wrote a Puju opera, "Visiting Sages in Li Mountain" (Lishan Fangxian), in 2005, and it was performed once by a local Puju opera troupe in Hongtong. In recent years, his hearing has deteriorated, and the temple association is trying to find a new person to receive outside visitors, especially high-level officials. However, no one from Lishan knows all the stories about Yao and Shun in the way Li does, and only Li can tell those stories coherently and convincingly.

In Yangxie, the local shè executors have been considered important inheritors (*chuancheng ren*) of local traditions in the process of safeguarding the intangible cultural heritage (Wang and Yan 2008, 1–2). Qiao Guoliang was an important shè executor and inheritor from 1965 to 1982 in the Yangxie Village temple; later Wang Wenhua took his turn and served as the shè head in South Yangxie from 1983 to 2004. Qiao Longhai was appointed by Wang Wenhua to serve as the Southern shè associate head in the early 2000s. Yan Zhenghong joined the general shè as a consultant in 2004, though he did not serve in any position in the local shè. Wang Kaiyuan was the associate shè head in South Yangxie from 1982 to 1988.

Dealing with the different affairs in the temples is not always easy, and this was especially true for Qiao Guoliang as a traditional literatus. During our interview on July 7, 2012, his grandson Quio Longhai told me: "[My grandpa] suffered a lot for serving aunties. [He] also got angry, angry at some people in the temple. He could not stand that someone did something very bad in the temple. [Some people] are not honest in many things when serving aunties, and they could not have behaved so badly. He was also very angry at it."

Because Qiao was an honest man, he did not want to spend any incense money collected at the temple for himself. Even though he wrote couplets for the temple, he did not have free meals there but intended to save all the money for temple reconstruction. However, not everyone in the temple thought and acted in this way, and some people tried to benefit from their service in the temple, sometimes even spending the incense money for themselves. Qiao was angry about this kind of behavior, but he could not stop them. Because of this, he did not really get along with his peers in the temple.

Despite the efforts Qiao Guoliang made to continue and to revive local traditions in the 1970s and 1980s, his contributions are not fully recognized in the village temple today. As Qiao Longhai said: "In the temple, to be honest, nowadays, all capable people move ahead to secure their personal gain . . . since my grandpa passed away, we do not have to compete for anything, and it doesn't matter." Qiao Longhai indicated that the temple affairs were now run by a group of new, "capable" people who did not participate in temple activities in the 1970s and 1980s and who did not really believe in the deities sincerely. In contrast, many old people who once fought fearlessly for the continuity of local rituals and beliefs during harsh political periods have been marginalized or even kicked out from the newly established temple reconstruction association.

Yan Zhenghong's case is different from Qiao Guoliang's, for he has actively participated in local temple activities only since 2004. Even though some old shè executors questioned how he became a consultant in the temple when he did not really believe in the deities, the old temple head Shao Caiwang supported him strongly and even provided funding for him to publish his booklet. Yan once served as the party secretary in North Yangxie, and he has certain cultural and political resources to build his social networks in local communities. Today his regular role in Yangxie Village temple is very similar to Li Xuezhi's in Lishan: to receive important outside visitors in the village temple, tell them the local legends, and introduce them to local culture. As with Li, Yan is also getting older, and so the Yangxie general shè have tried to find a young man to replace him. However, none of the young people have enough time and enough local knowledge for these responsibilities, especially since most of them have moved to big cities.

During my fieldwork in Yangxie, I observed Yan Zhenghong's main work at the temple fairs from the twentieth day to the twenty-ninth day of the fourth lunar month (May 29 to June 7), 2013. Yan was the leader of a literature and theatrical performance coordination group (*wenyi diaoyan zu*, 文艺调演组), and his main responsibilities included making public propaganda about temple fairs, composing new couplets for all temple halls and doors, communicating with local sponsors of regional opera performances at temple fairs and collecting money from them, receiving opera troupes, negotiating with sponsors and troupes to decide which plays would be performed every day, and preparing daily opera posters (*xibao*, 戏报), which announce the names of sponsors and their sponsored plays.

Yan Zhenghong used to compose an elegiac address (*jiwen*, 祭文) to praise Emperor Yao's virtues and achievements for the annual ceremony to celebrate Emperor Yao's birthday on the morning of the twenty-eighth day of the fourth lunar month in the Old Temple of Tang Yao, but his address was not used in 2013. He usually wrote the essay in classical Chinese and particularly imitated the style of rhapsody or poetic exposition (*fu*, 赋), a genre of Chinese rhymed prose popular in the Han dynasty. This ancient form of writing was not easy for ordinary people to understand, and the temple head decided to invite a new guest speaker to give the elegiac address in 2013. This speaker wrote his presentation in colloquial Chinese, which was well received by the audience.

Although Yan Zhenghong was active in the running of temple activities, his younger peers sometimes criticized him as being inefficient. In 2013, forty-eight households sponsored an opera performance at the temple fairs in Yangxie, and two opera troupes were invited to perform. I met a young man from the Temple Fair Office who directly criticized Yan for not listing all the sponsors' names on the opera poster. When Yan saw me, he forced a smile and said that he was too old to manage everything efficiently and that it was probably time for him to fully retire. In contrast with Li Xuezhi, Yan was not an authoritative figure—he did not have a strong sense of self-confidence and consequently was not likely to present himself in a way that would lead others to highly respect and obey him. Still, he had some authority in representing local traditions to outside audiences and in organizing some work for the temple reconstruction association.

Pei Beiji's role was ambiguous in the Southern shè and the general shè. In 2013 he was named the associate leader of the atmosphere group (*fenweizu*, 氛围组) at temple fairs. In theory, the job of this group was to create an all-encompassing atmosphere for the temple fairs, but in practice they merely ran errands for others. Pei also used to lead the Yangxie band of drums and gongs, and he trained many village women to play for the reception during the third day of the third lunar month. However, because he did not really study with the old people who were the masters of the local Awe-Inspiring Gongs and Drums, they always criticized his performance.

Wang Kaiyuan was a capable man, and he was an active member of the VIP guest reception group (*guibin jiedai zu*, 贵宾接待组) at temple fairs. Because of his sincere service, he got to know some officials and folklorists and became their good friend. He drew on his networks to increase business for his own restaurant and also to build his personal fame in local communities. After he passed away in June 2009, his significance faded away, and new actors emerged to actively participate in local traditions.

Folk Literati and Local Mazi

Folk literati in Hongtong also actively interact with other important local social actors, such as *mazi*, in rituals and processions at temple fairs and other religious festivals. In this interactive process, some folk literati have shaped multiple identities for themselves in their communities, and some have even become *mazi*. *Mazi* are practitioners who convey messages for local deities and heal through the power of supernatural spirits, and they remain active in Hongtong (Yao 2010). Among the eight important folk literati that I examine, three of them are conceptualized as *mazi* by their village fellows or themselves. Qiao Guoliang became an apprentice (*dizi*) of Tongtian Erlang in his later years;[4] in that capacity, he tried to cure villagers' illnesses through the power of the two aunties, though his main goal was to collect stories of the two aunties and represent those stories in writing. Pei Beiji followed the model of Qiao and claimed to be a *mazi*, again with the primary purpose of serving the deities by writing down their stories. Han Xiaomao was originally an amateur Daoist, primarily serving the Jade Emperor to cure sickness for locals. While promoting the receiving of aunties as an element of China's national intangible cultural heritage in 2007, Han began collecting sources for a manuscript on local traditions. Qiao's and Pei's roles as *mazi* have influenced their representations of local traditions, while Han stated that he purposefully drew on written sources to reconstruct local history.

On July 17, 2012, I interviewed Li Descheng, one of Qiao Guoliang's good friends, in West to the Sacred Temple Village; he was sixty-nine years old at the time. Li served as *dizi* to the deities, and in his words, the apprentice "is always accompanying the deities" (*yizhi peiban zhe shen de ne*). His action is interpreted as "using his voice to relay a message for the deities" (*ding shen*). Li and his old masters are the apprentices of Tongtian Erlang, and they serve as both ritual specialists and healers in the local area. According to Li, Qiao became an apprentice of Tongtian Erlang when he practiced the annual ritual procession of receiving aunties by himself in the 1970s. Because this custom was illegal at the time, few villagers participated in it, but some apprentices of deities received him in West to the Sacred Temple Village during the annual ritual processions because the beliefs of Ehuang, Nüying, and Tongtian Erlang were very strong there. Every time he arrived at the village, Qiao stayed with the apprentices and asked to "see" the deities and "hear" their words. Since West to the Sacred Temple was far from Yangxie, it was inconvenient for him to go there whenever he or his fellows encountered such problems as sickness or personal crisis. Eventually, when he was in his late forties, Qiao became an apprentice of Tongtian Erlang, and he served as a ritual specialist and healer in Yangxie.

Today most old people who practice the local traditions in Lishan still remember Qiao Guoliang and know that he was loyal and sincere to Ehuang and Nüying. Li Desheng even commented that this kind of person would never be found again in Hongtong. Li was aware that Qiao devoted his life to writing "Biographies of Ehuang and Nüying," and he and his old masters had even contributed to the completion of this manuscript. Li said that Qiao stayed with him and his old masters whenever he came to the village, and they usually were up the whole night talking about everything related to Yao and Shun and Ehuang and Nüying. Li regretted that Qiao passed away too early; he believed that Qiao had worked too hard to finish the manuscript, but he also thought that Ehuang and Nüying now had Qiao to serve them in heaven and that it was a happy ending for Qiao.

In "Biographies of Ehuang and Nüying," Qiao Guoliang records many miraculous events and describes how local apprentices conveyed messages from the deities and helped the local people resolve all kinds of problems. Interestingly, these supernatural legends are intertwined with real history, such as the text in the eighth section that narrates the story of Ehuang and Nüying helping Chinese Nationalist troops defeat the Japanese soldiers during the Second Sino-Japanese War (see chap. 2). His narratives also highlighted his interaction with other local actors to reconstruct these local beliefs. In the final chapter of his manuscript, Qiao particularly describes his experiences of interacting with apprentices of deities in Lishan:

> After the older generation of people in our village passed away, I took over and went to the mountain to receive the two aunties with my third son, Jinming, on the third day of the third lunar month every year. At the beginning, I got in touch with lots of *shenhan* [male spiritual mediums] and *shenpo* [female spiritual mediums] one after another in the mountain. However, based on what they said, and after exploring its meaning, something was not right. Finally I got to West to the Sacred Temple Village and met Sun Sanlong and Guo Gen'er. These two men introduced me to Bao'er's wife. Afterward, on the third day of the third lunar month every year, my third son and I only went to Shenli Temple to burn incense and then returned to West to the Sacred Temple Village. In the evening, these two men accompanied me to visit Bao'er's wife. Bao'er's wife became the apprentice of Tongtian Erlang when she was eighteen years old; every time when people prayed for children and asked for predictions of their fortunes,

they got a response if they sincerely prayed, and it was miraculous. Therefore, I went to West to the Sacred Temple and did not go anywhere else. I remember that one year (the exact date is unclear), on the evening of the third day of the third lunar month, Sanlong and Gen'er accompanied me to Bao'er's house. I saw Tongtian Erlang and asked something about temple reconstruction. Tongtian Erlang then said that the Shenli Temple would be reconstructed only when the Yangxie temple was successfully rebuilt. When this was said, there was no news [about temple reconstruction] in Yangxie. Later, after many years, Yangxie temple was not rebuilt until 1988. Based on this event, sometimes I remember that what Tongtian Erlang said is miraculous. (Qiao 1998, section 11)

Obviously, Qiao strongly believed in the miraculous power of Tongtian Erlang, who served the two aunties. Although many local people claimed to be the apprentices of the deities, he only believed Bao'er's wife. I do not know how this female apprentice conveyed the sacred message for Tongtian Erlang in her house on the evening that Qiao recorded, but this message strongly affected Qiao and motivated him to mobilize local people to rebuild village temples.

Pei Beiji designated Qiao Guoliang's sacred role as a "civil apprentice" or a "cultural apprentice" (*wen dizi*) during my interview with him on May 3, 2013. Pei said that the local apprentices of deities were divided into "civil apprentices" and "martial apprentices" (*wu dizi*); the former represented the deities in order to spread and record their stories, whereas the latter used special martial arts and magical skills to serve the deities in rituals, processions, and other events. Pei also viewed himself as a civil apprentice, defining it as "literati representatives of the deity" (*shen de wenren daibiao*). He believed that the deities conveyed the stories to the apprentices in their dreams, rather than the apprentices themselves creating the tales. Pei commented that Qiao's manuscript was the most convincing one of the local literati's works, primarily because of Qiao's role as a civil apprentice of the deities. Thus, Qiao's identification as a spiritual medium empowered him to represent local traditions with more authority.

The division between civil apprentices and martial apprentices is not always clear-cut in local contexts, and it is particularly ambiguous in Han Xiaomao's case. Han Xiaomao was originally a martial apprentice of the Jade Emperor, the top deity in popular Daoism, and he would use a red-hot iron rod to hit his body without harm to show the miraculous power of the deity. In addition to his role as a martial apprentice in public, he fit into the category of civil apprentice because of his personal representation of local history and beliefs. Unlike Pei Beiji, Han did not state that his manuscript was conveyed by the deity in his dreams; instead, he emphasized that he had written and edited his work deliberately. Han clearly stated that his role model was Sima Qian, the influential Han dynasty historian.[5] Like Sima Qian, he visited many places and talked with different people when compiling his sources. Moreover, he was aware that there was not enough substantial evidence to prove the existence of Yao and Shun; what he could do, though, was to collect a variety of sources about local history. The *kao* (textual critique) in his manuscript title (2007) indicates that he used the methodology of textual research adopted by traditional literati to reconstruct local history and that he understood the limits of such methodology.[6] He represented his own role as that of a scholar rather than of a "literati representative of the deity."

Qiao Guoliang, Pei Beiji, and Han Xiaomao had multiple identities within their communities, and their role as apprentices of deities was as important as their role as folk literati. There is a large group of apprentices serving different deities in Hongtong; their practice tends toward local beliefs and folk medicine, and they remain an integral part of local traditions and village society (Yao 2010). The full survey of this important group is beyond the scope of this chapter, and my main concerns here are with the intertwined roles of folk literati and sacred apprentices as well as with the influence the role of sacred apprentices has on folk literati's representations of local traditions.

Spiritual mediums have been an important component of local cults and beliefs from ancient times up to the present in China, and they have had important roles in society by providing healing, fortune-telling, and other services (Kang 2006). However, the literati were often prejudiced against spiritual mediums, and they questioned illegal popular beliefs not recognized by the state in old times, even though they might secretly visit mediums who were devoted to these popular beliefs. Considering the contentious and ambiguous relationship between literati and spiritual mediums in the past, there has been no record to show that literati might become mediums themselves. My research and case studies in Hongtong provide us with new evidence highlighting the complex interrelationship between folk literati and spiritual mediums, and therefore I have been able to offer a new perspective of these relationships, especially when the two roles are merged together in one person.

Contested Localization of History and Beliefs

Like historian Sima Qian, folk literati in Hongtong regard the age of Yao and Shun as the real beginning of Chinese cultural history, and they intend to situate Yao and Shun stories in their own communities. In this process of local contextualization of history, folk literati represent controversial and even contradictory discourses. For instance, Liu Baoshan intended to legitimatize the idea that Shun's hometown was in Wan'an, whereas Li Xuezhi attempted to prove that Shun was born at Sage King Village and plowed in present-day Lishan. The controversies and conflicts among these folk literati shape and are shaped by the tensions among their native areas and village temples. Most of the folk literati that I study had to confront the dilemma caused by the lack of substantial evidence, and they had to draw on their own imaginations to deal with such a dilemma, an act that of course often raised more problems than it solved. In local devotion, we can thus see numerous layers of local discourses and traditions.

The creative process of representing local history and beliefs was clearly illustrated by Yan Zhenghong in our interview on April 20, 2014. He compiled the booklet "Anecdotes of Ehuang and Nüying" (Huangying yishi) for the Yangxie Village temple, and in his work he made Yangxie the birthplace of both Ehuang and Nüying. He explained to me how he had arrived at this conclusion:

> As for the birth of Yao's two daughters, [I] did not first consider that Yao's two daughters were born in Yangxie. In my first draft, the older daughter was born in Yidu Village. . . . Because one goat gave birth to a *xie*, Yao came here; he came here to see it. Then, Yao was connected to this place. If the goat had not given birth to a *xie*, Yao would not have come here to see it, and he would not have moved here later on. I did not consider this in my first draft. In my second draft, it was written that *da gugu* [old aunt] Ehuang was not born here, while *xiao gugu* [little aunt] Nüying was born here. Also, I wrote that on the day the *xie* was born, [Yao] took his wife here, with some officials; he took his wife to come to Yangxie to see this strange animal. After seeing it, he thought that this place was great in feng shui, and he looked around the village. When he looked around, his wife gave birth to his

second daughter. This was written in my second draft. In my third draft, I have a guiding idea. For example, Yao's history, legends of the Three Sovereigns and Five Emperors, if you check them in official history sources, none of them was there. They were oral legends, weren't they? Moreover, Director Yang once said there were many places that did not have a spectacular site but created one. That is, there was no tourism site; people created a tourism site. Why could we not emancipate our ideas and make this thing well rounded? When I wrote my third draft, I included the idea that both daughters were born in Yangxie. This is how I kept revising it.

Why did I write it like this? I think there is logic in it when I wrote it like this. On the eighteenth day of the sixth lunar month, the goat gave birth to the *xie*; on that day Yao's wife came. His wife did not go outside the village that day. She gave birth to her first daughter when she stayed in one ordinary peasant's house. Two to three years later, Yao returned here from his palace. He recalled the place where the goat gave birth to the *xie*, it was great in *feng shui* there; he had not gone there for a long time, and he wanted to visit there. These are what I have imagined. His wife also said that she wanted to go there, then they went there. They went there, went to the place where the *xie* was born. His wife was about to give birth; this time his second daughter, Nüying, was born. It was on the ninth day of the ninth lunar month. Ehuang was born on the eighteenth day of the sixth month; Nüying was born on the ninth day of the ninth month. Their birthdays were fixed like this. This is how I revised it step by step. I may still have those old drafts, you can see. The first draft, the second draft, the third draft, I think, it became more and more faithful. Of course, is it more and more fitting into historical development? Is history really like this? I do not know. As for the ancient history in the past, there are no particularly detailed records, and no written records, are there?

The concept of "creating landscape" (*zao jing*) was crucial in the advice Director Yang (Yang Biyun) gave to Yan, and it showed Yang's understanding that tourism sites can be invented. As for the historical site in Yangxie, it is widely believed that the *xie* was born there during Yao's age and that Nüying was born near the place where the *xie* was born. Yan repeated this plot and made Yangxie Ehuang's birthplace too. He thought that his creation was logical in certain ways and that personal imagination should be allowed because there were no written records to elucidate what really happened in the ancient past.

Even though Yan Zhenghong could defend himself in his creative remaking of local history and stories, his invention was not well received in Yangxie. Three hundred copies of his booklet were printed in 2012, and most of them were damaged by the flood in February 2013. Few people have read the work, and those who have done so did not have positive feedback. Wang Wenhua, the old shè head in South Yangxie, problematized Yan's creation, saying: "This does not make any sense; it's nonsense." Some villagers said that Yan did not participate in local temple activities in the early years when local traditions were stigmatized as "feudal superstitions," and they questioned how Yan became an important consultant in the Yangxie temple reconstruction association in the middle 2000s and how he was able to publish his booklet. Many thought that what Yan represented in his booklet sometimes did not accord with accumulated local knowledge and practice.

It is not easy to evaluate Yan Zhenghong's role in local cultural production and the reception of his work. As Wang Wenhua once said: "It depends on one's personal preference and standpoint." In other words, the evaluator's perspective determines the resulting attitude toward folk literati and their work. Although Wang disagreed with Yan about his innovative fabrication of some local history and stories, Shao Caiwang (who died in early 2015), the old head of the temple reconstruction association in Yangxie, and Yang Biyun, the director of the temple reconstruction association in Lishan, strongly supported Yan. Although other folk literati in Hongtong might have more cultural resources or influences than Yan, they did not have the same social networks. Social networks are thus important factors that shape and reflect folk literati's cultural production and reception.

When confronting the lack of evidence, most folk literati have drawn on their own imagination to localize history and legends in their own communities, and their fabrications sometimes cause problems. In some cases, these folk literati have contradicted one another in their representations of local traditions, especially when they situate local traditions in their native areas and village temples. Many new tensions arise from this dynamic process, and local traditions are constantly changing in both practice and discourse. As the Hongtong folk literati have exerted their innovative agency in reconstructing, contradicting, and negotiating local traditions, they have expressed themselves across the complicated social network they share with those around them, and their work allows us to understand what matters within local communities.

Folk Literati and Tradition

In this chapter, I have discussed how folk literati have been designated as a dynamic social group within local communities and how their roles have been differentiated and evaluated, depending primarily on the evaluator's standpoint. In addition, I illustrate how folk literati have negotiated with one another when transmitting and reproducing local traditions and how their roles have been contested across time and space. The construction and differentiation of folk literati themselves is an ongoing process, one that is intertwined with the changing cultural process of remaking local traditions. The interrelationship between tradition and folk literati is very complicated. On the one hand, folk literati are capable of reproducing local tradition in a creative way. On the other hand, preexisting knowledge and practice of local tradition dictates the extent of folk literati's agency and action. The remaining question is how tradition may be conceptualized and reproduced in this contested process.

Dorothy Noyes identifies three main conceptualizations of tradition in Western scholarship: "tradition as a communicative transaction, tradition as a temporal ideology, and tradition as communal property" (Noyes 2009, 233). She concludes by proposing that "scholars explore yet another working definition of tradition: the transfer of responsibility for a valued practice or performance." This definition is constructed primarily from the perspectives of "performers" instead of ordinary practitioners. As Noyes writes:

> Performers may hope to hand on their knowledge to inheritors authorized by blood or formal affiliation, but above all they look for those who will be willing and competent to do the work. That hand-to-hand transfer we may take as a metaphor for the transmission of metaknowledge along with the practice itself: what it means, how it is to be used, everything that is shaven off when it is packaged as a product or an entry in a database.
>
> Recall the Roman requirement of conscious intention on the part of both giver and receiver. In that touching of hands, real or virtual, responsibility is assumed towards both past and future as personified in particular individuals. The receiver must respect, but the giver

must let go. The constraint is thus mutual, as is the room for maneuver. (Noyes 2009, 248)

Following the definition of tradition as "the transfer of responsibility," I propose that tradition be conceptualized as the transfer of appreciation, an ability to understand the meaning or importance of a valued practice or cultural process. For the transmission of metaknowledge and practice, ordinary participants and practitioners should be able to appreciate the values, meanings, and functions, regardless of whether this full awareness or understanding reflects and is shaped by internal motivations, external forces, or both.

When tradition is conceptualized as a dynamic process of the transfer of appreciation, the roles of a variety of local actors come into play. I have analyzed how folk literati accumulate their cultural sources and build their social networks when remaking local tradition. The view of their roles in their communities depends on how deeply they are able to appreciate local beliefs and history and how effectively they are able to represent that understanding in writing. The appreciation of ordinary participants and practitioners is also important in the process of transmitting and reproducing local rituals, legends, and beliefs. Different levels of appreciation shape and reflect the active agency of individuals and folk groups. This appreciation assumes an understanding of our past in the present and an ability to create a future that aligns with the past. As folklorists, we start with this appreciation as we move forward to explore the changing dynamics of cultural production and reproduction.

The concept of tradition as a process of the transfer of appreciation is closely intertwined with the attitudes, feelings, values, and beliefs that people have about their own traditions or those of other people. Individual attitudes toward tradition may keep changing within particular contexts and time periods, and they can be explored through participant observation and interviews elicited by folklorists. The positive attitudes toward their own tradition and deep appreciation of its value and significance make folk literati an important social group that can continue, transmit, and transform local tradition and bind local communities together. Positive attitudes toward tradition are crucial to shape the identification of folk literati and local communities and to foster hope for a sustainable future. The cultural protection becomes possible because of the appreciation of individuals, groups, and communities and because of the transfer of that appreciation across time and space.

Notes

1. This is based on an informal discussion one day in the summer of 2012.

2. This is based on my interview with Han Xiaomao in Wan'an on August 7, 2012.

3. *The Records of the Listener* is a collection of fantastic stories compiled by the Song period writer Hong Mai. Hong had always been interested in popular stories about paranormal dreams, omens, gods, and ghosts, and therefore he began to write them down. The title of the book is based on one sentence in the old book *Liezi*, in which a certain Yi Jian wrote down stories he heard. The original size of *The Records of the Listener* was 420 scrolls (*juan*). It is divided into four parts ("Records I–IV," *Jiazhi, Yizhi, Bingzhi,* and *Dingzhi*), of which each is divided into ten collections (*ji*, 集) (Inglis 2006).

4. Tongtian Erlang specially served Ehuang and Nüying and was also known as their royal son. According to local legends, Tongtian Erlang was a native of Wang Jia Ping Village, not far from present-day Lishan. He fell from a tree when he was twelve years old and died; he was then adopted by Ehuang and Nüying in the netherworld and later stayed with them in the present-day temple in Lishan. Tongtian Erlang is considered miraculous in Hongtong, and his base temple is believed to be located in West to the Sacred Temple Village.

5. Han's statement was recorded in our interview on August 7, 2012.

6. *Kaozhengxue*, or "teachings of research and proof" (考证学), was developed by a group of Confucian scholars during the Qing dynasty (1644–1911). A lot of them lived during the reigns of the Qianlong 乾隆 (1736–95) and the Jiaqing 嘉庆 (1796–1820) emperors, so their school is also called the Qian-Jia School (乾嘉学派). These scholars emphasize the scientific and intellectual method of textual critique and lexical research to discern between originals and forgeries and to collect fragments of lost texts.

6

MAKING INTANGIBLE CULTURAL HERITAGE

Folklore, Tradition, and Power

I N THE 2000S, THE PROJECT TO PROTECT INTANGIBLE cultural heritage (ICH) had spread all over China, greatly contributing to the growth of Chinese folklore studies in this new century. Most Chinese folklorists have participated in this project, and the field of folklore studies itself has been reshaped in this new context. In this chapter, I examine the dilemma faced by Chinese folklorists in the safeguarding of ICH and address the contentious local responses to ICH protection in Hongtong in the late 2000s and early 2010s. I combine both top-down and bottom-up approaches to examine how local people who participate in the annual ritual procession of receiving aunties have interacted with officials, scholars, and committees who are in charge of ICH protection at county, city, provincial, and national levels, and how they have responded to the safeguarding of ICH on the ground, with a focus on shifting actors and power relations in the process of heritage making within the local and national contexts. In particular, I examine shifting power relations among shè, the temple reconstruction associations, and the local state in the process of protecting local traditions as ICH in Hongtong. I argue that the heritage-making process has not empowered the key folk institutions and folk literati to protect local traditions with and for local people but instead has disempowered the folk literati and put local communities at the bottom of the power relationship. How might the role of folk literati be recognized and acknowledged officially by the state in the safeguarding of ICH in China? How might the state return the power of cultural preservation to individuals, groups, and local communities on the ground? The answers to these questions remain open.

Folklore Studies and Intangible Cultural Heritage in China

The definition of intangible cultural heritage (ICH) promoted by UNESCO overlaps with the idea of folklore in general; folklorists have laid a good foundation for the construction of this concept, and they have also made great contributions to its development and promotion worldwide (An 2008). When the concept of ICH was introduced in China, Chinese folklorists were soon recruited as professionals in the national campaign to protect ICH. A large number of them were asked to serve on the Steering Committee of Intangible Cultural Heritage nationally, provincially, regionally, and locally, and scholars from other fields also joined with them to serve this national goal. In the process of protecting ICH, some Chinese folklorists emphasize the difference between ICH and folklore, some stress that the concepts are interchangeable, and others highlight the overlapping parts of these two concepts. In addition to these different interpretations of ICH and folklore, they also confront the dilemma in practice. My goal here is to track the relationship between politics and folklore in modern China and to examine how Chinese folklorists have constructed and explained ICH both in public and in their academic research in recent years. In the process I illustrate how interpretations and representations of folklore and ICH are formed, whose knowledge counts and why, who speaks and deploys "truth" and toward what end, and what is at stake.

In China, the "discovery" of folklore and the development of folklore scholarship grew out of a chaotic time of foreign aggression, internal disorder, and dissatisfaction with Confucianism, a moment of severe political and military crisis (Hung 1985). Chinese intellectuals believed that the Confucian tradition stifled the progress of China and that the corrupt bureaucratic system increased the deterioration and disaster. Because of the intellectuals' engagement and devotion, the traditional political system was overthrown in the 1911 Revolution, and the new Republic of China (1912–49) was established. Within the new ideological and political order, Chinese scholars attempted to find an alternative ideology to guide China and ensure its prosperity, one that wasn't based on Confucianism or Westernization. In their search for new ideas, the intellectuals "discovered" the folk and their culture. In 1918 several talented scholars at National Peking University launched the Chinese folk literature movement, which aimed to collect folk literature throughout the country and exalt the culture and spirits of the folk (Hung 1985; Liu 2006). These young scholars, including Liu Fu (1891–1934), Zhou Zuoren (1885–1967), and Gu Jiegang (1893–1980), shared a romantic view of the common people, especially the peasants who lived in rural areas. They assumed that the folk were simple, innocent, natural, sincere, and steadfast; their life was harmonious, easy, and cheerful; and their minds represented the pure national spirit. In their collecting activities, the scholars gave high priority to the oral literature that contained anti-Confucian themes. For instance, the journal *Folksong Weekly (Geyao zhoukan)* published many folk songs about love.[1] The songs displayed an air of openness, boldness, simplicity, and earnestness, and they were full of rebellion against Confucian moral values, in which people struggled for unfettered love. The songs also contained explicit, at times obscene, descriptions of sex. Since the collection of such songs was an act of defiance against traditional mores, the scholars attached particular importance to this work (Hung 1985).

Chinese intellectuals also stressed the importance of social reform in the 1920s. In 1923 the Custom Survey Society of National Peking University was founded with the intent to abolish backward customs and beliefs that were regarded as essential parts of Confucian ways. Although the Custom Survey Society was disbanded in the middle of 1924, social reform through education resumed two years later with the establishment of the Chinese Mass Education Movement in Dingxian (Eminov 1975). However, these activities and the movement did not focus on the folk and their activities, and people's everyday lives did not change in an obvious way during this period.

Political change often had an influence on folklore studies and the conception of folklore in modern China. After the death of Chinese nationalist leader Sun Yat-sen (1866–1925), China was divided into two parts, with the Nationalist Party ruling the south of China and various military warlords taking power in the north. The internal political pressures and struggles of this period forced many scholars to leave Peking for the south. This move led to the disbandment of the Folksong Research Society and the demise of *Folksong Weekly* at National Peking University in 1925. The scholars continued the folk literature movement in the south, expanding it into a Chinese folklore movement with a focus on folk literature as well as folk customs, festivals, beliefs, and so on. The center of folklore studies was shifted to Sun Yat-sen University in Canton from 1927 to 1934 (Eminov 1975). The political and social uses of folklore were strengthened during this period, with folklore being seen not only as a subject for investigation but also as a means to glorify the national spirit and propel social changes. National Peking University restored its eminence in folklore studies in 1935, but its reign was soon suspended with the outbreak of the Second Sino-Japanese War in 1937 (Eminov 1975).

The Communist Party of China (CPC) developed its political and ideological attitude toward folklore quite early. In the 1930s, folktales, folk songs, folk drama, folk dance, and other folkloric genres were utilized for political and ideological ends in the "liberated" areas ruled by the CPC. At the crucial 1942 Yan'an Forum on Art and Literature, Mao Zedong presented his important lecture about Chinese art and literature, including folk literature, and he overstated the political and ideological aspects of art and literature in an unprecedented way (Liu 2006). In Mao's opinion, art and literature were primarily ideological expressions, and he stated that artists and writers should create works based on the social life of the folk, including workers, peasants, and soldiers, with the guidance of Marxism. He emphasized that art and literature in this new era should focus on revolutionary content and develop new forms. Mao continued the focus on the folk, their culture, and the anti-Confucian spirits in the Chinese folk literature movement.

The political and social uses of folklore were executed to extremes, especially after the establishment of the People's Republic of China in 1949. In 1963 Mao Zedong launched the Socialist Education Movement in China, with the primary emphasis on restoring ideological purity, reinfusing revolutionary fervor into the CPC as well as its officials and people, and intensifying class struggle. When local officials carried out such a movement in rural areas, they found that the common people enjoyed listening to all kinds of folktales and stories. They thought stories might be used as an effective method to spread the Socialist Education Movement and to influence the common people in a structured way. Thus, the ongoing storytelling activities among the folk were "discovered" by the political leaders, and they began to serve political and ideological purposes. Accordingly, new stories were created, and the New Story Movement soon spread throughout the country (You 2012). These new stories were derived from folktales and other kinds of traditional narratives; however, ideological viewpoints dominated the content. This New Story Movement ended in 1966 when the Socialist Education Movement was terminated and universally supplanted by the Cultural Revolution (1966–76).

During the Cultural Revolution, folklore studies as a subject was dismantled in China, and folk culture itself was also strongly attacked. Folklorists who survived the Cultural Revolution—those who had begun studying folklore in the 1920s, when Chinese folk traditions were discovered from a romantic perspective—went to great lengths to revive folklore studies and train young folklorists starting from the early 1980s. After two decades' worth of work, Chinese folklore studies returned to its regular track (Wu 2007), and while folklore studies was a tiny academic field, with only one PhD program at Beijing Normal University as well as several MA programs nationwide in the 1990s, the influence from the safeguarding of ICH all over China helped it to spread quickly to other universities and institutions in this new century. At least eleven new PhD programs were founded,[2] and there are at least forty-four MA programs in folklore studies throughout China today.[3] Many research centers for ICH were also established at universities and research institutions. Most Chinese folklorists have actively participated in this national campaign to protect ICH, and the field of folklore studies has been reconstructed within this new context. Wu Bing'an (2007), an important Chinese folklorist and influential leader on the Steering Committee of Chinese National Intangible Cultural Heritage, points out that this national campaign changed the marginal status of Chinese folklore studies and made it a popular and well-regarded field in contemporary China. From the 1990s, in the official categories of academic disciplines, folk literature was a third-level discipline in the first-level discipline of literature and a third-level discipline in the second-level discipline of folklore studies, while folklore studies was a second-level discipline in the first-level discipline of sociology (Gao 2008).[4] However, by 2009, Chinese folk literature had become a second-level discipline in the first-level discipline of literature, and cultural anthropology and folklore studies had become a second-level discipline in the first-level discipline of ethnic studies and culture studies.[5] While China's emphasis on ICH greatly contributed to the rise of Chinese folklore studies in the 2000s, the field is not perfectly suited to its role in safeguarding ICH. For instance, Wu points out that Chinese folklorists haven't created sound theories and methodology to support this national campaign. As for the concepts of ICH and folklore, Wu further stresses that they are not defined in the same domain; instead they are constructed in different fields for different purposes, although they have overlapped each other to a degree. Wu views ICH as a concept for practical work instead of a subject for academic research. He emphasizes that no matter how powerful the concept of ICH is, it should not be a substitute for the concept of folklore (Wu 2007).

Wu Bing'an's differentiation between ICH and folklore has been widely accepted by Chinese folklorists (Shi 2009), and his statement is a critique of the widespread phenomenon of replacing folklore with ICH at some universities and research institutions. With the impact of the ICH campaign, some centers for folklore studies were renamed as centers for ICH, while some folklore programs were also reshaped or even substituted in this new context. For instance, Sun Yat-sen University has a long tradition of the study of traditional operas, folk literature, and folklore. In December 2002, the programs in these fields were reshuffled and the new Institute of Chinese Intangible Cultural Heritage was established at the university. Today this institution is a leading force in the study of Chinese ICH. However, not all substitutions of ICH for folklore have been successful, and the Center for Folk Literature Studies at the Central China Normal University is a case in point. This center used to offer an important program in folk literature studies in China, one that was founded and maintained for thirty years by Liu Shouhua (b. 1935), a respected scholar in folk literature and narratives. After the establishment of the Center for Intangible Cultural Heritage, the old Center for Folk Literature Studies was shut down, the former traditions of folk literature studies at the university came to an end, and folklorists there have had to conduct research in the new field of ICH instead. This transformation is regarded as "a disastrous hit" on Chinese folklore studies by Shi Aidong (2009, 13), and it shows the negative impacts of the ICH campaign on Chinese folklore studies.

Shi Aidong (2009) examines the dilemma that folklorists are confronted with in safeguarding ICH. In his opinion, this is a national political movement instead of a cultural or folkloric movement. He argues that folklorists' full participation in it will make them lose their independence in pursuing academic goals, that the suspension of regular folklore studies will further lower the significance of Chinese folklore studies in the academic world, and that the abandonment of fundamental research and existing research traditions will stifle folklore studies. He further notes that when the whole campaign of safeguarding ICH comes to an end, folklorists will face a big dilemma in regular research. From the intellectual history of folklore studies in China, Shi concludes that every academic campaign, such as the campaign for safeguarding ICH, is paid for by a dramatic decline in academic research, which is a heavy cost.

Chen Jinwen (2009) seconds Shi's argument, pointing out that local politicians and activists have used folklorists to control cultural resources and obtain regional benefits from the ICH campaign. He argues that in reality folklorists did not advise local people to protect folk traditions but were manipulated by local people to fulfill their goals. In addition, some folklorists overstate the authenticity of folklore and totally ignore its dynamics, which indicates the weakness of folklore studies itself (Chen 2009). Chen opposes folklorists' full participation in the ICH campaign, and he suggests that Chinese folklorists should conduct good research for purely academic goals.

Chinese folklorists face a dilemma similar to the one that American folklorists were confronted with in the 1970s and 1980s. Beginning in the late 1960s and continuing into the 1970s, as public folklore began to develop in the United States, folklorists who taught and conducted academic research at universities felt that both popularization and public folklore blurred the boundaries of pure folklore scholarship and siphoned off intellectual talent—they were seen as diminishing the reputation of academic folklore studies (Kirshenblatt-Gimblett 1988; Lloyd, You, and Ding 2013). However, Barbara Kirshenblatt-Gimblett problematizes the arbitrary dichotomy between academic and public folklore and justifies the legitimacy of public folklore in the field (1988). Over time, the wall that once existed between academic folklorists and public folklorists in the United States has been taken down, and some cross back and forth between academic research and public work during their careers (Lloyd, You, and Ding 2013). The ICH work of Chinese folklorists could be conceptualized as public folklore by definition, although there is no such term in Chinese folklore studies. The participation in the ICH project has made Chinese folklorists communicate with a broader public and pushed them to also become involved in making policies and serving communities nationally, provincially, regionally, and locally (Sun 2017).

The National ICH Framework and the Administrative System

The ICH movement in China is primarily led by the government, with the Ministry of Culture and the National Bureau of Cultural Relics as the two major national institutions in charge of cultural heritage policies and practices. After the ratification of the UNESCO Convention for the

Safeguarding of the Intangible Cultural Heritage in 2003, a special organization was established in China; in 2008 it officially became the Intangible Cultural Heritage Division (*feiwuzhi wenhua yichan si*) under the supervision of the Ministry of Culture (Bodolec 2012; Zhang 2014). It originally had three sections—Management (*guanli chu*), Protection (*baohu chu*), and the General Secretariat (*bangong shi*)—to fulfill its various tasks (Bodolec 2012, 252). In 2017, the division was restructured to include four sections: General Office (*zonghe chu*), Planning Office (*guihua chu*), Management Office (*guanli chu*), and Communication Office (*chuanbo chu*).[6] The main responsibilities of this institution are defined as follows: "Drafting the policies of ICH protection as well as relevant laws and regulations; drafting the plans to protect national ICH representative elements; organizing and carrying out the work of ICH protection, and taking charge of the application, nomination, evaluation, and designation of national ICH representative elements; implementing the transmission and popularization of excellent national Chinese culture" (Intangible Cultural Heritage Division, 2017).

In addition, the China Intangible Cultural Heritage Protection Center (CICHPC) (*Zhongguo feiwuzhi wenhua yichan baohu zhongxin*) was officially established in the Chinese Academy of Arts (*Zhongguo yishu yanjiuyuan*) by the Ministry of Culture in 2006. The central government set up this institution to protect China's native traditions in the performing arts, cuisine, rituals, festivals, and other forms of culture, and its main responsibilities are stated as follows: "Undertaking the specific work on the national ICH protection, fulfilling the policy consultation on ICH protection; organizing the census work nationwide; guiding the implementation of the protection plans; conducting theoretical research on ICH protection; holding academic activities, exhibitions, performances, and public activities; exchanging, promoting and propagating the achievements and experiences of protection work; organizing and implementing the publication of research results, personnel training, and other responsibilities" (CICHPC 2006).

In general, after China ratified UNESCO's 2003 ICH Convention, the state used the existing mechanisms of the government system to reshape the administration system at the national, provincial, prefecture, and county levels to engage in ICH protection. In this system, the national policies are carried out and implemented from top to bottom, whereas it is required that the ICH elements to be protected must be established from bottom to top, which means that any ICH item must be selected, declared, and approved at the county and prefecture levels first, and then at the provincial level, before entering the national-level protection system (Zhang 2015). Under this framework, the national Intangible Cultural Heritage Division and the CICHPC are in charge of ICH protection nationwide, while provincial ICH divisions (*feiyi chu*) and ICH protection centers (*feiyi baohu zhongxin*), some of which are established in the system of Cultural Affairs Bureaus, are the direct administrators in thirty-one provinces, autonomous regions, and municipalities, as well as in the Xinjiang Production and Construction Corps. ICH offices (*feiyi chu* or *feiyi ke*) and protection centers at the prefecture level and the county level are in charge of implementation (Zhang 2015; CICHPC 2016; Kuah and Liu 2017). From provincial to county level, some ICH divisions, offices, and protection centers are "independent" (*duli*) institutions in charge of ICH management work, whereas others are "listed" (*guapai*) institutions, which are established in the existing institutions but have new labels or brands as ICH units (CICHPC 2016). Moreover, in the past decade the Ministry of Culture has encouraged the construction of experimental eco-cultural protection zones (*wenhua shengtai baohu shiyan qu*) as well as ICH transmission centers (*chuanxi zhongxin*) and transmission spots (*chuanxi dian*) in these zones. By 2016, the Ministry of Culture supported 18 national-level experimental eco-cultural protection zones to build 62 ICH transmission centers and add 287 ICH transmission spots (Luo and Gao 2017, 24). The Ministry of Culture also named 100 national-level ICH productive protection example bases (*shengchan xing baohu shifan jidi*), and 653 example bases were established at the provincial level (Luo and Gao 2017, 24–25). These places assume an important function in the ICH protection on the ground. In March 2018, the Ministry of Culture and Tourism was formed in China foregrounding the importance of tourism. The association of culture and tourism reveals the central government's ultimate goal to use culture to develop the economy.

It is worth noting that the Chinese government attached importance to folk culture protection before the UNESCO 2003 ICH Convention. In 1984 the Ministry of Culture, the State Ethnic Affairs Commission (*Guojia minzu shiwu weiyuanhui*), and the Chinese Folk Literature and Arts Research Society (*Zhongguo minjian wenyi yanjiuhui*), which was renamed the Chinese Folk Literature and Art Association (*Zhongguo minjian wenyijia xiehui*) in 1987, jointly launched the "Three Collections of Chinese Folk Literature" (*Minjian wenxue santao jicheng*) project (An and Yang 2015). The three collections in this project include folk stories, folk songs and rhymes, and folk proverbs. Folk stories include myths, legends, folktales, fairy tales, jokes, and other prose narratives. The participants of this project first collected stories, folk songs, and proverbs in villages, then compiled parts of the material into volumes for each county; the county collections were then compiled into volumes for each province. According to reported statistics, between 1984 and 1990 more than two million people took part in the surveying and collection of folk literature (Yang and An 2005, 14). In total, 1.84 million folktales, 3.02 million folk songs and ballads, and 7.48 million proverbs were collected from all over the country (Liu 2006, 711). By September 2009, all the province-level collections (298 titles [*juan*] and 440 volumes [*ce*]) were published (Liu Shouhua 2009). In 2010, county-level volumes began being processed for publication (Zhang 2010).

China has a long history of multiethnic culture, and the oral tradition created by generations of Chinese people from all ethnic groups has been regarded as the "precious treasure" of Chinese culture. With the rapid development of modern society, it is claimed that many traditions have gradually changed and even disappeared. The primary goal of the "Three Collections of Chinese Folk Literature" project is to save and preserve those cultural treasures before they disappear, while also contributing to the transmission and continuity of those old traditions and providing important sources for academic research in the fields of folk literature and folk arts, and even for creative writing.

The project resonates with the folk literature movement in many ways, but its large scale is unprecedented. Indeed, it has been praised as the construction of "the national cultural Great Wall" (*minzu wenhua changcheng*) (Liu Shouhua 2009), and the project has provided a strong foundation for the current national campaign to protect ICH in China. Cultural officials at the national, provincial, municipal, and county levels were all mobilized to investigate, collect, and document folk literature; the same administrative system has been mobilized again to serve the national purpose of cultural preservation in this new century. In order to train people to fulfill these tasks, the Chinese Academy of Arts and the CICHPC produced a handbook in 2007 explaining how to collect living traditions in the field. For example, for a theater piece, the handbook illustrates a variety of tasks, such as how to record the piece; how to survey it; how to explore vital questions such as who the art form's master is, who the disciples are, and how it's transmitted; and even simple things like how to properly use video recorders.

Not only has a lot of time and expertise been put into ICH protection, but the governments at different levels have also invested a lot of money. From 2011 to 2015, 1.637 billion yuan was invested by the provincial-level governments (including the Xinjiang Production and Construction Corps) all over the country, with 1.019 billion yuan by the municipal-level governments and 1.237 billion yuan as special financial funds by the county-level governments (CICHPC 2016). In 2015 alone, 387.19 million yuan was spent as special funding for ICH protection by all provincial-level governments in China, with 309.31 million yuan by the municipal-level governments and 321.22 million yuan by the county-level governments (CICHPC 2016). Some special funds were used to protect ICH elements and support "representative transmitters" with stipends at all levels, and some were used for special projects. For example, the government of Zhejiang Province assigned 3 million yuan from the special ICH funds to preserve ancient books and assigned 5 million yuan to protect Kunqu, one of the oldest extant forms of Chinese opera, listed as one of the Masterpieces of the Oral and Intangible Heritage of Humanity by UNESCO since 2001. Some governments also set up special funds for a Cultural Heritage Day to sponsor various activities and propagate the safeguarding of ICH (CICHPC 2016).

With the rapid development of China's ICH campaign, the study of ICH protection has emerged as a newly shaped discipline, and many universities and research institutions have established specialized organizations or agencies in it (Wang Xianzhao 2010; Sun 2017). Some of these agencies are independent research centers at the universities and institutions, while others are formed under certain cultural administrative departments in the governments, jointly established by cultural or economic agencies within universities and research institutions, or shaped by nongovernmental organizations (NGOs) or local communities (Wang Xiaozhao 2010). For example, since 2004 more than thirty universities have initiated and strengthened the disciplinary development of ICH preservation and research, and of these, at least nine universities have clearly made plans for disciplinary development and training (Wang Xianzhao 2010). These research agencies often have national, regional, and local research projects related to ICH protection, and they are in charge of training researchers on ICH.

Despite its rapid development, the new discipline of ICH studies has not been fully developed, and the training of high-quality researchers for ICH protection is still a challenging problem. Wang Xianzhao (2010) points out that in the process of safeguarding ICH it is important not only to protect and cultivate transmitters of various traditions but also to train good researchers of ICH. He defines *researchers of ICH* as a large academic research group, including full- and part-time researchers; professionals in research institutions, higher education institutions, governments, and NGOs; and independent researchers. Overall, these researchers are individuals who study certain subjects in the ICH project. Nowadays the poor quality of ICH researchers has increasingly restricted China's ICH protection, and the question of how to correctly understand and rationally coordinate human resources on ICH studies has become an unavoidable problem. Wang proposes that researchers of ICH should have interdisciplinary, dynamic, and collaborative training so that they can play a strong role in ICH protection.

In his article "Protecting Intangible Cultural Heritage: A Dilemma of Chinese Folklore Studies," An Deming (2008) explores the dilemmas and controversies of the ICH movement in contemporary China, noting that the big problem in this national movement is the formation of new cultural hegemonies and hierarchies and that the national list of ICH lies at the core of controversies and conflicts. As mentioned in the introduction, the State Council issued the official document "Recommendations on the Strengthening of the Safeguarding of China's Intangible Cultural Heritage" in March 2005. According to this document, the objective of the project is to establish a national system for protecting ICH all over China so that precious and endangered ICH with high historical, cultural, and scientific value can be effectively preserved, transmitted, and developed. One of its main tasks is to make the Representative List of Intangible Cultural Heritage of Humanity at the national, provincial, municipal, and county levels, and the national representative list is supposed to be approved and released by the State Council. The national list of ICH corresponds to the program of "The Proclamation of Masterpieces of the Oral and Intangible Heritage of Humanity" launched by UNESCO in 2000. This list is the main motivation for different institutions, communities, groups, and individuals to get involved in the project. Unexpectedly, the making of this list has aroused many conflicts over ICH among different communities and groups. For certain cultural items or events, there have been various claims of ownership from different areas in China, and therefore the proclamation of ICH reinforced local tensions and conflicts (An 2008). In the following section, I will draw on my ethnographical work to explore this problematic issue, highlighting the shifting actors and power relations in the safeguarding of ICH on the ground.

Local Tradition Promoted as China's National ICH

In 2005, after the State Council issued its "Recommendations on the Strengthening of the Safeguarding of China's Intangible Cultural Heritage" to specify local governments' obligations to protect ICH, the People's Government of Shanxi Province (*Shanxi sheng renmin zhengfu*) also released their "Recommendations on the Strengthening of the Safeguarding of ICH in Our Province" (*Shanxi News* 2010), and in December 2006, the Provincial Department of Culture (*sheng wenhua ting*) followed up with the establishment of the Shanxi ICH Protection Center (CICHPC 2017). This center has three offices: the General Office (*zonghe bangongshi*), the Application and Project Management Office (*shenbao yu xiangmu guanli ke*), and the Technology Office (*jishu ke*). The main responsibilities of this protection center include drafting the overall plan and the step-by-step implementation plan for ICH protection in Shanxi Province; formulating technical standards and working regulations; taking charge of discovering, rescuing, researching, and protecting provincial ICH elements and collecting data on them; managing projects at all levels; tracking and evaluating the implementation of projects; undertaking specific work on the nomination and declaration of ICH elements at provincial and national levels; guiding and training ICH practitioners and staff on the ground; and establishing and managing Shanxi ICH data and archives (CICHPC 2017). Overall, this center drafted the guidance, principles, goals, and tasks of ICH protection and management in Shanxi and took charge of their implementation.

After the Intangible Cultural Heritage Law was enacted in China in 2011, an Intangible Cultural Heritage Ordinance in Shanxi Province (*Shanxi sheng feiwuzhi wenhua yichan tiaoli*) was approved by the Thirty-First Meeting of the Standing Committee of the Eleventh People's Congress in Shanxi Province in September 2012; it came into force on January 1, 2013 (*Huanghe News* 2012). The ordinance provided legal support for the safeguarding of ICH in Shanxi Province. With promotion by the governments at all levels, as of the end of 2016 there were 116 national-level ICH elements in Shanxi, with 168 protection units (*baohu danwei*), and the province was ranked third nationwide. Moreover, there were 403 provincial-level ICH elements in Shanxi, with 723 protection units, 1,534 municipal-level ICH elements, and 4,010 county-level ICH elements (CICHPC 2016; *Sina News* 2017). As for designated culture bearers ("representative transmitters") of ICH, there are 106 at the national level, 815 at the provincial level, 1,855 at the municipal level, and 3,520 at the county level. Since 2006, the governments at all levels have invested 255 million yuan in ICH protection in Shanxi Province (*Sina News* 2017). Throughout the province, 128 ICH cultural exhibition venues (*wenhua zhanshi changguan*) and 322 transmission centers (*chuanxi suo*) have been established. These places have become important platforms for demonstrating local culture and transmitting local traditions in Shanxi (CICHPC 2016; *Sina News* 2017).

As noted earlier in this chapter, the establishment of the ICH elements of individuals, groups, or communities must be done from the bottom to the top, which means that any elements at one level must be previously declared and approved by the lower level (Zhang 2015). By drawing on my ethnographic case study, we can examine this selection process of ICH elements from bottom to top, with a particular focus on the process of the promotion of *Hongtong zouqin xisu* as the ICH element from county-level up to national-level.

Hongtong Zouqin Xisu was inscribed in the Provincial Representative List of ICH in Shanxi Province in 2006, and in 2008 it was included in the second list of items of China's national ICH (see introduction). The success of its designation as national ICH was fostered by the collaboration among local communities, officials, and folklorists. The local tradition was studied earlier by Chinese folklorist Chen Yongchao (b. 1966) when he conducted his dissertation fieldwork on the living legends of Yao and Shun in Hongtong in 2000. In 2006, Zhou Xibin, the Communist Party Secretary in Ganting Town at that time, saw the term *intangible cultural heritage* on the ticket of "Naxi Ancient Music" (*Naxi guyue*, 纳西古乐)[7] when he visited one of his friends during the Spring Festival. After finding out more about ICH and the lists, he decided that the local tradition in Yangxie (which is a part of Ganting Town) deserved to be listed both on the national and the UNESCO ICH lists. Therefore, he mobilized the local people to apply for its inclusion on the national list, and Wang Chunliang, the director of the Hongtong County Cultural Bureau (*wenhua guan*), became one of his core partners.[8]

Zhou Xibin first mobilized local officials to study the important documents about ICH national policies, including "Recommendations on the Strengthening of the Safeguarding of China's Intangible Cultural Heritage"

(State Council 2005a) and "Circular on the Survey of Intangible Cultural Heritage" (Ministry of Culture 2005). The town-level government in Ganting made study plans for officials and arranged special lectures regularly on Mondays, Wednesdays, and Fridays (Wang Chunliang 2009). In March 2006, the ICH Protection Leading Group (*lingdao zu*) and ICH Protection Center (*baohu zhongxin*) were established in Hongtong County. Li Junhu, the assistant to the county head, became the leader of the Leading Group. The Hongtong County ICH Protection Center was established in the County Cultural Bureau, and Wang Chunliang served as the director of this newly established center.

On the second day of the third lunar month in 2006, the Ganting Town government launched the opening ceremony of receiving aunties in the Old Temple of Tang Yao in Yangxie, marking the beginning of ICH protection work in Hongtong. Zhou Xibin invited a variety of journalists, writers, and cultural celebrities from regional to national levels to participate in the annual ritual processions of receiving aunties on the third day of the third lunar month; they were also invited to reflect on the experience in essays that were collected and published in a volume he edited (Zhou 2006). With the promotion of officials and local communities, receiving aunties became the second element of ICH in Hongtong County, and the Hongtong County ICH Protection Center also nominated it as an ICH element at the provincial level.

On July 6, 2006, the Provincial Department of Culture issued a "Notice on the Declaration of Elements of Provincial-Level Intangible Cultural Heritage" (*guanyu shenbao sheng ji fei wuzhi wenhua yichan baohu xiangmu de tongzhi*), with the application deadline on September 30 (*Shanxi News* 2010). In order to prepare for the application materials, a survey team was formed in Hongtong. Li Junhu was the team leader, and Yan Hanyu (director of the Bureau of Culture and Sports in Hongtong County), Zhou Xibin (secretary of the Party Committee of Ganting Town), and Cheng Yanping (secretary of the Party Committee of Wan'an Town) served as the vice directors of the survey team. Other leading members of the survey team included Wang Chunliang, Yang Ruiping (vice secretary of the Party Committee of Ganting Town), Li Baoyu (vice mayor of Ganting Town), Wei Xiaoping (secretary of the Party Committee of South Yangxie Village), and Yan Quansheng (secretary of the Party Committee of North Yangxie Village). The team members included retired officials in Yangxie, shè executors in Yangxie and Lishan, and some staff from the Hongtong County ICH

Protection Center (Wang Chunliang 2009). On the same day that the notice was issued, a survey-launching ceremony was held in the Old Temple of Tang Yao in Yangxie, and Wang Chunliang, Yan Zhenghong, Wang Kaiyuan, and many other villagers from Yangxie joined the team to conduct a survey on the local tradition of receiving aunties. The survey took sixty-eight days, and the team of fourteen people visited more than thirty villages along the routes of the annual ritual processions. They talked with more than two hundred people and recorded interviews with thirty-three individuals. In addition, the team investigated 55 temples, more than 40 vernacular dwellings, 54 stone steles, 7 old trees, and 402 objects in the region. Eventually, they collected more than twenty objects, made several eight-hour videos, took more than two thousand pictures, and recorded data with more than ten thousand characters (Wang Chunliang 2009, 328). In particular, they discovered the 1674 stele established in the Temple of Ehuang and Nüying in Wan'an, which recorded the "public property" in the temple, and the 1788 stele in the same place that commemorated the celebration of Ehuang's birthday on the eighteenth day of the sixth lunar month and the celebration of the birthday of the Goddess of Fertility (*zisun shengmu*) on the twentieth day of the third lunar month in the same temple (Li et al. 2008). The team also collected more than seven hundred couplets in local village temples, more than one hundred poems on Yao and Shun as well as Ehuang and Nüying, notations for ten music pieces of Awe-Inspiring Drums and Gongs, and more than thirty legends and folktales (Wang Chunliang 2009).

Since July 2006, the Hongtong County ICH Protection Center has convened three evaluation meetings and has invited experts at county level, municipal level, and provincial level to review the applications. All these meetings laid a good foundation for ICH applications and declarations at higher levels. In late 2006, the Shanxi provincial government announced the first list of provincial ICH elements, and *Hongtong zouqin xisu* was included in it, under the folklore category. This was only the beginning of a long process of ICH application at the national level (Wang Chunliang 2009).

In early 2007, Zhou Xibin managed to contact Liu Kuili (b. 1934)—committee member of the Bureau of Academic Divisions of Chinese Academy of Social Sciences, deputy director of the Expert Committee on National Intangible Cultural Heritage Protection (*Guojia feiwuzhi wenhua yichan baohu zhuanjia weiyuanhui*),[9] and also the president of the China Folklore Society (*zhongguo minsu xuehui*) at that time—in addition to other folklorists, to request help for the local people in completing the application materials. Chen Yongchao, who by this time was a professor at Beijing University, volunteered to help, and he took his students to record the local traditions during the annual ritual processions of receiving aunties on the third day of the third lunar month. The Beijing University research team included two graduate students, Zhong Jian and Sun Chunfang, and two undergraduate students, Wang Yao and Yao Huiyi. At that time I was working as an assistant editor for *Forum on Folk Culture* (*minjian wenhua luntan*), a flagship journal in Chinese folklore studies, after I graduated from the MA program in folk literature at Beijing University in 2005, and I was also invited to join the team. We conducted our first fieldwork in Hongtong from April 16 to April 22, 2007, using participant observation, interviews, and video to record the local annual ritual processions of receiving aunties. After our fieldwork, the research team wrote a detailed field report, which was published in *Forum on Folk Culture* (Chen et al. 2007). This field report first describes the whole process in which Yangxie villagers receive aunties, from the second day to the fifth day of the third lunar month, and then explores how local people regard Yao and Shun's legends as real history and how they use this history to construct local beliefs. The researchers also analyzed the use of an invented kinship system to construct relationships among people in the region, and the secular beliefs toward ancient sage-kings Yao and Shun as well as Ehuang and Nüying (Chen et al. 2007).

The same research team went back to conduct further fieldwork on the twenty-eighth day of the fourth lunar month that year. Wang Chunliang organized the first competition of Awe-Inspiring Drums and Gongs and also invented the ceremony to celebrate the birthday of Emperor Yao in the Old Temple of Tang Yao. After going back to Beijing, Chen Yongchao and his students finished the application materials and a documentary in mid-August. Wang Chunliang, Yang Ruiping, and Wei Xiaoping went to Beijing to discuss the applications in late August, and they finished printing the application texts on August 30. The Shanxi Provincial Government approved the declaration on September 15, and the Shanxi ICH Protection Center then recommended it to the national ICH Protection Center (Wang Chunliang 2009).

After the application was submitted, Li Junhu brought some officials to Beijing and convened three meetings on *Hongtong zouqin xisu* at Beijing University. Liu Kuili, Song Zhaolin (researcher at the National Museum of China, member of the Expert Committee of National ICH Protection),

Xing Li (professor in the Chinese Department at Minzu University of China, member of the Expert Committee of National ICH Protection), Gao Bingzhong (professor in Anthropology and Sociology at Beijing University, member of the Expert Committee of National ICH Protection), Yin Hubin (researcher at the Chinese Academy of Social Sciences), Zhou Minghua (associate researcher at the Chinese Academy of Social Sciences), Chen Lianshan (associate professor at Beijing University), Wang Juan (associate professor at Beijing University), Chen Yongchao, Wang Yao, and Zhong Jian attended these conferences (Wang Chunliang 2009). In order to promote the influence of *zouqin xisu* among Chinese folklorists, Zhou Minghua even organized a cultural salon for it with the initiative from Liu Kuili.

With the strong support from folklorists, *Hongtong zouqin xisu* was approved by the Steering Committee of Chinese National Intangible Cultural Heritage, but it disappeared from the tentative second list of national ICH elements released by the State Council in early 2008. No one knew for sure what had happened, but according to rumor, the application was rejected by a senior official in the Ministry of Culture who thought that there were too many sacrifice scenes in the documentary of *zouqin xisu*. After receiving the news, Zhao Zhongyue, the director of Shanxi Provincial ICH Protection Center, immediately notified Wang Chunliang and asked him to organize a project counterappeal group (*xiangmu kangsu zhuanti zu*) to petition against the exclusion of *zouqin xisu* in the national ICH list during the public comment period. The Hongtong County ICH Protection Center, the Shanxi Provincial ICH Protection Center, and metropolitan folklorists all sent their appeals of the decision to the national ICH Protection Center (Wang Chunliang 2009). Hongtong cultural officials and village representatives went to Beijing during the Spring Festival and collaborated with folklorists to argue vociferously for its inclusion on the basis that it is a long, nearly uninterrupted tradition. Finally, on June 7, 2008, *Hongtong zouqin xisu* was inscribed on the second national ICH list.

At this point Zhou Xibin, the initiator of the whole project, was eager to further promote the local tradition by nominating it for UNESCO's ICH Representative List. However, he was soon appointed deputy head of Hongtong County, after which he left his town-level position. The inscription of *Hongtong zouqin xisu* on the UNESCO list became the ultimate goal for a few folk literati in Yangxie who had actively participated in the ICH application; today whenever outside scholars visit for research purposes, they share this dream with them in hopes of gaining their support.

When I conducted my fieldwork in Yangxie in 2012 and 2013, two folk literati asked me to assist them in achieving this goal, but no one has yet put forth the effort, and *Hongtong zouqin xisu* is still not nominated for the UNESCO list.

On-the-Ground Responses: A New Element in Local Conflicts

During my fieldwork in Hongtong, I interviewed many local people, and when asked if they knew what ICH and UNESCO were, most could not answer my questions. Only a few local officials and folk literati knew of ICH, and they explained that this foreign term had entered local discourse in 2006 when people were mobilized to assist in the ICH application. Yan Zhenghong interpreted ICH as "invisible history and legends," distinct from "material objects." When describing *Hongtong zouqin xisu*, Yan emphasized that contemporary people practiced it in reality, not in imagination, because it had been handed down for many generations. Yan regarded the local ICH as the region's cultural treasure, which could stimulate local people to stay together harmoniously. Wang Wenhua regarded ICH as the local tradition handed down for more than four thousand years, and *long history* (*niantouduo*) became a key phrase in local interpretations of ICH. However, for most ordinary people, ICH was a foreign term remote from their knowledge and discourse. They similarly had no knowledge of UNESCO and its relationship to ICH.

The discourse on ICH has intensified the preexisting gap between local officials and ordinary people, and this gap is sometimes expressed ironically during public celebrations. In 2008, for example, Liu Kuili and Chen Yongchao led some graduate students to conduct follow-up fieldwork in Yangxie and sponsored a performance of local opera at the temple fair. The temple fair office invited the two folklorists to give a short talk onstage before the sponsored performance. Wang Chunliang suddenly jumped onstage. He was quite drunk, and he began talking at great length. At one point, he said: "What is ICH? Do you know it? Not only do you not know what ICH is, but even your grandpa and grandma do not know." An elderly woman sitting in the audience responded: "Your grandma is sitting here." This woman was no relation to him, but she was expressing, with irony, the audience's dismissal of this cultural official's arrogant speech. For her, the definition of ICH did not matter; her concern was with the live performance of local opera. She wanted to stop the "silly" speech and proceed with the performance.

From my fieldwork, I have concluded that knowledge of ICH and UNESCO is not significant in the daily lives of most ordinary people. Those who were mobilized to assist in the ICH application expected to receive a large amount of money from the central government to use however they wished within their local communities. However, many express that they have yet to receive any funds, even after the success of the ICH application on the national level. When I interviewed Wang Chunliang about the financial situation in August 2012, he explained that the Ministry of Culture sent money to the Culture Department at the provincial level, but this department could not figure out how to distribute the money it had received for a number of different ICH projects in the region. In the end, it decided to evenly distribute the high interest from the ICH funds (allocated by the state from 2009 to 2012) among all national ICH elements in Shanxi. Accordingly, approximately 430,000 yuan (around 70,000 US dollars) was assigned to the *Hongtong zouqin xisu* project in November 2012 and received by the Hongtong County ICH Protection Center. This was problematic because the tradition is shared by different communities in Hongtong, and people from Yangxie, Lishan, and Wan'an have all played important roles in continuing the tradition. These communities are located in different towns, and none of them had enough power to establish the protection center, which was crucial for the ICH safeguarding project. Moreover, the ICH application had fueled local conflicts between the communities, and they found it hard to reach any agreement. The local government thus authorized the Hongtong County ICH Protection Center to be the representative institution to protect *Hongtong zouqin xisu*. After receiving the money, however, the center did not distribute it to local temple reconstruction associations, which was what most local people had hoped; instead Director Wang Chunliang planned to build a folklore transmission center (*minsu chuanxi suo*) for *Hongtong zouqin xisu*. Wang's decision disappointed local people, who tried to get the money back for temple affairs.

The local conflicts among Yangxie, Lishan, and Wan'an did not begin with the ICH application, but they were certainly exacerbated in the process. In 2007, when Yangxie and Lishan collaborated to apply for the national ICH listing, Wan'an was excluded. This exclusion is one episode in a long-standing feud between villagers in Wan'an and Yangxie. Yan Zhenghong (2007a) provided some history of this feud with his account of the hail disaster discussed in chapter 5. Yan states that in 1991 he led Yangxie temple executors, in coordination with temple executors from other places, to change the festival date from the twenty-eighth day of the fourth lunar month to ten days earlier, resulting in the participating villages suffering heavy hail, an event that many local people interpreted as miraculous retribution from the deities for changing the date. Residents of Wan'an had not wanted to change the date; they also claimed that they had not received the official notification and that the name of their village was not listed in the notification. Additionally, Yan had been in charge of coordinating many receptions for official and unofficial visitors when the local tradition was publicly revived in the 1990s. In 1993, Zhao Yu led a film team to the area to make a documentary about the local tradition (see chapter 5). They shot plenty of footage in Yangxie and Lishan, but they did not even go to Wan'an. People from Wan'an did not believe that this avoidance of their community was the choice of the documentary crew; rather they thought that it was due to Yan's arrangements.

In order to solve the long-existing conflicts, local ritual specialists, shè executors, and temple reconstruction association leaders met on September 9, 2007, at a meeting chaired by Yang Biyun (Yan 2007a). Most participants expressed the idea that they should distinguish the goddesses' affairs from human affairs, and they proceeded to hold a ritual to address the conflict. All the important ritual specialists in the area attended the meeting, and some of them performed the ritual, which enabled them to speak for the two goddesses. They said that it was the two goddesses' sacred order that Wan'an was merely a place for resting horses and eating meals. Wan'an temple heads had to obey the order.

Through the meeting described above, local communities made use of sacred rituals and supernatural powers to solve conflicts that were exaggerated by the ICH recognition. Although Wan'an tried to promote its cultural status within the local tradition, reconstructing its own discourse, people still had to respect the existing social interaction between different communities. Local belief systems were invoked in order to define the tradition. In other words, ICH became a subject of conflict and dispute that was resolved by the belief in the very tenets that made up the ICH. The disputes may have been exacerbated by outside issues, but the solution was ultimately local.

Conflicts over Representative Transmitters

China's national lists of ICH are complemented by national lists of representative transmitters, and the intensive and complicated competition to become the latter in the process of application has made the ICH project controversial in local contexts. Between 2007 and 2011 the Ministry of Culture assessed and published four lists of representative transmitters of national ICH elements: the first included 226 people, the second 551, the third 711, and the fourth 498, a total of 1,986 (Zhang 2015; CICHPC 2016).[10] There are also representative transmitters of ICH elements at the provincial, municipal, and county levels, and by 2016 the provincial-level representative transmitters had reached 14,928 in number (CICHPC 2016). In accordance with the Ministry of Culture's 2008 official document "Interim Measures of the Designation and Administration of Representative Transmitters of National-Level Intangible Cultural Heritage Elements" (*guojia ji feiwuzhi wenhua yichan xiangmu daibiaoxing chuanchengren rending yu guanli zanxing banfa*), *representative transmitters* are defined and designated as follows:

> [They are] designated by cultural administrative departments of the State Council, carrying the responsibilities of the transmission and protection of national-level Intangible Cultural Heritage items, and are commonly viewed as representative, authoritative, and influential transmitters. . . .
>
> Those who meet the following conditions may apply for, or be recommended as, representative transmitters of national-level Intangible Cultural Heritage items:
>
> (1) mastering and inheriting an item of national-level Intangible Cultural Heritage;
> (2) in a certain area or field being commonly reviewed as representative and influential;
> (3) actively engaging in activities of [cultural] transmission, and training following practitioners.
>
> Those who are engaged in collecting, collating, and studying resources on Intangible Cultural Heritage should not be designated as representative transmitters of national-level Intangible Cultural Heritage items. (Ministry of Culture 2008)

Overall, *representative, authoritative,* and *influential* are three keys terms to designate those official transmitters, and the cultural administrative departments of the State Council, such as the Ministry of Culture, have absolute power to decide who these representative transmitters are. In reality, the designation of representative transmitters aroused all kinds of tensions and conflicts in local communities. In particular, the competition and friction between the representative transmitters and other tradition practitioners have been exacerbated, and the motivations of ordinary practitioners are severely undermined in the process (Huang, Zhao, and Wu 2013).

In Hongtong the local communities had warring opinions on the designation of representative transmitters, and no one became a representative transmitter at the national level, even though two individuals were designated as representative transmitters at the provincial level. Those two provincial-level representative transmitters were Shao Caiwang, the general shè head in Yangxie and also the head of the temple reconstruction association there, and Li Yinzi, the former director of the temple reconstruction association in Lishan. They both were in their sixties when they were designated as provincial-level representative transmitters in 2009. Although Li Xuezhi should have applied for the designation from the beginning, local cultural officials thought that he probably would not live long enough to receive funding in subsidy from the government since he was in his eighties at that time, and Li Yinzi was instead recommended for the application first. However, Li Yinzi lost his honored title after the controversial debt crisis broke out in Lishan in 2010, and Li Xuezhi was added as a representative transmitter afterward.

Most of the folk literati that I highlight in my research are actually excluded from the designation of representative transmitters in the ICH projects because they were and are actively engaged in collecting and compiling resources on local traditions and in representing local traditions in writing. They have played an essential role in the process of transmitting and producing local traditions. Some of them are commonly viewed as representative, authoritative, and influential in local communities, but they were also excluded from the application process primarily because they usually did not have enough power in the administrative system of ICH protection. The two candidates for the designation were the most powerful executors in local temple reconstruction associations; they were recommended by the Hongtong County ICH Protection Center primarily because they were the heads of local folk organizations. If there had been no debt crisis in Lishan, Li Xuezhi would never have had the chance to be designated a representative transmitter, even though he devoted much of his life to rebuilding local temples and continuing local traditions. As for other folk literati, they still carried their responsibilities of cultural transmission and production, even without any official designation. However, that continuance of responsibilities has not always been the end result—for example, in Guangchang the designation of a single performer in an opera troupe as a representative transmitter made other performers fight against him and further undermined their motivation to perform traditional operas; it also led to the troupe almost disbanding because of the intensive conflicts caused by the designation (Huang, Zhao, and Wu 2013, 38–39).

Although the designation of representative transmitters did not weaken the transmission of local traditions on the ground in my case study, it did exaggerate existing tensions between local village communities. For instance, the fact that nobody from Wan'an was designated as a representative transmitter raised some problems in the region. The candidates were nominated by the Hongtong County ICH Protection Center after local traditions were inscribed as an item of national-level ICH in 2008. Wang Chunliang discussed the nominations with Zhou Xibin, who later became a deputy head of Hongtong County. They decided to nominate the shè heads from Yangxie, Lishan, and Wan'an as representative transmitters of *Hongtong zouqin xisu*, and Wang Chunliang then sent out notifications to the town-level governments and asked them to tell candidates to submit their application forms before the deadline. He did send the notification to Du Dongxi, the shè head in Wan'an, but Du did not submit his application by the deadline and thus lost his candidacy.

Wan'an residents had different stories about why their shè head lost the designation of representative transmitter. During my stay in Wan'an in August 2012, some shè executors told me that they did not get the notification from the Hongtong County ICH Protection Center, while others said that they did get the notification several days before the deadline but that the head didn't have enough time to prepare the application materials. Some even said that the notification was sent late on purpose. I interviewed Du Dongxi in Wan'an on August 11, 2012, and he said that the notice was sent to the party secretary in Wan'an Town, who then called him and asked him to submit the application. Du said that other candidates were asked to go to the Hongtong County ICH Protection Center and fill out the application forms there, but nobody had told him to do that. He thought that some people from Yangxie had made trouble during the application process, and they attempted to nominate two candidates from Yangxie, thus excluding him from the nomination. The nomination itself aggravated the tension between Yangxie and Wan'an, and the conflicts were not easily resolved in the short term.

Among folk literati, Wang Kaiyuan did prepare his application for the designation of representative transmitter at the national level, but his application ended after his sudden death on June 10, 2009. During my stay with his older son Wang Wei's family in summer 2012, Wang Wei showed me his father's application form. In it, Wang Kaiyuan highlighted his experience and achievements:

1. In 1982 he and his village fellows (including Wang Wenhua, Xue Dongcai, and Qiao Guoliang) mobilized local residents to resume the annual ritual processions of receiving aunties on the third day of the third lunar month, and they were detained for fifteen days because the local tradition was still viewed as feudal superstition at that time.
2. With Wang Wenhua and Chen Baozhu, he organized the purchase of a divine sedan chair, twenty-four ritual instruments, and two divine whips in 1984.
3. In 1986, he mobilized ordinary people to make donations to rebuild the temple of the aunties.
4. He arranged accommodation and various other issues during the annual ritual processions of receiving aunties on the third day of the third lunar month every year from 1983. He also collected many photos, videos, books, household items, and production tools along the route.
5. From 2006 to 2008, he assisted Zhou Xibin in editing the book *The Customs of Yao and Shun Living up to Today* (2006) and assisted Li Xuezhi in editing the book *Lishan Where Shun Plowed Was in Hongtong* (2009).
6. In January 2008, he applied to the Trademark Office under the State Administration for Industry and Commerce (SAIC) for the trademark *xie zhi* (獬豸).
7. From 2006 to 2008, he assisted in the survey and ICH applications at the municipal, provincial, and national levels.

In addition to his personal experience and achievements, Wang Kaiyuan is well known in the area because of his close relationship with folklorists. In the letter of condolence to Wang's family on June 11, 2009, Chen Yongchao spoke for many folklorists when he celebrated Wang's support of their work and highly praised his great contribution in promoting local tradition as China's national ICH element:

Since the spring of 2007, we have conducted research on the activities of Yangxie villagers for three years; during the process, we have received great help and wonderful care from Mr. Wang and thus have developed a very deep friendship with him. Every time [we visited the village], he treated us in his house and served as our guide during our fieldwork. He always tried his best to fulfill all our needs to conduct research. He came to Beijing twice in 2008, and we also had pleasant meetings and memorable conversations. The last meeting with Mr. Wang only happened eighteen days ago, when we were done with our fieldwork on the "welcoming *niangniang*" during the twenty-eighth day of the fourth lunar month. Mr. Wang sent us to Linfen [train station], and that unexpectedly became our last farewell. We feel very sad in our hearts because we lost a knowledgeable teacher and a thoughtful close friend. His sound and smile seem to be still around, and he will forever live in our hearts. . . . It is with the great efforts of many warm-hearted and compassionate people like Mr. Wang Kaiyuan that the activities of receiving aunties and welcoming *niangniang* were successfully approved as a national-level ICH element. . . . While we are still grieved, we strongly believe that the activities of receiving aunties and welcoming *niangniang* that Mr. Wang Kaiyuan had participated in during his lifetime will continue year after year, and the traditional folkloric activities in Yangxie will be renowned in the whole country and even in the whole world. Mr. Wang's name will forever be recorded in history; his distinguished merit and immortal spirit will always be remembered.

Although Wang Kaiyuan did not obtain any official designation from the state, his personal stories and his contribution are recorded in Chen Yongchao's work (2010, 2015). Chen (2015) questions the definition of *representative transmitters* and argues that this particular designation excludes those ordinary people who tell Yao and Shun's legends in both rituals and daily lives in local communities. Instead, he uses the term *traditional practitioners* to refer to all those who share these legends (Chen 2015, 129). I agree with his analysis on the limitation of the designation, but I think we couldn't really avoid this term in our research, and the study of this particular designation reveals the unbalanced power relations on the ground.

The designation of representative transmitters fulfills UNESCO's efforts to emphasize the important role of indigenous communities, groups, and individuals in the production and protection of ICH, but the local communities do not have the power to say who should get the designation. In the face of bureaucratic administration, those who have power and sources get the tickets to enter the system, whereas most ordinary people are sidelined. Numerous individuals like Wang Kaiyuan make history and contribute to the success of ICH protection in China, but only a few harvest the benefits from it.

Shifting Actors: Shè, the Temple Reconstruction Associations, and the Local State

In the process of heritage making, global, national, regional, and local actors interact and compete with one another, which can cause a series of transformations that disempower old owners and users. This dynamic is clearly shown in the edited volume *World Heritage Angkor and Beyond: Circumstances and Implications of UNESCO Listings in Cambodia* (Hauser-Schäublin 2012b), in which an interdisciplinary group of scholars illustrate the hierarchical relationships and problematic tensions among local peoples, new heritage owners, and international tourism businesses, as well as their corresponding practices and goals in Angkor, Cambodia. The contributors to this volume demonstrate how the local population is placed at the bottom of this complex of power relationships and how the situation deepens preexisting inequalities.

My case study reveals a similar process: attempts at safeguarding ICH in Hongtong County have caused a series of transformations that disempower local communities and people. The town-level government played a crucial role in promoting local tradition as an element of national ICH, and local people were mobilized to fight for this goal. They expected to receive a large amount of money from the state after the heritage status was approved. However, so far they have received little, despite the fact that it cost them a great deal to achieve the ICH status: the local temple reconstruction association in Yangxie supported the ICH application and paid partial costs of 420,000 yuan (around 68,404 US dollars).[11] What is worse, in the process of ICH application and protection, the power struggles between the local government and the temple reconstruction associations have been intensified. As mentioned above, the Hongtong County ICH Protection Center represented itself to the local people as an institute to protect local heritage, and it obtained absolute power to manage the money sent from the state. Therefore, the Yangxie temple reconstruction association did not have enough power to get the money and manage it at its discretion. At the end of 2012, the temple heads met with Wang Chunliang about the situation, and

Wang responded in an unhelpful manner: "We managed protection, we also managed transmission of tradition, and it was none of your business" (*Baohu shi women, chuancheng ye shi women, bu ai ni men de shi*). Shao Caiwang told me this story when I interviewed him on May 1, 2013; he and the other temple heads tried to ask for help from Zhou Xibin to solve the problem. Unfortunately Shao died suddenly in the Old Temple of Tang Yao in Yangxie on February 19, 2015, during the Spring Festival, the Chinese New Year; later, Wang Huguan took over and became the new general shè head. On June 5, 2016, I asked Wang Wei to talk with Wang Huguan to get an update on the ICH funds. The new head said that *Hongtong zouqin xisu* received 430,000 yuan as ICH protection funding, and the County ICH Protection Center took 130,000 yuan. On paper, the Yangxie general shè got 150,000 yuan, the Lishan general shè received 100,000 yuan, the Wan'an general shè got 30,000 yuan, and the Xiqiao Zhuang general shè received 20,000 yuan. However, because the Lishan general shè was faced with a debt crisis, it eventually took 150,000 yuan, and as a result, the Yangxie general shè actually only got 100,000 yuan. After getting the money, the Yangxie general shè used it to pay some of its debts and also to engage in some construction at the temple, building fireproofing facilities and drilling wells, among other things.

The finances managed by the general shè are primarily derived from incense donation money (*bushi*) collected in the temples, although there is also income from renting out space to vendors at the temple fairs. This money is public knowledge in local communities because the income and expense figures are posted at the main temple hall at the end of every lunar month and also at the end of the annual temple festival. For instance, the temple income and expense figures were posted at the entrance to the Old Temple of Tang Yao after the ten-day temple festival celebrating Emperor Yao's birthday on the twenty-eighth day of the fourth lunar month in 2013 (see table 6.1).

Although the branch shè executors on duty coordinate the temple affairs during the annual temple festival, it is the general shè that manages the incense donation money and publicizes these figures as a way to make the temple famous—the amount of incense donation money collected is seen as an indication of the efficacy of the deities.

The temple income is usually enough to balance the running costs in a year, as long as there are no costly construction projects. The ten-day temple festival usually draws a large majority of the annual donation income

Table 6.1. Economics of Yangxie Temple Fairs. Monetary totals are in yuan.

2013 年庙会收支情况公示 Temple Income and Expenses at the Temple Fairs in 2013			
收入 **Income**		支出 **Expenses**	
庙堂集资 Donations at the temple halls	384,164.5	伙食费 Food	12,539.8
摊位收入 Income from vendors	104,060	招待费 Receiving guests	47,119
电费收入 Electricity fees charged (from vendors)	13,385	水电费 Water and electricity	16,928
社团捐资 Donations from social groups or institutions	41,400	管理费 Administration	5,531
		戏款 Hiring opera troupes	45,000
赞助戏款 Donations sponsoring opera performance	94,700	其它 Others	63,122.5
合计 In total	637,709.5	合计 In total	190,240.3
余额 Remaining sum	446,369.2	唐尧故园 The Old Temple of Tang Yao	
			July 15, 2013

for the Old Temple of Tang Yao in Yangxie, and it makes the fame of the temple. Some local people also visit the temple on a daily basis, especially during the first and fifteenth days of every lunar month; the donations on a normal day can be as low as 20 yuan, and those for a normal month can be around 4,500 yuan. In addition to the costs of running temple fairs, a large amount of incense donation money is used to rebuild the temples and repair old buildings, and the general shè is in charge of managing the donations for temple expansion and repair projects.

Money has become a sensitive issue in the process of heritage making, and it has caused conflicts between the general shè and the local state. It is ironic that the local tradition was "protected" and transmitted primarily by the newly established Hongtong County ICH Protection Center instead of by members of the communities who have long practiced it. Of course, the conundrum here is that the protection center has not historically contributed to the tradition but is now charged with safeguarding it; in contrast, the shè and temple reconstruction associations that have maintained the tradition have no voice in the safeguarding process. Yangxie general shè covered the costs of the sixty-eight-day survey in 2006 and paid the bills for the ICH application at the national level in 2007 and 2008. It also accommodated visitors, including officials, scholars, journalists, and ICH division staff, when they came to participate in local activities in Yangxie starting in 2006. Moreover, different local state agents interacted with the general shè during the ICH project, and the latter covered the costs. However, the heritage-making process has not empowered this folk institution to protect local tradition with and for the local people; it has instead disempowered it and put local communities at the bottom of the power relationship, exaggerating preexisting inequalities. The ICH project thus became a means for the local ICH division to exploit the local population and harvest the profits from the state. This process of local disempowerment helped to shape some fundamental precepts of the "heritage regime" (Bendix, Eggert, and Peselmann 2012).

In the "Comparative Assessment" to the volume *Heritage Regimes and the State*, Chiara De Cesari (2012) highlights the "ambiguous" and "conflicted" relationship between many local civil society organizations dedicated to heritage preservation and the local UNESCO or ICH office, which may be viewed as allied with local authorities. De Cesari states that UNESCO frequently ends up reinforcing the power and reach of the nation-state and its bureaucracy, which is contradictory to its own principle of involving local communities and grassroots groups in heritage making—particularly as stated in the 2003 ICH Convention. Contrary to UNESCO's goal of establishing a common heritage for humanity, the process of heritage making frequently gives rise to numerous tensions and conflicts (De Cesari 2012). My research is critical to this issue because it is a study of local, regional, and national conflicts regarding a pre-UNESCO stage of ICH discourse. The conflicts I have observed among the people on the ground are caused by UNESCO despite the fact that this ICH has not even been nominated for the UNESCO list. In other words, even though the ICH in question has not been nominated for the UNESCO list, the UNESCO Convention itself set off a chain of events and national lists that ultimately had a profound effect on the communities involved.

In the process of protecting ICH on the ground, the alliance between discourse, practice, and power has not come to an end but has reappeared in a new form. My question is not simply about who owns tradition and heritage or how it is conceived locally. From a practical dimension, I am interested in how tradition and heritage can be transmitted and promoted respectfully with the active participation of local communities. With regard to the question of respect, Michael F. Brown (2003, 10) suggests that we should not ask "Who owns native culture?" but "How can we promote respectful treatment of native cultures and indigenous forms of self-expression" within our everyday lives? All of us, native and non-native alike, have a stake in decisions about the control and transmission of tradition and heritage, for those decisions will determine the future health of our natural and cultural world.

Overall, cultural forms travel through time and space across social networks, and folklorists are concerned with cultural stability, variation, reproduction, and reconstruction. In the national campaign to protect ICH in China, the complex and problematic relationships between the ICH movement and folklore are becoming central to the contemporary dilemma Chinese folklorists face. How may folklorists conciliate mutually contradictory discourses and practices of ICH protection and fully serve the ultimate goal of keeping local traditions active and lively? How might the role of folk literati and other individuals be recognized and acknowledged officially by the state in the safeguarding of ICH? How might the state return the power of cultural reproduction and protection to individuals, groups, and local communities on the ground? Chinese folklorists are still seeking answers to these questions, and what follows from their search is an ongoing process of shaping, shifting, and sharpening new disciplinary configurations and theoretical commitments, without the loss of complex truth in practice and in reality.

Notes

1. The first issue of *Folksong Weekly* came out in December 1922. The magazine was sponsored by the Folksong Research Society, which was established at National Peking University in 1920, following on from the Bureau for Collecting Folksongs (initiated in 1918).

2. The data is collected at Folklore Forum, especially with reference to http://www.chinesefolklore.org.cn/forum/viewthread.php?tid=25379, accessed on October 10, 2017.

3. The data is collected at Folklore Forum, but the full list can be found at https://zhidao.baidu.com/question/11475077.html, accessed on October 10, 2017.

4. According to "National Standards for Disciplinary Classification and Code of the People's Republic of China," issued by the State Bureau of Technical Supervision, there are 62 first-level disciplines or discipline groups, 676 second-level disciplines or discipline groups,

and 2,382 third-level disciplines. For more information, please refer to http://dean.pku.edu.cn /urtpku/yjxk.html, accessed on September 21, 2018.

5. Please refer to http://dean.pku.edu.cn/urtpku/yjxk.html, accessed on September 21, 2018.

6. Refer to the division's official introduction at http://www.mcprc.gov.cn/gywhb/jgsz /bjg/201111/t20111121_278093.html, accessed on October 26, 2017.

7. *Naxi guyue* is the traditional music of the Naxi ethnic group in southwestern China. It is a kind of ritual music intertwined with local religions and has been represented as a "living fossil" of traditional Chinese music (Rees 2000, 4–5).

8. On August 5, 2012, I interviewed Zhou Xibin about the detailed process of ICH application.

9. The Expert Committee on National Intangible Cultural Heritage Protection was established on July 13, 2006, and its main tasks include the creation of the ICH protection program, the creation and implementation of the ICH census, the review and administration of a national-level directory, and the approval of national-level ICH elements and representative transmitters, among other responsibilities (Luo 2008).

10. From 2008 onward, specialized national-level representative transmitters received funding of 8,000 yuan per person per year in subsidy, which was raised to 10,000 yuan (1,625 US dollars) in 2011 (Zhang 2015).

11. The total costs for the ICH application are unknown. From 2006 to 2008, the local government invested a lot of money to invite cultural celebrities, scholars, journalists, and other visitors to experience the annual ritual processions of receiving aunties in Hongtong in an effort to make the fame of the local traditions more public. The temple reconstruction association in Yangxie coordinated almost all of the activities and paid for most of the costs for research, the preparation of the application forms and materials, and the reception.

CONCLUSION

THIS BOOK PRESENTS AN ETHNOGRAPHIC AND CULTURAL ANALYSIS of the role of folk literati in cultural transmission and reproduction as well as in the contested process of tradition reconstruction and heritage making on the ground in contemporary China. Villagers in Hongtong, Shanxi, China, have practiced the local folklore of receiving aunties for many years, and it has been promoted as China's ICH since 2008. Within this context, various social actors have competed and negotiated with each other in the remaking of local tradition, and these social actors include shè, temple reconstruction associations, folk literati, local cultural institutions, the national government, and UNESCO. By exploring how folk beliefs, annual ritual processions, and temple fairs surrounding the receiving of aunties have been banned, revived, reproduced, and run by shifting social actors in contemporary China, this book provides a nuanced understanding of the dynamic process of remaking tradition, producing culture, and protecting heritage on the ground. I highlight the role of contemporary folk literati in the process of reconstructing and representing local history, legends, and beliefs, and I analyze the shifting power balances between shè, temple reconstruction associations, and the local state in the promotion and safeguarding of local tradition as ICH.

Folk literati are similar to what Merrill Kaplan conceptualizes as "amateur scholars" (2013, 143) or what John H. McDowell thinks of as "folk folklorists" (2016, 114). What makes folk literati unique in the Chinese context is their strong responsibility of cultural transmission, production, and reproduction within a community context. They actively participate in the annual ritual processions of receiving deities and in temple fairs, and they record their own history, myths, legends, and beliefs in their own terms. In their practice, the division between folklorists and informants is blurred. On the ground, it is folk literati and numerous other individuals who keep incense burning and keep local tradition alive. However, their role in the process of heritage making is not fully recognized by intellectuals and the state. The anonymous and semi-anonymous individuals have done the actual work in tradition revival and heritage protection, and their agency should not be elided in both discourse and practice.

The many kinds of ritual specialists—known as *mazi* or *dizi*—who actively participate in folk beliefs and festivals (though they provide their services for a fee) form another social group in local communities. Because of their specialized training and broad social network, these ritual specialists have played an important role in practicing folk beliefs and shaping local knowledge. However, they have diverse backgrounds and social statuses, and villagers have differing opinions toward their roles (Yao 2010). Furthermore, this social group has never been homogeneous, and the conflicts between them have been shaped by the tensions among different communities and have also shaped the frictions within local communities. My highlighting of the actions of folk literati does not undermine the significance of *mazi* and their practice, for without the latter it would be impossible for other actors to mobilize the support of ordinary villagers.

The discourse and practice of ICH protection have affected the field of folklore studies significantly (Kuutma 2016), expanding the field by enriching the meanings of key words such as *tradition, heritage,* and *intangible* (Zhang and Zhou 2017, 134). In this process of "conceptual shift," should the term of *folklore* be abandoned and replaced with other new terms such as *ICH*? If the term *ICH* "carries more weight and presumably alternative power, does it also entail an ontological shift to 'a brave new world'? Or is this just semantic quibbling?" (Kuutma 2016, 41) The disciplinary change and renaming has taken place all over the world (Kuutma 2016), and the universal concept of folklore has been situated and remade within various contexts in different regions and periods (Bendix and Hasan-Rokem 2012). In the transformation from the study of the "science of tradition" to the rise of ICH, the Europe-centered paradigm and concepts have dominated in research (Kuutma 2016), but the Eurocentric landscape is challenged by the geopolitical shift in this new "Asian century" (Logan and Aygen 2015, 411). How is the transformation from tradition to heritage situated in China? How do Chinese folklorists contribute to the discussion of ICH discourse and practice? Does the concept of ICH create a new category in the Chinese context? Or is it just semantic renaming? Zhang and Zhou (2017) provide an insightful perspective on the relationships between folklore studies and the ICH movement in China as well as the interactions between folklore and heritage. Overall, the ICH movement has contributed to the development and expansion of folklore studies in China and enabled folklorists to be involved in the process of identifying, evaluating, and protecting ICH elements at all levels. It has also built a bridge between Chinese folklorists and their international colleagues as well as between folklorists and scholars in other disciplines. Folklorists' research on folk beliefs has contributed to their legitimization in China (Zhou 2017a), and many aspects of folk cultures that were once suppressed have also obtained legitimate status in public domains (Gao 2017). In addition, with major contributions from folklorists, traditional festivals (for example, Spring Festival, Qingming Festival, Dragon Boat Festival, and Mid-autumn Festival) have been included in the official holiday system in China (Xiao 2017). In Chinese folklore studies, the concepts of both folklore and ICH coexist—the former is viewed as a subject for academic research, whereas the latter is used for practical work (Wu 2007). Juwen Zhang (2017) highlights the concepts of *coexistence* (*gongcun*) and *harmonization with differences* (*heerbutong*) in Chinese culture, and on the basis of these ideas, he invents the concept of *culture self-healing mechanism* (*wenhua ziyu jizhi*) to recapitulate the essentials of cultural continuity and ICH practices in China. But he holds an essentialist view toward cultural traditions, and he does not explore further the vernacular perspectives on ICH protection on the ground. This book contributes to the growing field of ICH studies in China by shedding light on the contested process of tradition reconstruction and ICH protection within local communities, specifically illustrating the important role of folk literati in cultural transmission and reproduction.

When studying the ICH movement in China, Gao Bingzhong emphasizes that it creates "new cultural concepts," "new laws," and "new public cultural policies" and thus "has changed, ended, and even subverted the concepts and logic of cultural revolutions in China since the 19th century" (2017, 167). Xiao Fang also situates the ICH movement within the context of Chinese cultural history from the late nineteenth century up to the present and emphasizes that it "represents a new stage of Chinese culture history" (2016, 79). My conclusion is different from theirs. My research shows that ICH protection has affected local communities profoundly, but some villagers still hold a strong sense of cultural continuity as conveyed in the vernacular expression "incense is kept burning." In the local villagers' understanding, the concept of ICH is really just a semantic renaming of the continuing of traditions they have engaged in all along.

Regardless of well-intentioned acts from governments and scholars (Maags and Holbig 2016), the identification, evaluation, and designation of ICH elements unavoidably turns them into objects for the purpose of safeguarding. Individuals, groups, and communities often became voiceless and invisible in this decision-making process (Oakes 2013). The ICH movement does not provide a "timely" venue for "alleviating domestic problems" (Zhang and Zhou 2017, 139); instead it exaggerates preexisting conflicts and tensions between local communities and the local state, as well as conflicts and debates within local communities. In Hongtong, the conflicts among shè and temple reconstruction associations in Yangxie, Lishan, and Wan'an center on the key issue about who the "leading actor" is in local traditions, and the ICH application exacerbated existing conflicts. In order to solve these conflicts, the heads of local temple reconstruction associations made use of sacred rituals and supernatural powers to unite local shè to serve deities. However, this local solution did not resolve the conflicts completely, and local tensions remain open for negotiation.

Although the ICH movement has provided a platform for Chinese folklorists to communicate with their international colleagues, the stage is still dominated by Western scholars (Bendix, Eggert, and Peselmann 2012; Foster and Gilman 2015; Adell, Bendix, Bortolotto, and Tauschek 2015). Chinese folklorists want to provide unique perspectives to the study of ICH discourse and practice in China in English scholarship (An and Yang 2015; Chen Zhiqin 2015; Zhang and Zhou 2017), but many questions remain unexplored at the time of the writing of this book. This book is only a study of one element of 1,372 national-level ICH elements and one of 13,087 provincial-level ICH elements in China (CICHPC 2016). There is still much to be done to create even a basic understanding of which ICH elements are at various levels, which important actors protect them, and how the ICH administrative system operates at different levels in different regions. Further research in different communities and on different cases is needed to understand the global-local interactions related to the ICH protection on the ground.

Currently, critical heritage studies is a rising interdisciplinary and transnational field, and scholars from different regions and disciplines have actively engaged in the research (Logan, Craith, and Kockel 2015). Further collaborative work is needed to study the different genres of ICH, including folk literature, traditional music, traditional dance, traditional opera, performing arts, traditional physical activities, games, acrobatics, traditional fine arts, traditional craft skills, traditional medicine, and folklore, as well as the complicated interactions among these genres in both China and beyond. In addition, transnational collaboration is necessary to help people from various backgrounds understand, cherish, and enjoy their own heritage in their own terms, no matter whether or not their heritage is recognized by the state or UNESCO.

Folk literati have carried on the cultural responsibility of continuing and recreating local tradition and heritage by their own choices and have also represented them in writing. Even though they may compete and disagree with one another, their great efforts have contributed to the binding together of local communities and the growth of a local tradition's prestige from the regional to the national, and even to the global. They actively write down local history, legends, and beliefs—sometimes at high cost to themselves—even though their work has not always been appreciated by local people. And although they have personal freedom to create expressive legends and stories, their creation is constrained by existing knowledge about and practice of local tradition as well as by the appreciation of their county fellows and outsiders (including scholars and officials at various levels). Unlike many literati in traditional China, who often had high social status, most folk literati have marginal status in their local communities, despite their great efforts to ensure that the incense is kept burning at local temples. My work sheds light on their important role in tradition revitalization and heritage protection, making their contributions more visible and accessible. In other words, folk literati are key figures in reconstructing and representing local tradition within local communities, and my study, focused on their significance and contribution, brings a new perspective to debates about the grassroots and individual agency in the reconstruction of tradition and the safeguarding of ICH in contemporary China.

APPENDIX

In Commemoration of the Reconstruction of the Shun Temple

Lishan [Li Mountain] stands forty kilometers to the west of the county seat, and according to legend it is the Lishan that Shun plowed on. Shun is Shun of Yu, the last of the five emperors in ancient China. His family name is Yao, his first name is Chonghua (double splendor), and he is the eighth-generation descendant of Huangdi (Yellow Emperor). Shun's father was a blind man, thus named Gusou (blind man). He was born in the hometown of Yu, and he married Wodeng; both were ordinary people. One year, the hometown of Yu was flooded, and they moved to Yuanqu; another year Yuanqu was flooded, and Gusou moved his family to Zhufeng, Hongtong. The following year, Shun was born. Because his eyes had double pupils, he was named Chonghua (double splendor); in addition, he was the second child of the family, and thus he was also named Zhonghua (second splendor). Born from the ordinary, he was intelligent and extraordinary. He had the eyes of a dragon and a square mouth, his face was dark, and he was more than two meters high. Shun's mother died when he was very young. His father remarried with Lady Han from Han Family Village, and Lady Han gave birth to a son, named Xiang, and a daughter, named Keshou. Shun's father was unprincipled, his stepmother insincere, and his stepbrother, Xiang, arrogant. They all tried to kill Shun, but he managed by his dutiful conduct to be reconciled to them, and he never by chance failed in his filial duty. Though they tried to kill him, they did not succeed. Shun was treated terribly by his parents, and he was exiled many times. He once made pots on the bank of the river, fished in Thunder Lake, and plowed on Lishan and other places. Finally he resided on Lishan, Hongtong, and frequently appeared in the drains between fields and in the fields; thus he was a person of Lishan.

When Shun was twenty years old, he was noted for his filial piety. Yao was old, and he saw firsthand that his own son Danzhu was unworthy of being the Son of Heaven or emperor. He once visited Xu You, Chao Fu, and other recluse sages, but he did not succeed. One day, he convened his officials together and discussed who would be the successor. The governors from the Four Mountains all brought Shun forward as a capable man. Yao believed them, and he visited Shun on Li Mountain. After meeting Shun, Yao saw his extraordinary look, then invited him to the court and put him in an important position. Moreover, Yao wed his two daughters to Shun to look after his internal affairs and had his nine sons live with him to look after matters on the outside. Shun was thirty at the time, and he began to assist Yao in governing the country from then on. When Shun plowed on Lishan, the inhabitants yielded the boundaries; when he fished in Thunder Lake, the men on the lake yielded to him the best places; and when he made pots on the bank of the river, the vessels from the place became the best in the world. If he dwelt in a place for a year, he formed a village; in two years it became a town, and in three a metropolis. Thus, Yao was touched by Shun's great virtues and outstanding talents. He then bestowed upon Shun linen robes and *qin* (zither), built for him granaries for millet and rice, and gave him cattle and sheep. Gusou was very jealous after seeing this, and he again tried to kill Shun. One day he sent Shun up to plaster the roof of the granary. Shun told his two wives about it, and his two wives said: "This is just their attempt to set you on fire. Make your clothes that of the magpie; dress as a bird. Go do this work." As Shun went up and repaired the granary, Gusou set fire to it from below, but Shun flew away like a bird, came down, and escaped with his life. Next Gusou had Shun dredge out the well. Shun told his two wives about it, and his two wives said: "Take off your clothes; dress as a dragon. Go do this task." When Shun had gone into the well, Gusou and Xiang filled up the well with earth. Shun dressed in the clothes of a dragon, became a dragon, and secretly came out from the other well. The two wells were the wells of Shun on Lishan. Shun fell in the well, and Gusou and Xiang rejoiced, thinking that Shun was without doubt dead. Xiang said: "The plot is mine. The oxen, sheep, and granary shall belong to my parents, while the shield, spear, *qin*, bow, and his two wives shall be mine." Xiang then went away into Shun's palace, and there was Shun playing on his *qin*. Xiang was stunned to see him and said: "I was just thinking of you, and getting very anxious."

"Quite so," said Shun, "and so you possessed yourself of all these things."

Shun again served his parents with filial piety, and he loved his brother as usual. Gusou and Xiang were not content. One day they invited Shun to drink alcohol with them so that when he got drunk, they could kill him.

Shun's two wives had him wash in the medicine pool; thereupon he set out and drank alcohol the whole day but did not become drunk. Gusou and Xiang tried to kill Shun three times, but they did not succeed. They thought that Shun must have holy virtues and get assistance from the gods. They gradually got along with Shun in harmony. Shun again served his parents, loved his brother, and became still more careful in his conduct. Yao thereupon tested Shun as to the five cardinal rules (*wudian* 五典), and the various officers were under control. Yao also sent Shun to the great plains at the foot of the mountains, and amid violent wind, thunder, and rain, he did not go astray. Yao then knew that Shun was fit to accept the empire, and being old, he caused Shun to act as the regent and went on a tour of inspection in the kingdom. Shun was promoted to the important position, and he served Yao for twenty years and acted as the regent for eight years. Yao died, and when the three years' mourning was over, Shun gave way to Danzhu on the south of the southern river. When the princes went to an audience at court, they did not present themselves before Danzhu but before Shun; those who had to try a lawsuit did not go to Danzhu but to Shun; and the singers did not sing in praise of Danzhu but of Shun. Shun said, "It is from heaven." Afterward he went to the capital and sat on the imperial throne.

Shun sat on the imperial throne, set his capital in Puban, and named his nation Yu; thus he was King Yu. Then he appointed the various officers, raised the eight talented sons of King Gaoyang to office, and made them superintend the land department and direct all matters, arranging them according to their seasons. He also raised the eight talented sons of King Gaoxin to office, employing them to spread throughout the country a knowledge of the duties pertaining to the five social relationships, for fathers became just, mothers loving, elder brothers sociable, younger ones respectful, and children dutiful; within the empire there was peace and harmony in both families and society. In addition, Shun banished the four wicked men to the four borders of the empire to manage hobgoblins. He banished Gong Gong to Youzhou (in the north), banished Huan Dou to Chongshan (in the south), killed the San Miao in Sanwei (Three Perils, in the west), and killed Gun on Yushan (Feather Mountain, in the east). After these four condemnations, all in the world submitted.

Now Yu, Gaoyao, and other officers from the time of Yao were all promoted to office, but they had no separate appointments. Shun then promoted Yu to be the master of the official works, directing political affairs; Gaoyao was the minister of justice, directing judicial affairs; Boyi was the master of rites, directing ceremonies in the ancestral temple; Chui was the master of works, directing all workmen; Yi was the imperial forester, superintending mountains and lakes; Qi was the ruler of the millet, directing agricultural affairs; Xie was the master of the multitude, propagating the five instructions (that they should be just, loving, friendly, respectful, and filial respectively); Long was the conveyer of words, directing guests and visitors; Kui was the director of music, directing music and dance. Shun also raised his brother Xiang to the rank of prince in Youshe. A variety of officers were appointed; all did their duties and obtained their achievements. Yu's great achievements consisted in making great cuttings through the nine hills, making thoroughfares through the nine swamps, deepening the nine rivers, and regulating the nine provinces, each of which by their officials sent tribute and did not lose their rightful dues. In a square of 5000 *li*, the boundaries reached the border areas and the wild domains. All within the four seas were grateful for King Shun's achievements; and Yu then performed the nine tunes, and the result was that strange creatures and phoenixes flew to and fro. Therefore, all within the world praised the virtues of the king, beginning from the days of King Shun of Yu.

When Shun was twenty years of age, he was noted for his filial piety; at thirty Yao raised him to office; at fifty he assisted in the administration of imperial affairs; when he was fifty-eight Yao died; after three years' mourning, when he was sixty-one, he sat on the imperial throne in Yao's stead. After he had occupied the imperial throne thirty-nine years, he went on a hunting expedition to the south, died in the desert of Cangwu, and was buried at a place called Lingling (broken hillocks) in the Jiuyi range in Jiangnan province. In his lifetime, Shun was as benevolent and virtuous as heaven, always keeping his people on his mind. After he died, people in Lishan were deeply grateful for his kindness and virtues. They built the temple for him and made his statues, making sacrifices in spring and autumn. The burning of incense and candles has been continued as the local custom for more than four thousand years. It is impossible to track the earliest date of construction of the temple in Lishan, but according to the records in the *Local Annals*, the temple was last rebuilt in the seventh year of the Tiansheng period (1029), during the Song dynasty, with a double-eave gabled roof, majestic and magnificent. It is a shame that it was burned by the Japanese army in 1942. In 1995, with the support of county-level officials, Lishan people laid the foundation and rebuilt the temple, and the whole project was completed in a year and a half. The architecture of the new temple excels in artistry over the one built in previous dynasties. The temple is magnificent, the place is splendid, the statues are distinctly made, and the paintings are brilliant. In any of these aspects, it could be reviewed as one of the best new constructions that imitate traditional architecture in Shanxi. Now it is completed, in order to let our descendants know how the emperor became a sage-king owing to his loyalty, filial piety, benevolence, and love and how he made great achievements and virtues beginning as an ordinary peasant, who plowed, sowed, made pottery, and fished, and progressing to a king. In order to transmit and promote the temple, and to honor our Chinese nation, I wrote this essay based on the original biography in ancient texts and folk legends, and inscribed it on the stele, hoping that it will last forever.

The Shun Temple Reconstruction Association in Lishan, Hongtong
Written by Li Xuezhi, Associate Director of the Shun Temple
Reconstruction Association in Lishan
Reviewed by Yao Dianzhong, Director of the Institute of Chinese
Classical Literature Studies, Chair of the Chinese Department,
at Shanxi University
Written with red ink for stone inscription by Wen Shouzhang
Inscribed by Pang Guanghong
Erected on September 13, 1996
(Wang et al. 2009, 784–85)

BIBLIOGRAPHY

Abrahams, Roger D. 1976. "The Complex Relations of Simple Forms." In *Folklore Genres*, edited by Dan Ben-Amos, 193–214. Austin: University of Texas Press.

Adell, Nicolas, Regina F. Bendix, Chiara Bortolotto, and Markus Tauschek, eds. 2015. *Between Imagined Communities and Communities of Practice: Participation, Territory and the Making of Heritage*. Göttingen Studies in Cultural Property. Göttingen: Universitätsverlag Göttingen.

Aikawa-Faure, Norika. 2009. "From the Proclamation of Masterpieces to the Convention for the Safeguarding of Intangible Cultural Heritage." In *Intangible Heritage*, edited by Laurajane Smith and Natsuko Akagawa, 13–44. London: Routledge.

Allan, Sarah. 1981. *The Heir and the Sage: Dynastic Legend in Early China*. San Francisco: Chinese Materials Center.

———. 1991. *The Shape of the Turtle: Myth, Art, and Cosmos in Early China*. Albany: State University of New York Press.

An Deming 安德明. 2008. "*Feiwuzhi wenhua yichan baohua: minsuxue de liang nan xuanze* 非物质文化遗产保护: 民俗学的两难选择" [Protecting intangible cultural heritage: A dilemma of Chinese folklore studies]. *Henan Social Sciences* 1: 14–20.

An Deming and Yang Lihui. 2015. "Chinese Folklore since the Late 1970s: Achievements, Difficulties and Challenges." *Asian Ethnology* 74 (2): 270–73.

Bauman, Richard, and Donald Braid. 1998. "The Ethnography of Performance in the Study of Oral Traditions." In *Teaching Oral Traditions*, edited by John Miles Foley, 106–22. New York: The Modern Language Association.

Ben-Amos, Dan. 1971. "Toward a Definition of Folklore in Context." *Journal of American Folklore* 331 (84): 3–15.

———. 1976. "Analytical Categories and Ethnic Genres." In *Folklore Genres*, edited by Dan Ben-Amos, 215–42. Austin: University of Texas Press.

———. 1984. "The Seven Strands of Tradition: Varieties in Its Meaning in American Folklore Studies." *Journal of Folklore Research* 21 (2–3): 97–132.

Bender, Mark. 2003. *Plum and Bamboo: China's Suzhou Chantefable Tradition*. Urbana: University of Illinois Press.

Bendix, Regina. 1989. "Tourism and Cultural Displays: Inventing Traditions for Whom?" *Journal of American Folklore* 102 (404):131–46.

———. 2009. "Heritage between Economy and Politics." In *Intangible Heritage: Key Issues in Cultural Heritage*, edited by Laurajane Smith and Natsuko Akagawa, 253–69. London: Routledge.

Bendix, Regina F., Aditya Eggert, and Arnika Peselmann, eds. 2012. *Heritage Regimes and the State*. Göttingen Studies on Cultural Property, vol. 6. Göttingen: Göttingen University Press.

Bendix, Regina F., and Hasan-Rokem, G., eds. 2012. *A Companion to Folklore*. Oxford: Wiley-Blackwell.

Birrell, Anne. 1993. *Chinese Mythology: An Introduction*. Baltimore: Johns Hopkins University Press.

———. 1994a. "Studies on Chinese Myth since 1970: An Appraisal, Part 1." *History of Religions* 33 (4): 380–93.

———. 1994b. "Studies on Chinese Myth since 1970: An Appraisal, Part 2." *History of Religions* 34 (1): 70–94.

Blank, Trevor J., and Robert Glenn Howard. 2013. *Tradition in the Twenty-First Century: Locating the Role of the Past in the Present*. Logan: Utah State University Press.

Blumenfield, Tami, and Helaine Silverman, eds. 2013. *Cultural Heritage Politics in China*. New York: Springer.

Bodolec, Caroline. 2012. "The Chinese Paper-Cut: From Local Inventories to the UNESCO Representative List of the Intangible Cultural Heritage of Humanity." In *Heritage Regimes and the State*, edited by Regina Bendix, Aditya Eggert, and Arnika Peselmann, 249–64. Göttingen: Göttingen University Press.

Bourdieu, Pierre. 1977. *Outline of a Theory of Practice*. Cambridge: Cambridge University Press.

———. (1980) 1990. *The Logic of Practice*. Cambridge: Polity Press.

———. 1984. *Distinction: A Social Critique of the Judgement of Taste*. Cambridge, MA: Harvard University Press.

Bourdieu, Pierre, and James Samuel Coleman. 1991. *Social Theory for a Changing Society*. Boulder, CO: Westview.

Bourdieu, Pierre, and Randal Johnson. 1993. *The Field of Cultural Production: Essays on Art and Literature*. New York: Columbia University Press.

Bourdieu, Pierre, and Jean Claude Passeron. 1990. *Reproduction in Education, Society, and Culture*. London: Sage in association with Theory, Culture & Society, Dept. of Administrative and Social Studies, Teesside Polytechnic.

Bramall, Chris. 2007. *Industrialization of Rural China*. Oxford: Oxford University Press.

Brandtstädter, Susanne, and Gonçalo D. Santos. 2009. *Chinese Kinship: Contemporary Anthropological Perspectives*. London: Routledge.

Bronner, Simon J. 1998. *Following Tradition: Folklore in the Discourse of American Culture*. Logan: Utah State University Press.

———. 2005. "Contesting Tradition: The Deep Play and Protest of Pigeon Shoots." *Journal of American Folklore* 470 (118): 409–52.

———. 2011. *Explaining Traditions: Folk Behavior in Modern Culture*. Lexington: University Press of Kentucky.

Brown, Michael F. 2003. *Who Owns Native Culture?* Cambridge, MA: Harvard University Press.

Brumann, Christoph, and David Berliner. 2016. *World Heritage on the Ground: Ethnographic Perspectives*. New York: Berghahn Books.

Byrne, Denis. 2009. "A Critique of Unfeeling Heritage." In *Intangible Heritage*, edited by Laurajane Smith and Natsuko Akagawa, 229–52. London: Routledge.

Cashman, Ray. 2011. "The Role of Tradition in the Individual: At Work in Donegal with Packy Jim McGrath." In *The Individual and Tradition: Folkloristic Perspectives*, edited by Ray Cashman, Tom Mould, and Pravina Shukla, 303–22. Bloomington: Indiana University Press.

Cashman, Ray, Tom Mould, and Pravina Shukla, eds. 2011. *The Individual and Tradition: Folkloristic Perspectives*. Bloomington: Indiana University Press.

Chan, Selina Ching, and Graeme S. Lang. 2007. "Temple Construction and the Revival of Popular Religion in Jinhua." *China Information* 21 (1): 43–69.

Chang, Hao. 1971. *Liang Ch'i-ch'ao and Intellectual Transition in China, 1890–1907.* Cambridge, MA: Harvard University Press.

Chang Jianhua 常建华. 2010. "Mingqing shiqi huabei zongzu de fazhan—yi Shanxi Hongtong Liu shi wei li 明清时期华北宗族的发展—以山西洪洞刘氏为例" [The development of north China clan in Ming and Qing Dynasty—A case study of LIU family of Hongtong in Shanxi]. *Qiushi xuekan* 2: 125–31.

Chang, Kang-i Sun. 1986. *Six Dynasties Poetry.* Princeton, NJ: Princeton University Press.

Chang, Kwang-chih. 1983. *Art, Myth, and Ritual: The Path to Political Authority in Ancient China.* Cambridge, MA: Harvard University Press.

Chao Gejin 朝戈金 et al. eds. 2016. *Zhongguo minsu xue nianjian* 2015 中国民俗学年鉴 2015 [Annual review of China folkloristics 2015]. Beijing: Zhongguo shehui kexue chubanshe.

Chau, Adam Yuet. 2006. *Miraculous Response: Doing Popular Religion in Contemporary China.* Stanford, CA: Stanford University Press.

———, ed. 2011. *Religion in Contemporary China: Revitalization and Innovation.* Milton Park, Abingdon: Routledge.

Cheek, Timothy. 2015. *The Intellectual in Modern Chinese History.* Cambridge: Cambridge University Press.

Chen Jianxian 陈建宪. 1998. "Jingshen huangxiang de yinhun zhi fan: 20 shiji zhongguo shenhuaxue huimou 精神还乡的引魂之幡: 20 世纪中国神话学回眸" [Spiritual flags of returning soul: Chinese mythology in the twentieth century]. *Hebei shifan daxue xuebao* 3: 190–96.

———. 2003. "Zouxiang tianye huigui wenben: Zhongguo shenhuaxue lilun fansi zhiyi 走向田野回归文本—中国神话学理论建设反思之一" [Going to the field and returning to the text: A reconsideration of the foundation of Chinese mythology theory]. *Minsu yanjiu* 4: 5–13.

Chen Jinwen 陈金文. 2009. "Feiyi baohu yu minsuxue yanjiu jian de lixiang guanxi bing shiji zhuangkuang 非遗保护与民俗学研究间的理想关系并实际状况" [The ideal relation between the safeguarding of the intangible cultural heritage and folklore studies and its real situation]. *Henan Social Sciences* 3: 7–10.

Chen Lianshan 陈连山. 2004. "20 shiji zhongguo shenhua xue jianshi 20 世纪中国神话学简史" [A brief history of Chinese mythology in the 20th century]. In *Xiandai xueshu shi shang de su wenxue* 现代学术史上的俗文学 [Popular literature in the modern intellectual history], edited by Chen Pingyuan. Wuhan: Hubei jiaoyu chubanshe.

Chen Shouxiang 陈绶祥. 1999. *Xin wenren hua yishu: wenxin wanxiang* 新文人画艺术: 文心万象 [The art of new literati: Ten thousand images of the literati mind]. Changchun: Jilin meishu chubanshe.

Chen, Xiaohong. 2015. "Tradition in Process: Framing Tradition in Cultural Preservation and Invention in Jixian in the Course of the Modernization of China." PhD diss., Indiana University, Bloomington.

Chen Yongchao 陈泳超. 2000. *Yao Shun chuan shuo yan jiu* 尧舜传说研究 [A study on the legends of Yao and Shun]. Nanjing: Nanjing shifan daxue chubanshe.

———. 2010. "Minjian chuanshuo yanbian de dongli xue jizhi 民间传说演变的动力学机制" [The dynamic mechanism of the changing of folk legends]. *Wen shi zhe* 2: 60–73.

———. 2015. *Beiguo shenqu de da niangniang—difang minjian chuanshuo shengxi de donglixue yanjiu* 背过身去的大娘娘—地方民间传说生息的动力学研究 [Old queen who turned her back: The dynamics of making local folk legends]. Beijing: Beijing daxue chubanshe.

Chen Yongchao, Jian Zhong, Chunfang Sun, Yao Wang, and Huiyi Yao. 2007. "Yangxie, Lishan san yue san 'jie gugu' diaocha baogao 羊獬、历山三月三 '接姑姑' 活动调查报告" [A report of a survey of the activities of 'receiving aunties' in Yangxie and Lishan on the third day of the third lunar month]. *Minjian wenhua luntan* 3: 59–69.

Chen Yongchao and Wang Yao 王尧. 2010. "Jiemei niangniang: zuowei youshen yishi zhicheng de yao shun chuanshuo 姐妹娘娘：作为游神仪式支撑的尧舜传说" [Sister goddesses: Legends of Yao and Shun supporting rituals of religious parade]. *Minzu wenxue yanjiu* 1: 5–17.

Chen, Zhiqin. 2015. "For Whom to Conserve Intangible Cultural Heritage: The Dislocated Agency of Folk Belief Practitioners and the Reproduction of Local Culture." *Asian Ethnology* 74 (2): 307–34.

Cheng Anxia 程安霞. 2011. "'Zou' chulai de 'qinqi' '走'出来的'亲戚'" [Making "relatives" by "walking"]. Diss., Minzu University of China, Beijing.

China Intangible Cultural Heritage Protection Center (CICHPC) (*Zhongguo feiwuzhi wenhua yichan baohu zhongxin* 中国非物质文化遗产保护中心). 2006. "Zhongguo feiwuzhi wenhua yichan baohu zhongxin jianjie 中国非物质文化遗产保护中心简介" [Introduction to China intangible cultural heritage protection center]. Accessed February 16, 2017. http://www.ihchina.cn/2/10313.html.

———. 2010. *Di'erpi guojia ji feiwuzhi wenhua yichan minglu jianjie* 第二批国家级非物质文化遗产名录简介 [Introduction to the second list of national intangible cultural heritage]. Beijing: Wenhua yishu chubanshe.

———. 2016. "Gedi guanche luoshi Zhonghua Renmin Gongheguo Feiwuzhi Wenhua Yichan Fa qingkuang pinggu baogao 各地贯彻落实《中华人民共和国非物质文化遗产法》情况评估报告" [The evaluation report on the implementation of the intangible cultural heritage law in People's Republic of China]. December 28. Accessed February 16, 2017. http://www.mcprc.gov.cn/whzx/ggtz/201702/t20170210_490717.html.

———. 2017. "Zhuanfang shanxi feiyi baohu zhongxin zhuren Zhao Zhongyue 专访山西非遗保护中心主任赵中悦" [An interview with Zhao Zhongyue, the director of Shanxi ICH Protection Center]. October 26. Accessed November 16, 2017. http://www.ihchina.cn/8/53915.html.

Chinese National Academy of Arts (*Zhongguo yishu yanjiuyuan* 中国艺术研究院) and China Intangible Cultural Heritage Protection Center (*Zhongguo feiwuzhi wenhua yichan baohu zhongxin* 中国非物质文化遗产保护中心), eds. 2007. *Zhongguo feiwuzhi wenhua yichan pucha shouce* 中国非物质文化遗产普查手册 [Handbook of Chinese intangible cultural heritage investigation]. Beijing: Wenhua yishu chubanshe.

Ching, Julia, and R. W. L. Guisso. 1991. *Sages and Filial Sons: Mythology and Archaeology in Ancient China*. Shatin, NT, Hong Kong: Chinese University Press.

Chow, Kai-wing. 2008. *Beyond the May Fourth Paradigm: In Search of Chinese Modernity*. Lanham, MD: Lexington Books.

Cooper, Eugene. 2012. *The Market and Temple Fairs of Rural China: Red Fire*. New York: Routledge.

Cresswell, Tim. 2004. *Place: A Short Introduction*. Malden, MA: Blackwell.

De Cesari, Chiara. 2012. "Thinking Through Heritage Regimes." In *Heritage Regimes and the State*, edited by Regina F. Bendix, Aditya Eggert, and Arnika Peselmann, 121–39. Göttingen: Göttingen University Press.

Dégh, Linda. 2001. *Legend and Belief: Dialectics of a Folklore Genre*. Bloomington: Indiana University Press.

Denton, Kirk A. 1996. *Modern Chinese Literary Thought: Writings on Literature, 1893–1945.* Stanford, CA: Stanford University Press.

———. 2014. *Exhibiting the Past: Historical Memory and the Politics of Museums in Postsocialist China.* Honolulu: University of Hawai'i Press.

DeWalt, Kathleen Musante, and Billie R. DeWalt. 2011. *Participant Observation: A Guide for Fieldworkers.* Lanham, MD: Alta Mira.

Diamond, Norma. 1988. "The Miao and Poison: Interactions on China's Frontier." *Ethnology* 27 (1): 1–25.

Dirks, Nicholas B., Geoff Eley, and Sherry B. Ortner. 1994. *Culture/Power/History: A Reader in Contemporary Social Theory.* Princeton, NJ: Princeton University Press.

Dorson, Richard M., ed. 1968a. *Peasant Customs and Savage Myths: Selections from the British Folklorists.* 2 vols. Chicago: University of Chicago Press.

———. 1968b. "What Is Folklore?" *Folklore Forum* 1 (4): 37.

———. 1972. "Introduction: Concepts of Folklore and Folklife Studies." In *Folklore and Folklife: An Introduction,* edited by Richard M. Dorson, 1–50. Chicago: University of Chicago Press.

DuBois, Thomas David. 2005. *The Sacred Village: Social Change and Religious Life in Rural North China.* Honolulu: University of Hawai'i Press.

Elias, Norbert. (1965) 1994. *The Established and the Outsiders: A Sociological Enquiry into Community Problems.* London: Sage.

———. 1983. *The Court Society.* Oxford: Blackwell.

Eminov, S. 1975. "Folklore and Nationalism in Modern China." *Journal of the Folklore Institute* 12 (2–3): 257–77.

Epstein, Maram. 2001. *Competing Discourses: Orthodoxy, Authenticity, and Engendered Meanings in Late Imperial Chinese Fiction.* Cambridge, MA: Harvard University Asia Center.

Fabian, Johannes. 1990. *Power and Performance: Ethnographic Explorations through Proverbial Wisdom and Theater in Shaba, Zaire.* Madison: University of Wisconsin Press.

Fairbank, Wilma. 1994. *Liang and Lin: Partners in Exploring China's Architectural Past.* Philadelphia: University of Pennsylvania Press.

Fang Shiming 方詩銘 and Wang Xiuling 王修齡. 1981. *Guben zhushu jinian ji zheng* 古本竹書紀年輯證. Shanghai: Shanghai Guji Chubanshe.

Feintuch, Burt. 2003. *Eight Words for the Study of Expressive Culture.* Urbana: University of Illinois Press.

Feld, Steven, and Keith H. Basso, eds. 1996. *Senses of Place.* Santa Fe, NM: School of American Research Press. Distributed by the University of Washington Press.

Feldman, Burton, and Robert D. Richardson. 1972. *The Rise of Modern Mythology, 1680–1860.* Bloomington: Indiana University Press.

Feuchtwang, Stephan. 2004. *Making Place: State Projects, Globalisation and Local Responses in China.* London: UCL.

Foster, Michael Dylan, and Lisa Gilman. 2015. *UNESCO on the Ground: Local Perspectives on Intangible Cultural Heritage.* Bloomington: Indiana University Press.

Gao Bingzhong 高丙中. 1994. *Minsu wenhua yu minsu shenghuo* 民俗文化与民俗生活 [Folk culture and folk life]. Beijing: Zhongguo shehui kexue chubanshe.

———. 2007. "Zuowei feiwuzhi wenhua yichan yanjiu keti de minjian xinyang 作为非物质文化遗产研究课题的民间信仰 [Folk belief as the subjects of intangible cultural heritage]. *Jiangxi shehui kexue* 3: 146–54.

———. 2008. "Zhongguo minsuxue sanshi nian de fazhan licheng 中国民俗学三十年的发展历程" [Chinese folklore studies in the past three decades]. *Minsu yanjiu* 3: 5–19.

———. 2013. "Zhongguo de feiwuzhi wenhua yichan baohu yu wenhua geming de zhongjie 中国的非物质文化遗产保护与文化革命的终结" [The conservation of China's intangible cultural heritage and the ending of culture revolutions]. *Kaifang shidai* 5: 143–52.

———. 2017. "The Social Movement of Safeguarding Intangible Cultural Heritage and the End of Cultural Revolutions in China." *Western Folklore* 76 (2): 167–80.

Gao, Jie. 2010. "Saving the Nation through Culture: The Folklore Movement in Republican China (1918–1949)." PhD diss., University of Western Ontario, Canada.

Geertz, Clifford. 1973. "Thick Description: Toward an Interpretive Theory of Culture." In *The Interpretation of Cultures: Selected Essays*, by Clifford Geertz, 3–30. New York: Basic Books.

———. 1983. *Local Knowledge*. New York: Basic Books.

Gerritsen, Anne. 2007. *Ji'an Literati and the Local in Song-Yuan-Ming China*. Leiden, Netherlands: Brill.

Gillin, Donald G. 1967. *Warlord: Yen Hsi-shan in Shansi Province, 1911–1949*. Princeton: Princeton University Press.

Grove, Linda. 2006. *A Chinese Economic Revolution: Rural Entrepreneurship in the Twentieth Century*. Lanham, MD: Rowman & Littlefield.

Gu Jiegang 顾颉刚. 1928. "Shengxian wenhua yu minzhong wenhua 圣贤文化与民众文化" [Sages' culture and people's pulture]. *Minsu zhoukan* 5: 17–22.

———. 1929. "Hunan Changben Tiyao Xu" 湖南唱本提要序 [Preface to an outline of Hunan song books]. *Minsu zhoukan* 64: 1–3.

———. 2010. *Gu Jiegang quan ji* 顾颉刚全集 [Completed works of Gu Jiegang]. 62 vols. Beijing: Zhonghua shuju.

Gu Jiegang and Wu Limo 吴立模. 1931. "Suzhou changben xulu 苏州唱本序录" [On Suzhou's song books]. In *Minsu xue jijuan* 民俗学集卷 [The collections of folklore studies], vol. 1.

Gu Jiegang et al., eds. (1926–41) 1982. *Gu shi bian* 古史辨 [Critique of Ancient (Chinese) History]. 7 vols. Shanghai: Shanghai Guji Chubanshe.

Hafstein, Valdimar T. 2012. "Cultural Heritage." In *A Companion to Folklore*, edited by Regina Bendix and Galit Hasan-Rokem, 500–519. Malden, MA: Wiley-Blackwell.

Han Xiaomao 韩小毛. 2007. "Tangyao Yushun Hongtong xian Shun xiang Wan'an jinshi ming kao 唐尧虞舜洪洞县舜乡万安金石铭考" [Textual research of inscriptions on mental utensils and stone tablets in Wan'an, the hometown of Shun, Hongtong county, during Tang Yao and Yu Shun's time]. Manuscript.

Handler, Richard, and Jocelyn Linnekin. 1984. "Tradition, Genuine or Spurious." *Journal of American Folklore* 97 (385): 273–90.

Hansen, Valerie. 1990. *Changing Gods in Medieval China, 1127–1276*. Princeton, NJ: Princeton University Press.

Hao, Zhidong. 2003. *Intellectuals at a Crossroads: The Changing Politics of China's Knowledge Workers*. Albany: State University of New York Press.

Hauser-Schäublin, Brigitta. 2012a. "Preah Vihear: From Object of Colonial Desire to a Contested World Heritage Site." In *World Heritage Angkor and Beyond: Circumstances and Implications of UNESCO Listings in Cambodia*, edited by Brigitta Hauser-Schäublin, 34–56. Göttingen: Göttingen University Press.

———, ed. 2012b. *World Heritage Angkor and Beyond: Circumstances and Implications of UNESCO Listings in Cambodia.* Göttingen Studies on Cultural Property, vol. 2. Göttingen: Göttingen University Press.

Hawkes, David, translator and introduction. (1985) 2011. Qu Yuan et al. *The Songs of the South: An Ancient Chinese Anthology of Poems by Qu Yuan and Other Poets.* London: Penguin Books.

Hill, Jonathan D., ed. 1988. *Rethinking History and Myth: Indigenous South American Perspectives on the Past.* Champaign: University of Illinois Press.

Hobsbawm, Eric. 1983. "Introduction: Inventing Tradition." In *The Invention of Tradition,* edited by Eric Hobsbawm and Terence Ranger, 1–14. Cambridge: Cambridge University Press.

Hobsbawm, Eric, and Terence Ranger, eds. 1983. *The Invention of Tradition.* Cambridge: Cambridge University Press.

Hofer, Tamás. 1984. "The Perception of Tradition in European Ethnology." *Journal of Folklore Research* 21 (3): 133–47.

Holbek, Bengt. 1992. "On the Comparative Method in Folklore Research." *NIF Papers* 3: 3–20.

Holcombe, Charles. 1994. *In the Shadow of the Han: Literati Thought and Society at the Beginning of the Southern Dynasties.* Honolulu: University of Hawai'i Press.

Holm, David. 1991. *Art and Ideology in Revolutionary China.* Oxford: Clarendon Press.

Hon, Tze-Ki. 1996. "Ethnic and Cultural Pluralism: Gu Jiegang's Vision of a New China in His Studies of Ancient History." *Modern China* 22 (3): 315–39.

Hong Mai 洪迈. (1123–1202). 1981. *Yijian zhi* 夷坚志 [The Records of the Listener]. Beijing: Zhonghua shuju.

Honko, Lauri. 1986. "Types of Comparison and Forms of Variation." *Journal of Folklore Research* 23 (2–3): 105–24.

Horigan, Kate Parker. 2010. "City of Sin?" Paper presented at the annual meeting of the American Folklore Society, October 13–16, in Nashville, TN.

Howard, Keith, ed. 2012. *Music as Intangible Cultural Heritage: Policy, Ideology, and Practice in the Preservation of East Asian Traditions.* Farnham, UK: Ashgate.

Hu Yinglin 胡应麟. 1958. *Shaoshi shan fang bi cong* 少室山房筆叢. Beijing: Zhonghua shuju.

Huang, Martin W. 1995. *Literati and Self-Re/presentation: Autobiographical Sensibility in the Eighteenth-Century Chinese Novel.* Stanford, CA: Stanford University Press.

Huang Meiling 黄美龄, Zhao Hongbao 赵红宝, and Wu Yuanyuan 吴媛媛. 2013. "Dui feiwuzhi wenhua yichan chuanchengren zhidu de sikao—yi guangchang mengxi weili 对非物质文化遗产传承人制度的思考—以广昌孟戏为例" (Reflections on the System of Transmitters of Intangible Cultural Heritage—A Case Study on Meng Opera in Guangchang). *Shenzhou wenhua* 2: 38–39.

Huangfu Mi 皇甫谧. 2000. *Diwang Shiji* 帝王世纪 [Records of Emperors and Kings]. Jinan: Qilu shu she.

Huanghe News. 2012. "'Shanxi sheng feiwuzhi wenhua yichan tiaoli' jiangyu 2013 nian yi yue yi ri zhengshi shixing 《山西省非物质文化遗产条例》将于 2013 年1月1日正式施行" [Intangible Cultural Heritage Ordinance in Shanxi Province will come into force on January 1, 2013]. December 7. Accessed November 21, 2017. http://news.ifeng.com/gundong/detail _2012_12/07/19951578_0.shtml.

Hung, Chang-tai. 1985. *Going to the People: Chinese Intellectuals and Folk Literature, 1918–1937.* Cambridge, MA: Council on East Asian Studies, Harvard University Press.

Hymes, Dell. 1975. "Folklore's Nature and the Sun's Myth." *Journal of American Folklore* 88 (350): 345–69.

Hymes, Robert P. 1986. *Statesmen and Gentlemen: The Elite of Fu-chou, Chiang-hsi, in Northern and Southern Sung*. Cambridge: Cambridge University Press.

Inglis, Alister David. 2006. *Hong Mai's Record of the Listener and Its Song Dynasty Context*. Albany: State University of New York Press.

Intangible Cultural Heritage Division (*feiwuzhi wenhua yichan si* 非物质文化遗产司). 2017. Accessed November 21, 2017. http://www.mcprc.gov.cn/gywhb/jgsz/bjg/201111/t20111121 _278093.html.

——— ed. 2016. *Material Vernaculars: Objects, Images, and Their Social Worlds*. Bloomington: Indiana University Press.

Jay, Jennifer. 1999. "Sima Qian." In *The Encyclopedia of Historians and Historical Writing* vol. 2, edited by Kelly Boyd, 1093–94. Chicago: FitzRoy Dearborn.

Jessup, Sarah Huntington. 2001. "Staging Traditional Chinese Opera in the Reform Era: Conflicting Local Identities in Modernization." PhD diss., University of Michigan.

Jiang Guanyun 蒋观云. (1903) 2002. "Shenhua lishi yangcheng zhi renwu 神话历史养成之人物" [Those people cultivated through the reading of myth and history]. In *Ershi shiji zhongguo minsuxue jingdian, shenhua juan* 二十世纪中國民俗學經典·神话卷 [Classics of Chinese folklore studies in the twentieth century—volume on myth], edited by Zhong Jingwen and Li Yuan. Beijing: Shehui kexue wenxian chubanshe.

Jin Yaoji 金耀基. 1966. *Cong chuantong dao xiandai* 从传统到现代 [From tradition to modernization]. Taibei: Taiwan shangwu yinshu guan.

———. 1984. *Zhongguo xiandai hua yu zhishi fenzi* 中国现代化与知识分子 [Chinese modernization and intellectuals]. Taibei: Shibao chuban gongsi.

Jing, Jun. 1996. *The Temple of Memories: History, Power, and Morality in a Chinese Village*. Stanford, CA: Stanford University Press.

Jing Zhankui 景占魁. 2008. *Yan Xishan zhuan* 阎锡山传 [Biography of Yan Xishan]. Beijing: Zhongguo shehui chubanshe.

Johnson, David G. 2009. *Spectacle and Sacrifice: The Ritual Foundations of Village Life in North China*. Cambridge, MA: Harvard University Asia Center.

Jones, Michael Owen. 1989. *Craftsman of the Cumberlands: Tradition & Creativity*. Lexington: University Press of Kentucky.

———. 2000. "'Tradition' in Identity Discourses and an Individual's Symbolic Construction of Self." *Western Folklore* 2 (59):115–41.

Jones, Stephen. 2004. *Plucking the Winds: Lives of Village Musicians in Old and New China*. Leiden, Netherlands: CHIME.

———. 2007. *Ritual and Music of North China: Shawm Bands in Shanxi*. Aldershot, UK: Ashgate.

Kaartinen, Timo. 2013. "Handing Down and Writing Down: Metadiscourse of Tradition among the Bandanese of Eastern Indonesia." *Journal of American Folklore* 126: 385–406.

Kang Baocheng 康保成, ed. 2011. *Zhongguo feiwuzhi wenhua yichan baohu fazhan baogao (2011)* 中国非物质文化遗产保护发展报告 (2011) [*Report on the safeguarding and development of Chinese intangible cultural heritage in 2011*]. Beijing: Shehui kexue wenxian chubanshe.

Kang, Xiaofei. 2006. *The Cult of the Fox: Power, Gender, and Popular Religion in Late Imperial and Modern China*. New York: Columbia University Press.

——. 2009. "Two Temples, Three Religions, and a Tourist Attraction: Contesting Sacred Space on China's Ethnic Frontier." *Modern China* 35 (3): 227–55.

Kaplan, Merrill. 2013. "Curation and Tradition on Web 2.0." In *Tradition in the Twenty-First Century: Locating the Role of the Past in the Present*, edited by Trevor J. Blank and Robert Glenn Howard, 123–48. Logan: Utah State University Press.

Kirshenblatt-Gimblett, Barbara. 1988. "Mistaken Dichotomies." *Journal of American Folklore* 101 (400): 140–55.

——. 1995. "Theorizing Heritage." *Ethnomusicology* 39 (3): 367–80.

——. 1998a. *Destination Culture: Tourism, Museums, and Heritage*. Berkeley: University of California Press.

——. 1998b. "Folklore's Crisis." *Journal of American Folklore* 441 (111): 281–327.

——. 2004. "Intangible Heritage as Metacultural Production." *Museum* 56 (1–2): 52–64.

Kuah, Khun Eng, and Zhaohui Liu, eds. 2017. *Intangible Cultural Heritage in Contemporary China: The Participation of Local Communities*. London: Routledge.

Kuutma, Kristin. 2016. "From Folklore to Intangible Heritage." In *A Companion to Heritage Studies*, edited by William Logan et al., 41–54. Wiley-Blackwell.

Lee, Ching Kwan, and Guobin Yang. 2007. *Re-envisioning the Chinese Revolution: The Politics and Poetics of Collective Memories in Reform China*. Washington: Woodrow Wilson Center Press.

Lee, Joseph Tse-Hei, Lida V. Nedilsky, and Siu Keung Cheung. 2012. *China's Rise to Power: Conceptions of State Governance*. New York: Palgrave Macmillan.

Lefebvre, Henri. 1991. *The Production of Space*. Oxford: Blackwell.

Leibold, James. 2006. "Competing Narratives of Racial Unity in Republican China: From the Yellow Emperor to Peking Man." *Modern China* 32 (2): 181–220.

Li Chunwen 李春文. 2012. "Huaxia Hongtong Lishan zhi 華夏洪洞歷山誌 [Gazetteer of Lishan, Hongtong, China]. Unpublished manuscript.

Li Guofu 李国富, Wang Rudiao 王汝雕, and Zhang Baonian 张宝年, eds. 2008. *Hongtong jinshi lu* 洪洞金石录 [Records on metals and stones in Hongtong]. Taiyuan: Shanxi guji chubanshe.

Li Hui 李辉 and Ying Hong 应红. 1999. *Shiji zhi wen: laizi zhishijie de shengyin* 世纪之问：来自知识界的声音 [The question of the century: The voice of intellectuals]. Zhengzhou: Daxiang Chubanshe.

Li Xueqin 李学勤. 1997. *Zouchu yigu shidai* 走出疑古时代 [Leave the "doubting antiquity" period]. Shenyang: Liaoning daxue chubanshe.

Li Xuezhi 李学智. 1995. "Cong Shun geng Lishan tan Yu Shun zhuanji 从舜耕历山谈虞舜传记" [Annals of Yu Shun starting from Shun plowed in Lishan]. *Hongtong wenshi ziliao* 8: 106–10.

——. 1997. *Yangxie Lishan lianyin zhuanji* 羊獬·历山联姻传记 [Records of connections between Yangxie and Lishan through sacred marriage]. Published booklet.

——, ed. 2009. *Shun geng Lishan zai Hongtong* 舜耕历山在洪洞 [Lishan where Shun plowed was in Hongtong]. Taiyuan: Sanjin chubanshe.

——. 2012. "Wo shi zenyang puxie Hongtong Lishan de 我是怎样谱写洪洞历山的" (How did I make Lishan, Hongtong?). Manuscript.

Li, Zehou, and Vera Schwarcz. 1983–84. "Six Generations of Modern Chinese Intellectuals." *Chinese Studies in History* 17 (2): 42–57.

Liang Huazhi 梁化之 (1906–49). 1951. *Liang dai zhuxi Huazhi wenji* 梁代主席化之文辑 [Literary collection of Liang Huazhi]. Taipei: Shanxi sheng zhengfu linshi banshichu.

Lin, Yi-min. 2001. *Between Politics and Markets: Firms, Competition, and Institutional Change in Post-Mao China*. Cambridge: Cambridge University Press.

Lincoln, Bruce. 2014. *Discourse and the Construction of Society: Comparative Studies of Myth, Ritual, and Classification*. 2nd ed. New York: Oxford University Press.

Lindahl, Carl. 2012. "Legends of Hurricane Katrina: The Right to Be Wrong, Survivor-to-Survivor Storytelling, and Healing." *Journal of American Folklore* 125 (496): 139–76.

Lingohr-Wolf, Susanne. 2011. *Industrialisation and Rural Livelihoods in China*. London: Routledge.

Linnekin, Jocelyn. 1991. "Cultural Invention and the Dilemma of Authenticity." *American Anthropologist* 93 (2): 446–49.

Liu Baoshan 刘宝山. 1990. *Yao Shun guxiang qing* 尧舜故乡情 [Love of Yao and Shun's hometown]. Published booklet.

———. 1995. "Yao Shun guxiang jianjie 尧舜故乡简介" [Introduction to Yao and Shun's hometown]. *Hongtong wenshi ziliao*(8): 98–105.

Liu, Junren. 1980. *Chūgoku rekishi chimei daijiten*. Tokyo: Ryōun Shobō.

Liu, Lydia He. 1995. *Translingual Practice: Literature, National Culture, and Translated Modernity—China, 1900–1937*. Stanford, CA: Stanford University Press.

———. 2012. "Translingual Folklore and Folklorics in China." In *A Companion to Folklore*, edited by Regina Bendix and Galit Hasan-Rokem, 190–210. Malden, MA: Wiley-Blackwell.

Liu Shouhua 刘守华. 2009. "Minjian wenxue baocang de kaijue yu jicheng—xi zhongguo minjian wenxue santao jicheng de jiazhi yu yingxiang 民间文学宝藏的开掘与继承—析中国民间文学三套集成的价值与影响" [The excavation and inheritance of folk literature treasures: Analysis on the value and influence of three collections of Chinese folk literature]. *Zhongguo yishu bao*, November 3. http://www.cflac.org.cn/ysb/2009-11/03/content_18119154.htm.

Liu Xiang 刘向. (18 BC) 2007. *Lienü zhuan* 列女传 [The Biographies of Exemplary Women]. Beijing: Beijing tushuguan chubanshe.

Liu Xiaochun 刘晓春. 2009. "Cong minsu dao yujing zhong de minsu: Zhongguo minsuxue yanjiu de fanshi zhuanhuan 从'民俗'到'语境中的民俗'—中国民俗学研究的范式转换" [From "folklore" to "contextual folklore": Shifting paradigm of Chinese folklore studies]. *Minsu yanjiu* 2: 5–35.

Liu Xicheng 刘锡诚. 2006. *20 shiji zhongguo minjian wenxue xueshu shi* 20世纪中国民间文学学术史 [The intellectual history of Chinese folk literature in the twentieth century]. Kaifeng: Henan daxue chubanshe.

Liu Yuqing 刘毓庆, ed. 2008. *Huaxia wenming zhi gen tanyuan: Jindongnan shenhua, lishi, chuanshuo yu minsu zonghe kaocha* 华夏文明之根探源: 晋东南神话, 历史, 传说与民俗综合考察 [Tracking the origins of Chinese civilization: Comprehensive research of myths, history, legends and folklore in southeastern Shanxi]. Beijing: Xueyuan chubanshe.

Lloyd, Timothy, Ziying You, and Ling Ding. 2013. "Meiguo gonggong minsuxue de guoqu, xianzai he weilai 美国公共民俗学的过去、现在和未来" [The past, present, and future of public folklore in America]. *Minsu yanjiu* 6: 30–41.

Loewe, Michael. 1982. *Chinese Ideas of Life and Death: Faith, Myth and Reason in the Han Period* (202 BC–AD 220). London: Allen & Unwin.

———. 1994. *Divination, Mythology and Monarchy in Han China*. Cambridge: Cambridge University Press.

Logan, William, and Zeynep Aygen. 2015. "Heritage in the 'Asian Century': Responding to Geopolitical Change." In *A Companion to Heritage Studies*, edited by William Logan et al., 410–25. Chichester, UK: Wiley-Blackwell.

Logan, William, Máiréad Nic Craith, and Ullrich Kockel, eds. 2015. *A Companion to Heritage Studies*. Chichester, UK: Wiley-Blackwell.

Lü Wei 吕微. 1999. "History of Chinese Myths." In *Zhonghua minjian wenxue shi* 中华民间文学史 [History of Chinese folk literature], edited by Qi Lianxiu and Cheng Qiang. Shijiangzhuang: Hebei jiaoyu chubanshe.

Luo Wei 罗微. 2008. "Country Report: China." International Partnership Programme for Safeguarding of Intangible Cultural Heritage: "Training Course for Safeguarding of Intangible Cultural Heritage," January 21–26, in Tokyo, Osaka, and Kyoto, Japan. Accessed December 13, 2017. https://www.accu.or.jp/ich/en/training/country_report_pdf/country_report_china_02.pdf.

Luo Wei and Gao Shu 高舒. 2017. "2016 nian zhongguo feiwuzhi wenhua yichan baohua fazhan yanjiu baogao 2016 年中国非物质文化遗产保护发展研究报告" [A report on the protection and development of China's intangible cultural heritage in 2016]. *Yishu pinglun* 4: 18–33.

Ma Changyi 马昌仪. 1992. "*Zhongguo shenhuaxue fazhan de yige lunkuo* 中国神话学发展的一个轮廓" [The outlined history of Chinese mythology]. *Minjian wenxue luntan* 6: 7–19.

———, ed. 1994. *Zhongguo shenhuaxue wenlun xuancui* 中国神话学文论选萃 [Selected works on Chinese mythology]. Beijing: Zhongguo guangbo dianshi chubanshe.

Ma Zhizheng 马志正. 2011. *Yao Shun yu gu Lishan yanjiu chuji* 尧舜与古历山研究初集 [A preliminary collection of research articles on Yao-Shun and old Lishan]. Beijing: Dizhi chubanshe.

Maags, Christina, and Heike Holbig. 2016. "Replicating Elite Dominance in Intangible Cultural Heritage Safeguarding: The Role of Local Government–Scholar Networks in China." *International Journal of Cultural Property* 23 (1): 71–97.

McDougall, Bonnie S., and Paul Clark. 1984. *Popular Chinese Literature and Performing Arts in the People's Republic of China, 1949–1979*. Berkeley: University of California Press.

McDowell, John H. 2016. Review of *Tradition in the Twenty-first Century: Locating the Role of the Past in the Present*, edited by Trevor J. Blank and Robert Glenn Howard. *Journal of American Folklore* 129 (511): 112–15.

McNeal, Robin. 2012. "Constructing Myth in Modern China." *Journal of Asian Studies* 71 (3): 679–704.

———. 2015. "Moral Transformation and Local Identity: Reviving the Culture of Shun at Temples and Monuments across China." *Modern China* 41 (4): 436–64.

Mencius and James Legge. 1970. *The Works of Mencius*. New York: Dover.

Messenger, Phyllis Mauch, and George S. Smith. 2010. *Cultural Heritage Management: A Global Perspective*. Gainesville: University Press of Florida.

Mißling, Sven. 2012. "A Legal View of the Case of the Temple Preah Vihear." In *World Heritage Angkor and Beyond: Circumstances and Implications of UNESCO Listings in Cambodia*, edited by Brigitta Hauser-Schäublin, 57–67. Göttingen: Göttingen University Press.

Ministry of Culture, P. R. China. 2005. "Guanyu kaizhan feiwuzhi wenhua yichan pucha gongzuo de tongzhi 关于开展非物质文化遗产普查工作的通知" [Circular on the survey of intangible cultural heritage]. Accessed November 22, 2017. http://www.ihchina.cn/3/10333.html.

———. 2008. "Guojia ji feiwuzhi wenhua yichan xiangmu daibiao xing chuancheng ren rending yu guanli zanxing banfa 国家级非物质文化遗产项目代表性传承人认定与管理暂行办法" [Interim measures of the designation and administration of representative transmitters of national-level intangible cultural heritage elements]. Accessed September 18, 2013. http://www.ihchina.cn/inc/detail.jsp?info_id=3062.

Miura, Keiko. 2012a. "From Property to Heritage: Different Notions, Rules of Ownership and Practices of New and Old Actors in the Angkor World Heritage Site." In *World Heritage Angkor and Beyond: Circumstances and Implications of UNESCO Listings in Cambodia*, edited by Brigitta Hauser-Schäublin, 97–119. Göttingen: Göttingen University Press.

———2012b. "World Heritage Making in Angkor: Global, Regional, National and Local Actors, Interplays and Implications." In *World Heritage Angkor and Beyond: Circumstances and Implications of UNESCO Listings in Cambodia*, edited by Brigitta Hauser-Schäublin, 10–31. Göttingen: Göttingen University Press.

Mould, Tom. 2005. "The Paradox of Traditionalization: Negotiating the Past in Choctaw Prophetic Discourse." *Journal of Folklore Research* 42 (3): 255–94.

Mueggler, Erik. 2001. *The Age of Wild Ghosts: Memory, Violence, and Place in Southwest China*. Berkeley: University of California Press.

Naquin, Susan. 2000. *Peking: Temples and City Life, 1400–1900*. Berkeley: University of California Press.

Noyes, Dorothy. 1995. "Group." *Journal of American Folklore* 108 (430): 449–78.

———. 2006. "The Judgment of Solomon: Global Protections for Tradition and the Problem of Community Ownership." *Cultural Analysis* 5: 27–56.

———. 2009. "Tradition: Three Traditions." *Journal of Folklore Research* 46: 233–68.

———. 2012. "The Social Base of Folklore." In *A Companion to Folklore*, edited by Regina Bendix and Galit Hasan-Rokem, 13–39. Malden, MA: Wiley-Blackwell.

———. 2016. *Humble Theory: Folklore's Grasp on Social Life*. Bloomington: Indiana University Press.

Oakes, Tim. 2000. "China's Provincial Identities: Reviving Regionalism and Reinventing 'Chineseness.'" *Journal of Asian Studies* 59 (3): 667–92.

———. 2006. "Culture Strategies of Development: Implications for Village Governance in China." *Pacific Review* 1 (19): 13–37.

———. 2013. "Heritage as Improvement: Cultural Display and Contested Governance in Rural China." *Modern China* 39 (4): 380–407.

Oring, Elliott. 2013. "Thinking through Tradition." In *Tradition in the Twenty-First Century: Locating the Role of the Past in the Present*, edited by Trevor J. Blank and Howard Robert Glenn, 22–48. Boulder: University Press of Colorado.

Ortner, Sherry B. 1984. "Theory in Anthropology since the Sixties." *Comparative Studies in Society and History* 26 (1): 126–66.

Overmyer, Daniel L. 2009. *Local Religion in North China in the Twentieth Century: The Structure and Organization of Community Rituals and Beliefs*. Leiden, Netherlands: Brill.

Owen, Stephen. 1992. *Readings in Chinese Literary Thought*. Cambridge, MA: Harvard University Press.

Pan, Hongli. 2006. "The Old Folks' Associations and Lineage Revival in Contemporary Villages of Southern Fujian Province." In *Southern Fujian: Reproduction of Traditions in Post-Mao China*, edited by Tan Chee-Beng, 69–96. Hong Kong: Chinese University Press.

Pei Beiji 裴北记. 2005–12. "Qiannian rongxian shenmi jie: E Ying zhuan 千年荣显神谜讦: 娥英传" [Discovering the mysteries of the deities with the glorious history of thousands of years: Biographies of Ehuang and Nüying]. Manuscript.

Peng, Mu. 2008. "Shared Practice, Esoteric Knowledge, and Bai: Envisioning the Yin World in Rural China." PhD diss., University of Pennsylvania.

Poon, Shuk-Wah. 2008. "Religion, Modernity, and Urban Space: The City God Temple in Republican Guangzhou." *Modern China* 34 (2): 247–75.

Popper, Karl R. 1965. *Conjectures and Refutations: The Growth of Scientific Knowledge.* New York: Basic Books.

Price, Maurice T. 1946. "Differentiating Myth, Legend, and History in Ancient Chinese Culture." *American Anthropologist* 48 (1): 31–42.

Qian Mingzi 潜明兹. 2008. *Zhongguo shenhuaxue* 中国神话学 [Chinese mythology]. Shanghai: Shanghai renmin chubanshe.

Qiao Guoliang 乔国樑. 1997–98. "E Ying zhuan 娥英传" [Biographies of Ehuang and Nüying]. Manuscript.

Qiao Zhongyan 乔忠延. 2000. *Yaodu shi jian* 尧都史鉴 [The History of the Capital of Yao]. Taiyuan: Shanxi guji chubanshe.

Redfield, Robert. 1956. *Peasant Society and Culture: An Anthropological Approach to Civilization.* Chicago: University of Chicago Press.

Rees, Helen. 2000. *Echoes of History: Naxi Music in Modern China.* New York: Oxford University Press.

———. 2012. "Intangible Cultural Heritage in China Today: Policy and Practice in the Early Twenty-First Century." In *Music as Intangible Cultural Heritage: Policy, Ideology, and Practice in the Preservation of East Asian Traditions,* edited by Keith Howard, 23–54. Farnham, UK: Ashgate.

Richter, Ursula. 1982. "Gu Jiegang: His Last Thirty Years." *China Quarterly* 90: 286–95.

Roddy, Stephen. 1998. *Literati Identity and Its Fictional Representations in Late Imperial China.* Stanford, CA: Stanford University Press.

Ruggles, D. Fairchild, and Helaine Silverman. 2009. *Intangible Heritage Embodied.* New York: Springer.

Said, Edward W. 1978. *Orientalism.* New York: Pantheon Books.

———. 1994. *Representations of the Intellectual: The 1993 Reith Lectures.* New York: Pantheon Books.

Sangren, P. Steven. 1995. "'Power' Against Ideology: A Critique of Foucaultian Usage." *Cultural Anthropology* 10 (1): 3–40.

———. 2012. "Fate, Agency, and the Economy of Desire in Chinese Ritual and Society." *Social Analysis* 56 (2): 117–35.

Scalapino, Robert A., and George T. Yu. 1985. *Modern China and Its Revolutionary Process: Recurrent Challenges to the Traditional Order, 1850–1920.* Berkeley: University of California Press.

Schneider, Laurence A. 1969. "From Textual Criticism to Social Criticism: The Historiography of Ku Chieh-kang." *Journal of Asian Studies* 28 (4): 771–88.

———. 1971. *Ku Chieh-kang and China's New History: Nationalism and the Quest for Alternative Traditions.* Berkeley: University of California Press.

Scott, James C. 1985. *Weapons of the Weak: Everyday Forms of Peasant Resistance.* New Haven, CT: Yale University Press.

———. 1990. *Domination and the Arts of Resistance: Hidden Transcripts.* New Haven, CT: Yale University Press.

———. 2013. *Decoding Subaltern Politics: Ideology, Disguise, and Resistance in Agrarian Politics.* New York: Routledge.

Scott, Janet Lee. 2007. *For Gods, Ghosts and Ancestors: The Chinese Tradition of Paper Offerings.* Seattle: University of Washington Press.

Shang, Wei. 2010. "The Literati Era and Its Demise (1723–1840)." In *The Cambridge History of Chinese Literature*, vol. 2, edited by Kang-i Sun Chang and Stephen Owen, 245–98. Cambridge: Cambridge University Press.

Shanxi News. 2010. "Shanxi sheng feiwuzhi wenhua yichan baohu gongzuo dashiji 山西省非物质文化遗产保护工作大事记" [Annals of intangible cultural heritage protection in Shanxi province]. June 1. Accessed November 14, 2017. http://www.reformdata.org/index.do?m=wap&a=show&catid=329&typeid=&id=22038.

Shanxi sheng zheng xie 山西省政协. 1981. *Yan Xishan tongzhi Shanxi shishi* 阎锡山统治山西史实. Taiyuan: Shanxi renmin chubanshe.

Sharman, Lyon. 1968. *Sun Yat-sen: His Life and Its Meaning, a Critical Biography.* Stanford, CA: Stanford University Press.

Shen Jie 沈洁. 2006. "'Fan mixin' huayu jiqi xiandai qiyuan '反迷信'话语及其现代起源" [The anti-superstition discourse and its modern origin]. *Shilin* 2: 30–42.

Shi Aidong 施爱东. 2009. "Xueshu yundong duiyu changgui kexue de fumian yingxiang—jian tan minsu xuejia zai feiyi baohu yundong zhong de xueshu dandang 学术运动对于常规科学的负面影响—兼谈民俗学家在非遗保护运动中的学术担当" [The negative effects of academic campaign on the regular research: Comments on the academic responsibilities of folklorists in the safeguarding of intangible cultural heritage]. *Henan Social Sciences* 3: 10–14.

Shi Nianhai 史念海. 1996. *Zhongguo gudu he wenhua* 中国古都和文化 [Chinese ancient aapitals and culture]. Beijing: Zhonghua shuju.

Silva, Francisco Vaz da. 2012. "Tradition without Ends." In *A Companion to Folklore*, edited by Regina Bendix and Galit Hasan-Rokem, 40–54. Malden, MA: Wiley-Blackwell.

Silverman, Helaine. 2011. *Contested Cultural Heritage: Religion, Nationalism, Erasure, and Exclusion in a Global World.* New York: Springer.

Sima Qian 司马迁. (91 BC) 1959. *Shiji* 史记 [The records of the grand historian]. 10 vols. Beijing: zhonghua shuju.

Sina News. 2017. "Feiwuzhi wenhua yichan baohu kan Shanxi 非物质文化遗产保护看山西" [Protection of intangible cultural heritage in Shanxi]. September 18. Accessed November 16, 2017. http://news.sina.com.cn/o/2017-09-19/doc-ifykynia8093526.shtml.

Smith, Laurajane, and Natsuko Akagawa. 2009. *Intangible Heritage: Key Issues in Cultural Heritage.* London: Routledge.

Song Hongjuan 宋红娟. 2009. "'Mixin' gainian de fasheng xue yanjiu '迷信'概念的发生学研究" [Phylogeny study of the conception of superstition]. *Sixiang Zhanxian* 3: 106–11.

State Council of the PRC. 2005a. "Guanyu jiaqiang woguo feiwuzhi wenhua yichan baohu gongzuo de yijian 关于加强我国非物质文化遗产保护工作的意见" [Recommendations on the strengthening of the safeguarding of China's intangible cultural heritage]. Accessed November 16, 2017. http://www.gov.cn/gongbao/content/2005/content_63227.htm.

———. 2005b. "Jiaqiang wenhua yichan baohu de tongzhi 加强文化遗产保护的通知" [Circular on the strengthening of protection for cultural heritage]. Accessed November 16, 2017. http://www.gov.cn/gongbao/content/2006/content_185117.htm.

Sun Huanlun 孙奂仑, Han Jiong 韩坰, Li Qinsheng 李琴声, and He Chunshou 贺椿寿 et al., eds. 1917. *Hongtong xianzhi* 洪洞县志 [Hongtong county annals]. 18 vols. Shanghai: Shangwu yinshuguan.

Sun Xingyan 孫星衍. 1986. *Shangshu jin gu wen zhushu* 尚書今古文注疏. Beijing: Zhonghua shuju.

Sun Yat-sen 孙中山. (1919) 1981–86. "Sanmin zhuyi 三民主义" [Three people's principles (draft)]. In Sun, 1981–86:5.185–96.

———. (1924a) 1981–86. "Minquan zhuyi 民权主义" [The principle of minquan]. In Sun, 1981–86: 9.184–96.

———. (1924b) 1981–86. "Minzu zhuyi 民族主义" [The principle of minzu]. In Sun, 1981–86: 9.241–54.

———. 1981–86. *Sun Zhongshan quanji* 孙中山全集 [Complete works of Sun Yat-sen]. 11 vols. Beijing: Zhonghua shuju.

Sun Zhengguo 孙正国. 2017. "Shiyunian lai zhongguo daxue feiyi chuancheng de shijian xingtai 十余年来中国大学'非遗'传承的实践形态" [Practices of the inheritance of intangible cultural heritage at Chinese universities during the past decade]. *Cultural Heritage* 1: 11–16.

Swartz, David. 1997. *Culture & Power: The Sociology of Pierre Bourdieu*. Chicago: University of Chicago Press.

Sydow, C. W. von. 1948. *Selected Papers on Folklore*. Copenhagen: Rosenkilde & Bagger.

Tan, Tian Yuan. 2010. *Songs of Contentment and Transgression: Discharged Officials and Literati Communities in Sixteenth-Century North China*. Cambridge, MA: Harvard University Asia Center.

Tauschek, Markus. 2012. "The Bureaucratic Texture of National Patrimonial Policies." In *Heritage Regimes and the State*, edited by Regina F. Bendix, Aditya Eggert, and Arnika Peselmann, 195–212. Göttingen: Göttingen University Press.

Tay, Lian soo. 1987. "Lun Gu Jiegang zhi xueshu licheng jiqi gongxian 论顾颉刚之学术历程及其贡献" [Discussion of the course and contribution of Gu Jiegang's academic work]. In *Gu Jiegang xueshu nianpu jianbian* 顾颉刚学术年谱简编 [Chronology of the academic activities of Gu Jiegang], 1–32. Beijing: Zhongguo youyi chubanshe.

Thurston, Timothy O'Connor. 2015. "Laughter on the Grassland: A Diachronic Study of A mdo Tibetan Comedy and the Public Intellectual in Western China." PhD diss., Ohio State University, Columbus.

Tian, Chang-wu. 1988. "On the Legends of Yao, Shun, Yu and the Origins of Chinese Civilization." *Chinese Studies in Philosophy* 19 (3): 21–68.

Tianying 天鹰. 1959. *1958 nian zhongguo minge yundong* 1958 年中國民歌运动 [Chinese folk song movement in 1958]. Shanghai: Shanghai wenyi chubanshe.

Tuohy, Sue. 1991. "Cultural Metaphors and Reasoning: Folklore Scholarship and Ideology in Contemporary China." *Asian Folklore Studies* 50 (1): 189–220.

UNESCO. 2003. "Text of the Convention for the Safeguarding of Intangible Cultural Heritage." Accessed December 15, 2017. https://ich.unesco.org/en/convention.

———. 2008. "Intangible Heritage Lists." Accessed April 13, 2012. http://www.unesco.org/culture/ich/index.php?lg=en&pg=00011.

———. 2017. "Browse the Lists of Intangible Cultural Heritage and the Register of Good Safeguarding Practices." Accessed December 15, 2017. https://ich.unesco.org/en/lists#tabs.

Utley, Francis Lee. 1965. "Folk Literature: An Operational Definition." In *The Study of Folklore*, edited by Alan Dundes, 8–20. Englewood Cliffs, NJ: Prentice Hall.

Wang Chunliang 王春亮. 2009. "Hongtong sanyuesan zouqin xisu shen yi shimo 洪洞三月三走亲习俗申遗始末" [How the custom of visiting sacred relatives in Hongtong became an element of intangible cultural heritage]. In *Shun geng Lishan zai Hongtong*, edited by Li Xuezhi, 325–32. Taiyuan: Sanjin chubanshe.

Wang Guowei 王国维. 1994. *Gushi xinzheng* 古史新证 [New attestation to ancient history]. Beijing: Qinghua daxue chubanshe.

Wang, Jinping. 2011. "Between Family and State: Networks of Literati, Clergy, and Villagers in Shanxi, North China, 1200–1400." PhD diss., Yale University.

Wang Kaiyuan 王开源. 2008. "Shenqin gudao ruhe gai 神亲古道如何改?" [How was the old procession route of sacred relatives changed?]. Unpublished essay.

———. 2009a. "Ergugu miao jiemi 二姑姑庙揭秘" [Discovering the mystery of the Temple of 'the Second Aunt']. In *Shun geng Lishan zai Hongtong*, edited by Li Xuezhi, 301–3. Taiyuan: Sanjin chubanshe.

———. 2009b. "Hexie chuancheng wuqian nian 和谐传承五千年 [Harmoniously transmitted for five thousand years]." In *Shun geng Lishan zai Hongtong*, edited by Li Xuezhi, 183–87. Taiyuan: Sanjin chubanshe.

Wang Kaiyuan and Wang Quansuo. 2007–9. "Ehuang Nüying chuanwen yishi 娥皇女英传闻轶事" [Legends and anecdotes of Ehuang and Nüying]. Unpublished manuscript.

Wang Kaiyuan and Yan Zhenghong. 2006. "Yiqu hexie minsu shihua 一曲和谐民俗史话" [A harmonious historical narrative of folklore]. In *Yao Shun zhi feng jin you cun*, edited by Zhou Xibin, 175–99. Beijing: Zhongguo xiju chubanshe.

———. 2008. "Yangxie gugu miao 1704 nian—2008 nian chuancheng ren 羊獬姑姑庙1704年—2008年传承人" [Chuancheng ren from 1704 to 2008 in the Temple of Aunts in Yangxie]. Unpublished essay.

Wang Wenzhang 王文章, Zhang Qingshan 张庆善, and Ma Shengde 马盛德, et al., eds. 2006. *Zhongguo feiwuzhi wenhua yichan baohu luntan lunwen ji* 中国非物质文化遗产保护论坛论文集 [A collection of papers of the forum on the protection of Chinese intangible cultural heritage]. Beijing: Wenhua yishu chubanshe.

Wang Xianzhao 王宪昭. 2010. "Shi lun feiwuzhi wenhua yichan yanjiu rencai de peiyang 试论非物质文化遗产研究人才的培养" [On the cultivation of researchers of intangible cultural heritage]. *Cultural Heritage* 4: 31–36.

Wang Xiaolian 王孝廉. 2005. *Zhongguo shenhua shijie* 中国神话世界 [The world of Chinese myths]. Taibei: hongye wenhua.

Wang Xuewen 汪学文 et al., eds. 2009. *San Jin shike daquan. Linfen shi Hongtong xian juan* 三晋石刻大全. 临汾市洪洞县卷. Taiyuan: Sanjin chubanshe.

Wang Yao 王尧. 2010. "*Minjian chuanshuo de neibu xieben yanjiu—yi Hongtong xian 'jie gugu ying niangniang' chuanshuo quan wei zhongxin* 民间传说的内部写本研究—以洪洞县'接姑姑迎娘娘'传说圈为中心" [A research on the interior written texts of folk legends: Based on the "welcoming aunties and receiving niangniang" legend circle in Hongtong]. MA thesis, Beijing University.

———. 2011. "Neibu xieben yu defang xing chuanshuo—yi Hongtong xian 'jie gugu ying niangniang' chuanshuo quan wei zhongxin 内部写本与地方性传说—以洪洞县'接姑姑迎娘娘'传说圈为中心" [Interior written texts and local legends: Based on the "welcoming aunties and receiving niangniang" legend circle in Hongtong]. *Minzu wenxue yanjiu* 5: 18–30.

Weatherley, Robert. 2006. *Politics in China since 1949: Legitimizing Authoritarian Rule*. London: Routledge.

Wei Chengsi 魏承思. 2004. *Zhongguo zhishi fenzi de fuchen* 中國知識份子的浮沉. Hong Kong: Oxford University Press.

Werner, E. T. C. (1922) 1986. *Ancient Tales and Folklore of China*. London: Bracken Books.

———. (1922) 1994. *Myths and Legends of China*. New York: Dover.

Wong, Wai Yip. 2011. "Defining Chinese Folk Religion: A Methodological Interpretation." *Asian Philosophy* 21 (2): 153–70.

Wu Bing'an 乌丙安. 2007. "Silu yu chulu: baohu fei wuzhi wenhua yichan rechao zhong de zhongguo minsu xue 思路与出路: 保护非物质文化遗产热潮中的中国民俗学" [Thought and outlet: Chinese folklore studies in the safeguarding of intangible cultural heritage]. *Henan Social Sciences* 2: 1–6.

Wu, Laura Hua. 1995. "From Xiaoshuo to Fiction: Hu Yinglin's Genre Study of Xiaoshuo." *Harvard Journal of Asiatic Studies* 55 (2): 339–71.

Xiao Fang 萧放. 2016. "Lun xin wenhua shi shiye xia de feiwuzhi wenhua yichan yundong 论新文化史视野下的非物质文化遗产运动" [Intangible cultural heritage movement in the vision of new culture history]. *Research on Heritage and Preservation* 1: 79–83.

———. 2017. "The Predicament, Revitalization, and Future of Traditional Chinese Festivals." *Western Folklore* 76 (2): 181–96.

Xiqiao Zhuang Miaoweihui 西乔庄庙委会 (Xiqiao Zhuang Temple Association). 2006. "Xiqiao Zhuang jianmiao jianshi 西乔庄建庙简史" [A brief history of building the temple in Xiqiao Zhuang]. Unpublished Essay.

Xunzi et al. 1996. *Xunzi* 荀子. Shanghai: Shanghai guji chubanshe.

Yan, Haiming. 2015. "World Heritage as Discourse: Knowledge, Discipline and Dissonance in Fujian Tulou Sites." *International Journal of Heritage Studies* 21 (1): 65–80.

Yan Xishan 阎锡山. 1968. *Yan Xishan zaonian huiyilu* 阎锡山早年回忆录. Taibei: Zhuan ji wenxue chubanshe.

Yan Zhenghong 闫正红, ed. 2007a. "Tangyao Guyuan huiyi jiyao 唐尧故园会议纪要" [Old Temple of Tang Yao meeting minutes]. Unpublished meeting records.

———, ed. 2007b. "Wan'an huiyi jiyao 万安会议纪要" [Wan'an meeting minutes]. Unpublished meeting records.

———, ed. 2012. *Huangying yishi* 皇英轶事 [Anecdotes of Ehuang and Nüying]. Booklet.

Yang Bojun 杨伯峻. 1960. *Mengzi yizhu* 孟子译注. 2 vols. Beijing: Zhonghua shuju.

———. 1980. *Lunyu yizhu* 论语译注. Beijing: Zhonghua shuju.

Yang, C. K. 1961. *Religion in Chinese Society: A Study of Contemporary Social Functions of Religion and Some of Their Historical Factors*. Berkeley: University of California Press.

Yang Kuisong 杨奎松. 2013. *Renbuzhu de "guanhuai": 1949 nian qianhou de shusheng yu zhengzhi* 忍不住的"关怀": 1949 年前后的书生与政治 [They couldn't help "caring": Intellectuals and politics before and after 1949]. Guilin: Guangxi shifan daxue chuban she.

Yang Lihui 杨利慧. 1997. *Nüwa de shenhua yu xinyang* 女娲的神话与信仰 [Myths and beliefs of Nüwa]. Beijing: Zhongguo shehui kexue chubanshe.

———. 1999. *Nüwa suyuan: Nüwa xinyang qiyuandi de zai tuice* 女娲溯源: 女娲信仰起源地的再推测 [Tracking the origin of Nüwa: Rethinking the birthplace of Nüwa beliefs]. Beijing: Beijing shifan daxue chubanshe.

———. 2011. "Performing Myth Today: A Field Study of the Renzu Temple Festival." In *China's Creation and Origin Myths: Cross-cultural Explorations in Oral and Written Traditions*, edited by Mineke Schipper, Ye Shuxian, and Yin Hubin, 238–60. Leiden, Netherlands: Brill.

———. 2015. "The Effectiveness and Limitations of 'Context' Reflections Based on Ethnographic Research of Myth Traditions." *Asian Ethnology* 74 (2): 363–77.

Yang Lihui and An Deming. 2005. *Handbook of Chinese Mythology*. Santa Barbara, CA: ABC-CLIO.

Yang Lihui, Xia Zhang, Fang Xu, Hongwu Li, and Yunli Tong. 2011. *Xiandai koucheng shenhua de minzuzhi yanjiu: yi sige Hanzu shequ wei ge'an* 现代口承神话的民族志研究: 以四个汉族社区为个案 [Ethnographic research of modern orally transmitted myths: Case studies in four Han communities]. Xi'an: shaanxi shifan daxue chubanshe.

Yang, Mayfair Mei-hui. 2000. "Putting Global Capitalism in Its Place: Economic Hybridity, Bataille, and Ritual Expenditure." *Current Anthropology* 41 (4): 477–509.

———. 2004. "Spatial Struggles: State Disenchantment and Popular Re-appropriation of Space in Rural Southeast China." *Journal of Asian Studies* 63 (3): 719–55.

———. 2011. "Postcoloniality and Religiosity in Modern China." *Theory, Culture and Society* 28 (2): 3–44.

Yao Huiyi 姚慧弈. 2010. "Yishi, shehui yu difang yulun—Hongtong xian 'jie gugu ying niangniang' zouqin huodong zhong de mazi yanjiu 仪式、社会与地方舆论—洪洞县 '接姑姑迎娘娘' 走亲活动中的马子研究" [Rites, community and local opinion: The study of Mazi in the 'receiving gugu and welcoming niangniang' activity in Hongtong county]. MA thesis, Beijing University.

Ye Peng 叶鹏. 2015. "Jiyu wenhu yu keji ronghe de woguo feiwuzhi wenhua yichan baohu jizhi ji shixian yanjiu 基于文化与科技融合的我国非物质文化遗产保护机制及实现研究" [Research on the protection mechanisms and their realization path of Chinese intangible cultural heritage based on the fusion of culture, science and technology]. PhD diss., Wuhan University, China.

Ye Shuxian 叶舒宪. 2005. "Zhongguo shenhuaxue bainian huimou 中国神话学百年回眸" [Outlined history of Chinese mythology]. *Xueshu jiaoliu* 1: 154–64.

Ye Tao 叶涛. 2009. *Taishan xiangshe yanjiu* 泰山香社研究. Shanghai: Shanghai guji chubanshe.

Yoshikawa Kōjirō. 1989. *Five Hundred Years of Chinese Poetry, 1150–1650*. Princeton, NJ: Princeton University Press.

You Ziying 游自荧. 2012. "Tradition and Ideology: Creating and Performing New *Gushi* in China from 1962 to 1966." *Asian Ethnology* 71 (2): 259–80.

———. 2015a. "Competing Traditions: Village Temple Rivalries, Social Actors, and Contested Narratives in Contemporary China." PhD diss., Ohio State University, Columbus.

———. 2015b. "Shifting Actors and Power Relations: Contentious Local Responses to the Safeguarding of Intangible Cultural Heritage in Contemporary China." *Journal of Folklore Research* 52 (2–3): 253–68. Reprinted in *UNESCO on the Ground: Local Perspectives on Global Policy for Intangible Cultural Heritage*, edited by Michael Dylan Foster and Lisa Gilman, 113–28. Bloomington: Indiana University Press.

Yu Shitang 余世堂 and Cai Xingren 蔡行仁 et al., eds. 1731. *Hongtong xian zhi: jiu juan* 洪洞县志: 九卷. 9 vols.

Yu Yingshi 余英时. 1982. *Shixue yu chuantong* 史学与传统 [History and tradition]. Taibei: Shibao wenhua gongsi.

———. 1984. *Cong jiazhi xitong kan zhongguo wenhua de xiandai yiyi: zhongguo wenhua yu xiandai shenghuo zonglun* 從價值系統看中國文化的現代意義: 中國文化與現代生活總論. Taibei: Shibao wenhua chuban shiye youxian gongsi.

———. 1987. *Shi yu zhongguo wenhua* 士与中国文化 [Shi and Chinese culture]. Shanghai: Shanghai renmin chubanshe.

———. 1992. *Zhongguo lishi zhuanxing shiqi de zhishi fenzi* 中國歷史轉型時期的知識分子. Taibei: Lianjing chuban shiye gongsi.

———. 1993. "The Radicalization of China in the Twentieth Century." *Daedalus* 122 (2): 125–50.

———. 1997. *Zhongguo zhishi fenzi lun* 中国知识分子论 [On China's intellectuals]. Zhengzhou: Henan renmin chubanshe.

———. 2004a. *Wenshi chuantong yu wenhua chongjian* 文史传统与文化重建. Beijing: Shenghuo, dushu, xinzhi sanlian shudian.

———. 2004b. *Yu Yingshi wenji* 余英时文集 [Collected works of Yu Yingshi]. 4 vols. Guilin: Guangxi shifan daxue chubanshe.

Yuan Ke 袁珂. 1984. *Zhongguo shenhua chuanshuo* 中国神话传说 [Chinese myths and legends]. Beijing: Zhongguo minjian wenyi chubanshe.

———. 1987. *Shenhua lunwen ji* 神话论文集 [Collection of papers on myth studies]. Taibei: Hanjing wenhua shiye youxian gongsi.

———. 1991. *Zhongguo shenhua shi* 中国神话史 [History of Chinese mythology]. Taibei: Shibao wenhua chuban qiye youxian gongsi.

———. 1993. "Forward." In *Chinese Mythology: An Introduction*, xi–xiii. Baltimore: Johns Hopkins University Press.

Yuan Ke, Kim Echlin, and Nie Zhixiong. 1993. *Dragons and Dynasties: An Introduction to Chinese Mythology*. London: Penguin Books.

Yung, Bell. 2008. *The Last of China's Literati: The Music, Poetry, and Life of Tsar Teh-yun*. Hong Kong: Hong Kong University Press.

Zeng Guoquan 曾國荃, Zhang Xu 張煦, and Wang Xuan 王軒, et al., eds. 1892. *Shanxi tongzhi* 山西通志. 184 vols.

Zhang, Boyu, with Yao Hui and Huib Schippers. 2015. "Report: The Rise and Implementation of Intangible Cultural Heritage Protection for Music in China." *World of Music* 4 (1): 45–60.

Zhang Chenxia 张晨霞. 2012a. "Di Yao yanjiu: cong diwang shengren dao shenhua he chuanshuo 帝尧研究: 从帝王圣人到神话传说" [Studies of Emperor Yao: From emperor and sage to myths and legends]. *Linyi daxue xue bao* 2: 34–39.

———. 2012b. "Jinnan Di Yao chuanshuo yanjiu 晋南帝尧传说研究" [A study on legends about Emperor Yao in the south of Shanxi province]. PhD diss., East China Normal University, Shanghai.

———. 2013. *Di Yao chuanshuo yu diyu wenhua*. 帝尧传说与地域文化 [Legends of Emperor Yao and regional culture]. Beijing: Xueyuan chubanshe.

Zhang, Juwen. 2017. "Intangible Cultural Heritage and Self-Healing Mechanism in Chinese Culture." *Western Folklore* 76 (2): 197–226.

Zhang, Juwen, and Xing Zhou. 2017. "Introduction: The Essentials of Intangible Cultural Heritage Practices in China: The Inherent Logic and Transmission Mechanism of Chinese Tradition." *Western Folklore* 76 (2): 133–49.

Zhang, Lijun. 2014. "Living with/in Heritage: Tulou as Home, Heritage, and Destination." PhD diss., Indiana University, Bloomington.

Zhang Qing 张青 and Lin Zhongyuan 林中园, eds. 1988. *Hongtong gu dahuaishu zhi* 洪洞古大槐树志. Taiyuan: Shanxi renmin chubanshe.

Zhang Qing 张青, Wang Gensheng 王根生, eds. 2005. *Hongtong xianzhi* 洪洞县志. Taiyuan: Shanxi chunqiu dianzi yinxiang chubanshe.

Zhang Yinlin 張蔭麟. (1925) 1982. "Ping jnren duiyu zhongguo gushi zhi taolun 評近人對於中國古史之討論" [Comments on the debates of Chinese ancient history in modern time]. In *Gushi bian*, vol. 2, 271–88. Shanghai: Shanghai guji chubanshe.

Zhang Zhenli 张振犁. 2009. *Zhongyuan shenhua yanjiu* 中原神话研究 [Myths of central China]. Shanghai: Shanghai shehui kexueyuan chubanshe.

Zhang Zhiyong 张志勇. 2010. "Zhongguo minjian wenxue santao jicheng jiang chuban xian juan ben 中国民间文学三套集成将出版县卷本" [County-Level volumes of three collections of Chinese folk literature will be published]. *Zhongguo yishu bao*, January 8. http://www.chinanews.com/cul/news/2010/01-08/2062367.shtml.

Zhao Fa 赵发. 2008. "Linfen zhanyi 临汾战役 [Battle of Linfen]." *Yaodu Wenshi* 15: 1–12.

Zhao Shiyu 赵世瑜. 1999. *Yanguang xiangxia de geming: Zhongguo xiandai minsu xue sixiang shi lun (1918–1937)* 眼光向下的革命：中国现代民俗学思想史论 (1918–1937) [Downward-sighted revolution: Discussion on the intellectual history of Chinese modern folklore studies, 1918–1937]. Beijing: Beijing shifan daxue chubanshe.

Zheng Tuyou 郑土有. 1995. *Guangong xinyang* 关公信仰. Beijing: xueyuan chubanshe.

Zhong Jingwen 钟敬文. 1982. *Zhong Jingwen minjian wenxue lunji* 钟敬文民间文学论集 [Essays on folk literature by Zhong Jingwen]. 2 vols. Shanghai: Shanghai wenyi chubanshe.

———. 1999. *Zhongguo minjian wenxue jiangyan ji* 中国民间文学讲演集 [Lectures on Chinese folk literature]. Beijing: Beijing shifan daxue chubanshe.

Zhong Jingwen and Li Yuan, eds. 2002. *Ershi shiji zhongguo minsuxue jingdian* 二十世纪中国民俗学经典 [Classics of Chinese folklore studies in the twentieth century]. 8 vols. Beijing: Shehui kexue wenxian chubanshe.

Zhong Zongxian 钟宗宪. 2006. *Zhongguo shenhua de jichu yanjiu* 中国神话的基础研究 [Basic studies of Chinese myth]. Taibei: Hongye wenhua shiye youxian gongsi.

Zhonggong shanxi shengwei 中共山西省委 (The CPC Shanxi Provincial Committee), Zhonggong linfen diwei 中共临汾地委 (The CPC Prefectural Committee), and Zhonggong linfen shiwei 中共临汾市委 (The CPC Municipal Committee). 1987. *Linfen gong jian* 临汾攻坚. Taiyuan: Shanxi renmin chubanshe.

Zhou Heping 周和平, ed. 2007. *Zhongguo feiwuzhi wenhua yichan baohu yanjiu* 中国非物质文化遗产保护研究 [Studies of Chinese intangible cultural heritage protection]. Beijing: Beijing shifan daxue chubanshe.

Zhou Minghua 邹明华. 2008. "'Wei' lishi yu 'zhen' wenhua: Shanxi Hongtong de huotai gushi chuanshuo '伪'历史与'真'文化：山西洪洞的活态古史传说" ['Unauthentic' history and 'authentic' culture: Living legends of ancient history in Hongtong, Shanxi]. *Wenxue Pinglun* 5: 123–28.

Zhou Xibin 周希斌, ed. 2006. *Yao Shun zhi feng jin you cun* 尧舜之风今犹存 [The customs of Yao and Shun living up to today]. Beijing: Zhongguo Xiju Chubanshe.

Zhou Xing 周星. 2013. "Minjian xinyang yu wenhua yichan 民间信仰与文化遗产" [Folk belief and cultural heritage]. *Wenhua yichan* 2: 1–10.

———. 2017a. "Folk Belief and Its Legitimization in China." *Western Folklore* 76 (2): 151–65.

———. 2017b. "'Shenghuo geming' yu zhongguo minsuxue de fangxiang '生活革命'与中国民俗学的方向" ['Life revolution' and the direction of Chinese folklore studies]. *Minsu yanjiu* 1: 5–18.

———. 2017c. "Shenghuo geming, xiangchou yu zhongguo minsu xue 生活革命、乡愁与中国民俗学" [Life revolution, nostalgia, and Chinese folklore studies]. *Minjian wenhua luntan* 2: 42–61.

Zhu, Yujie. 2015. "Cultural Effects of Authenticity: Contested Heritage Practices in China." *International Journal of Heritage Studies* 21 (6): 594–608.

INDEX

ZIYING YOU is Visiting Assistant Professor of Chinese Studies at the College of Wooster. She is editor (with Lijun Zhang) of *Chinese Folklore Studies Today: Discourse and Practice* (Indiana University Press, 2019) and of a special issue for the journal *Asian Ethnology*, titled *Intangible Cultural Heritage in Asia: Traditions in Transition.*